Ballet & Modern Dance

A Concise History

Third Edition

Ballet & Modern Dance

A Concise History

Third Edition

Jack Anderson

A Dance Horizons Book
PRINCETON BOOK COMPANY, PUBLISHERS

The photographs of the Kirov Ballet and the Bolshoi Ballet are reprinted from *The Russian Ballet: Past and Present* by Alexander Demidov, translated by Gary Daniels. Translation copyright © 1977 by Doubleday, a division of Bantam Doubleday Dell Publishing Group, Inc.

Excerpt from *Isadora Duncan, The Russian Years* by Ilya I. Schneider, translated by David Magarshock, copyright © 1963 by Macdonald & Company (Publishers) Ltd., reproduced by permission of Harcourt Brace Jovanovich, Inc.

LIBRARY OF CONGRESS CATALOGING IN PUBLICATION DATA
Names: Anderson, Jack, 1935–
Title: Ballet & modern dance : a concise history / Jack Anderson.
Other Titles: Ballet and modern dance
Description: Third edition. | Trenton, NJ : Princeton Book Company, Publishers, [2018] | "A Dance Horizons book." | Includes bibliographical references and index.
Identifiers: ISBN 9780871273963
Subjects: LCSH: Ballet—History. | Modern dance—History.
Classification: LCC GV1787 .A467 2018 | DDC 792.8/09--dc23

Interior design and composition by Mulberry Tree Press.

Cover photograph by Andreas H. Birkigt of Uwe Scholz's *Bach Kreationen*. Photo courtesy of the photographer.

Cover design by Alessia Lorea Studio.

A Dance Horizons Book
Princeton Book Company, Publishers
15 West Front Street, Trenton, NJ 08608

Contents

Acknowledgments

The author wishes to thank the following people for assistance, information, and suggestions over the years that have contributed to this book: The staff of the Dance Collection of The New York Public Library, Régine Astier, Edwin Bayrd, Ingrid Brainard, Mary Clarke, Selma Jeanne Cohen, George Dorris, Gage and Richard Englund, Camille Hardy, Henley Haslam, Ellen Kavier, Dally Messenger, Frank W.D. Ries, Christena L. Schlundt, Marian Smith, Kathrine Sorley Walker, Walter Terry, and Catherine Turocy. Special thanks go to the late Barbara Palfy, who besides being an exemplary, and delightful, editor, conscientiously compiled the previous edition's "Short Profiles" section, on which the present listings are based.

Preface

The past is unchangeable, although history may often change, if by "history" we mean the way we record and interpret past events. New data is uncovered. Hypotheses are validated or discarded. Reputations rise and fall. As a result all history books, no matter how authoritative they may seem, can offer only tentative accounts.

My first dance history, *Dance,* appeared in 1974 as a volume in the "World of Culture" series published by Newsweek Books in association with Arnoldo Mondadori Editore; it was a lavishly illustrated introduction to dance history for the general reader.

It was succeeded by the first edition of *Ballet and Modern Dance: A Concise History* in 1986. Now, I offer this revision. The text has been expanded and, in making changes and additions, I have been influenced by—and I remain grateful to—all the readers of this book and the teachers who have used it in their classrooms who have made suggestions about it to me and my publisher. Other textual changes have been prompted by fresh historical data that have come my way.

In *Ballet and Modern Dance: A Concise History* I have tried to meet the needs of both students and inquisitive dancegoers through a narrative focused on the development of Western theatrical dance—specifically ballet and modern dance—since the Renaissance, incorporating the most recent scholarship. The text is illuminated by excerpts from primary sources. Although intended to be entertaining as well as enlightening, the book seeks a greater objective—to emphasize the value of dance history as a field of study.

The result is a book that I hope will prove useful in dance history classes, theatre history classes, and survey courses in the performing arts in general. However, I also hope it will delight and inform any dance lover who is curious about the contours of dance at other times and in other places as well as in our own time.

—Jack Anderson

Ballet & Modern Dance

A Concise History

Third Edition

1

The Pleasures of Dance History

DANCE IS THE MOST PERISHABLE OF THE ARTS. It is forever in danger of vanishing. Many choreographers do not attempt to preserve their dances; some would not know how to go about doing so. Even today, when we have films and videotapes in addition to systems of dance notation, important works remain unrecorded. Usually dances are preserved—if they are preserved at all—only in the memory of the artists who perform them. But memory is fallible, and steps can easily be changed or forgotten.

No wonder, then, that dance historians often feel frustrated. Desiring to learn about a famous work of the past, they may discover that although copies of its musical score exist along with scenery and costume designs and reviews of the first performance, what is irretrievably lost is the choreography—the aspect of the production which, presumably, was most responsible for making that work a success.

One might be tempted to ask, What's the use? Why bother? Why study dance history at all? The past cannot be changed and we cannot live in the past; we can only live in the present. Moreover, our attempts to learn about dance's past are continually disrupted by the way dance works slip into oblivion.

Nevertheless, there are reasons why the study of dance history can be both useful and inspiring—and a pleasure as well. The more one knows about anything, the better one understands it, and with understanding may come increased respect and love. Dance was not invented this morning; its origins go back to the earliest days of human beings on this earth. Individual dances may fade and die, yet the art lives on. And the kinds of dances that existed in the past have helped to shape the dances that exist today.

From a knowledge of the dances of the past, one may develop a measure of power over the dances of the present. From a knowledge of the kinds of problems dancers and choreographers faced generations, or even centuries, ago and how they tried to solve those problems, one can learn about—and learn from—their successes and failures. Thus young choreographers may be granted insights into their own creative processes and may become aware of ways of choreographing and thinking about dance that they can use to their own advantage. Theatergoers may be better able to appreciate the kinds of dances they see at performances and understand the traditions from which they derive. Indeed, a knowledge of dance history may cause dancers, choreographers, and audiences to realize that they are heirs to great traditions. Because they understand those traditions, they need not feel bound or intimidated by them. The knowledgeable dancer or choreographer is able to choose either to work consciously within a tradition or to defy tradition and go off on a new creative path. If with knowledge comes power, knowledge also grants freedom.

The study of dance history helps one see how amazingly similar and yet how marvelously different people of the past were compared with men and women of today. In some ways, the human condition never changes. People in any country and historical period are born, attain maturity, and die. They feel hunger and pain, make love and war, and organize themselves into families and societies. All people work and play. All ask questions about, and tremble with awe before, the majesty of the universe. All weep. All laugh. All dance.

Over the centuries, certain choreographic concerns recur with fascinating regularity. It is occasionally even possible to see in choreographic styles of the past prefigurations of current trends. A historian may find some of today's supposed choreographic innovations to be simply fresh restatements of ideas that have long preoccupied choreographers.

If dance history can remind us of how similar people may be at heart, it can also make us aware of the remarkably different ways in which people can express themselves. Dance history calls one's attention both to the universality of certain human feelings and to the particular ways in which those feelings are expressed. Dance history reminds us of mankind's cultural and social diversity.

It is evident then that dance history involves more than listings of names and dates. Dances do not make themselves; people make them. People, in turn, are influenced by the societies in which they live. Therefore the study of dance history must also include some examination of the social and cultural background from which choreographic styles have emerged. Dance can be shaped by politics, economics, and philosophy; similarly, it can be influenced by fashions in clothing and standards of etiquette. The way, as custom decrees, that men and women shall live and work offstage may do much to determine the way they will dance together on stage. The judgments pronounced upon dance by religious leaders will also affect the art's development. And because dancers usually perform in some sort of decorated space to some sort of accompaniment, the history of dance is closely tied to the history of art, drama, music, and architecture. In fact, to study the way people dance usually involves studying much about the way they think and live.

As one looks back upon them, the dancers of the past prove to be fascinating people who lived colorful, even tumultuous lives. They were people fully as sensitive and intelligent, and as capable of folly and error, as the dancers and choreographers of today. In all ages, dancers have taken some sort of class, they have longed for great roles, they have gossiped and squabbled and complained about dingy dressing rooms. And they have danced their hearts out on great stages and small. Many famous dancers of the past would surely still be acclaimed today; others might puzzle us. The studio and stage may always be, to some extent, familiar places for dancers in any age or clime. Yet the works rehearsed and performed in those spaces may be unfamiliar because they reflect the way artists in a specific society think about the world.

If one can no longer have the pleasure of knowing those vanished dancers and choreographers personally, one can still acknowledge them as artistic ancestors. They bequeathed their dance discoveries to the dancers who came after them. Even now, as today's dancers make their own discoveries, the ghosts of old dancers are standing behind them, looking over their shoulders, applauding their triumphs, and sighing sympathetically over their failures.

However, before we can feel comfortable in the presence of these theatrical ghosts, we must have some understanding of how to watch dances, particularly dances from other eras.

Dances require viewers to have keen eyes, for movements fly quickly by. Viewers must also possess sharp minds capable of discerning how a multitude of separate steps may cohere into a meaningful artistic whole. Although comparisons of works can often be instructive and intellectually stimulating, a dance must first be appraised on its own terms. Viewers should ask themselves, what is this dance? Of what kinds of movements does it consist? Why are they arranged in this manner? Just what does the choreographer seem to be trying to do here?

A dance crammed with steps is intrinsically neither better nor worse than a kinetically austere one; virtuosity is not necessarily better than simplicity. What matter are the effects of motion—and, often, of emotion as well—created by the specific steps a choreographer has chosen.

Having gained a sense of a work's nature and aesthetic intent, viewers should next decide how well that work was realized. Was the choreography consistently imaginative and communicative? Or was it deficient in some way? Perhaps it was needlessly repetitive. Or it may have failed to clarify important points of the story or basic theme. Viewers must also decide how much or little the production was affected by the performances of the dancers and the contributions of the composer and designer.

It is important to remember that all dance forms are constantly changing. Modern dance is protean by its very nature. And even though ballet often boasts of its glorious heritage and its academic method of training, it, too, has changed—and often radically—from century to century. Indeed, even today, ballet lovers in various countries may have quite different expectations of ballet as an art. A great ballet choreographer of the past might be amazed, or positively horrified, to behold many works accepted as ballets without question by twenty-first century audiences. Similarly, one of our own choreographers might be mystified by some of the qualities that were prized by choreographers in the past.

More than steps develop over the centuries. Throughout history, ideas about what themes, plots, moods, or emotions are appropriate for dance have been changing constantly. And conceptions of the degrees of slimness, plumpness, dignity, or vivacity that are appropriate for the dancing body have sometimes come and gone almost like fads in high fashion.

The more someone knows about the history of dance, theatre, music, and art, the better prepared that person will be to appreciate the revival of a work from the past. But companies staging such works could also help audiences come to terms with their offerings by indicating in their program notes precisely what they intend their productions to be. Are they attempts to revive a work step by step as accurately as possible? Are they evocations of the essential spirit of a work that do not necessarily duplicate its exact steps? Or do their productions consist of a contemporary choreographer's flights of fancy inspired by some theme from the past?

A knowledge of dance history can make spectators as well as performers proud of being involved with dance. It can make all of us realize that dance is a great art to which dedicated people have devoted their lives and talents. Like all that is mortal, dancers may perish; dance itself lives and its traditions are passed on, sometimes falteringly, sometimes with confidence. The dancers who assemble on the world's stages tonight are the inheritors of those traditions. The wisdom of centuries of dance training may be summed up in the way their bodies move. Yet, thanks to the imagination of choreographers, every time the curtain rises a new chapter of dance history may begin.

Related Readings

The Dance of Life

Dancing and building are the two primary and essential arts. The art of dancing stands at the source of all the arts that express themselves first in the human person. The art of building, or architecture, is the beginning of all the arts that lie outside the person; and in the end they unite. Music, acting, poetry proceed in the one mighty stream; sculpture, painting, all the arts of design, in the other. There is no primary art outside these two arts, for their origin is far earlier than man himself; and dancing came first.

That is one reason why dancing, however it may at times be scorned by passing fashions, has a profound and eternal attraction even for those one might suppose farthest from its influence. The joyous beat of the feet of children, the cosmic play of philosophers' thoughts rise and fall according to the same laws of rhythm. If we are indifferent to the art of dancing, we have failed to understand, not merely the supreme manifestation of physical life, but also the supreme symbol of spiritual life.

The significance of dancing, in the wide sense, thus lies in the fact that it is simply an intimate concrete symbol of a general rhythm, that general rhythm which marks, not life only, but the universe, if one may still be allowed so to name the sum of the cosmic influences that reach us. We need not, indeed, go so far as the planets or the stars and outline their ethereal dances. We have but to stand on the seashore and watch the waves that beat at our feet, to observe that at nearly regular intervals this seemingly monotonous rhythm is accentuated for several beats, so that the waves are really dancing the measure of a tune. It need surprise us not at all that rhythm, ever tending to be moulded into a tune, should mark all the physical and spiritual manifestations of life. Dancing is the primitive expression alike of religion and of love—of religion from the earliest human times we know of and of love from a period long anterior to the coming of man. The art of dancing, moreover, is intimately entwined with all human tradition of war, of labour, of pleasure, of education, while some of the wisest philosophers and the most ancient civilizations have regarded the dance as the pattern in accordance with which the moral life of men must be woven. To realise, therefore, what dancing means for mankind—the poignancy and the many-sidedness of its appeal—we must survey the whole sweep of human life, both at its highest and its deepest moments.

(Havelock Ellis, *The Dance of Life*. Boston: Houghton Mifflin, 1923, pp. 36–37; also in Cobbett Steinberg, ed., *The Dance Anthology*. New York: New American Library, 1980, pp. 238–239)

A Dance Reconstructor Comments

A good researcher is basically a detective. For dance, finding the notation is the starting point. Then come the seemingly extraneous but utterly essential questions of context. Where was this dance first performed? What dancer or what theatrical character performed the dance? Are there any contemporary descriptions of it or of the events surrounding it? Who was in the audience? Was the dance intended to celebrate the king's birthday, or was it meant to satirize the monarchy? The answer to any of these questions may affect the very heart of the work. . . .

In the late-seventeenth and eighteenth centuries, meaning and symbolism were at the heart of every artistic statement. Thus the gestures of the dance from the period must not be read as abstract movements in space, but rather as a carefully designed science of motions conveying specific emotional and psychological states of the human spirit.

. . . so much has changed and continues to change ever more rapidly that the final task of the reconstructor's art is to deal with changes in aesthetic and world view, to understand the values of different times and different peoples. It is natural for any period or people to exalt itself as modern or advanced, in a kind of cultural blindness that is best held in check by reminders of important human expressions from other times and places. The dancer, the choreographer, the audience, and the dance's content existed in a different sociopolitical and philosophical context. For example, a bow or reverence was not necessarily an act of humility or subjugation; more often, it was a civilized acknowledgment of another person's dignity and divinity, which all possessed no matter what their station in life (and which is acknowledged far too little in our own time!). . . .

Perhaps the most interesting challenge for today's reconstructor is to avoid twentieth-century Puritanism in the presentation of historical dance. Our times, which in the name of freedom or social truth have variously rejected everything from sets and costumes to plot, moral, form, wigs, and even makeup, leave us very poor in traditional arts, which are crowded with all these things. Many reconstructions have been seen that present a very rich time solely in terms of an abstract science of steps. We serve the artists of the past very poorly by giving such a restricted version of their lives and work.

(Catherine Turocy, "Going for Baroque," *Dance Magazine,* June 1989, pp. 32, 34)

Catherine Turocy is the artistic director of the New York Baroque Dance Company.

The Importance of Dance Notation

One of the most pressing challenges with which we are confronted is to invent and notate dance-works of value so that they can be performed anywhere over and over again. Much of the decline in enthusiasm for dance, which at times has flared up so brightly, is due to the fact that one hardly catches sight of the dancer's movement—no matter how powerful and magnificent it is—before it disappears irrevocably into nothingness, unless it is written down in notation like literature and music.

What would we know today of Homer, Shakespeare and Goethe, if their works had not been written down? What do we know of the music of Orpheus, or Pythagoras? Nothing, except that it enchanted animals and human beings. But with the invention of music-notation, music began to blossom, and the works of a Bach, a Beethoven and a Wagner could fortunately be preserved. What do we know of the art of dance in the past? A few pictures and statues give us an inkling of the beauty of the movements. A few notes written in old forms of dance notation which we can barely decipher inform us about some court dance-steps of the last two centuries. But an effective, serviceable notation, able to render the many faces of dance, has yet to be created and made universally applicable. I have paved the way for this and I shall develop it still further. The dances of a Pavlova have already been buried with her. Must we also lose the works of our present dance-generation?

(Rudolf von Laban, *A Life for Dance*, trans. by Lisa Ullmann. London: Macdonald and Evans Ltd., 1975, pp. 183–184)

A Dance Historian at Work

For the theatre historian the daily press is an essential source. If reliable light is to be shed on a period of theatre history, there is no substitute for the plodding hard work that is involved in assembling basic information, for it is only through direct and exhaustive familiarity with contemporary material and the ability to make a balanced personal assessment that one can hope to re-create the past without distortion. There are, of course, other qualities that are indispensable in a ballet historian: an understanding of activities and trends in other branches of the theatre, a mastery of the social scene, familiarity with the literature and art of the period, and of music and how composers regarded writing for the ballet, and the directions in which the thought of the time was moving. Because of these many facets, and because every age views history in a different perspective, there can perhaps be no such thing as the ideal dance historian or the definitive dance history. . . .

An historian's life is never a dull one, for his world is continually expanding as he conjures up figures out of the past who appear to him almost as real as his flesh-and-blood contemporaries. In the hall of our flat is a large and very lovely photograph of Virginia Zucchi, and one evening, as I was quietly working at my desk, I heard Ann [Hutchinson Guest] greeting some of her students who had come to see her notation materials. One of them noticed the picture and commented on it.

"That," said Ann in a very matter-of-fact tone, "is the woman my husband is in love with."

I could sense the moment of awful embarrassment that followed this remark, until Ann, with perfect timing, released the tension.

"But don't worry," she added. "You see, she has been dead these forty years."

I smiled. Only an historian, I thought, can lead a double life with such impunity!

(Ivor Guest, *Adventures of a Ballet Historian: An Unfinished Memoir.* New York: Dance Horizons, 1982, pp. 17, 106)

This aerial view of the beautifully preserved Greek theatre at Epidaurus, dating from the 4th century B.C., shows the close relationship of the semicircular dancing space to the 14,000 spectators. *Photograph by Raymond V. Schoder, SJ.*

2

Glimpses of the Past

A S LONG AS MEN AND WOMEN HAVE LIVED upon this earth, they have danced. The art of movement is among the oldest of the arts. That is not really surprising, for so much about us is in perpetual motion. Rivers run, tides ebb and flow, leaves on trees and grass blades in a meadow all bend or tremble in the wind. The seasons pass. Day gives way to night, and night to a new day. Just as people are always aware of the movement around them, so their bodies may instinctively respond to situations through movement before their minds and tongues have been able to verbalize a response. We cringe with fear, throw up our hands in surprise, or reach out to clasp someone we love. Moving through a world that is itself in motion, people have always danced out their feelings about that world. The origins of dance are rooted in the prehistoric past. Long before dance became a complex art, people delighted in swaying, circling, and stamping out rhythms, just as small children still do. Aware of the movement of the forces of nature, prehistoric peoples moved in ways they hoped would appease those forces or give them new powers of their own. Hunters danced before going off to pursue game, warriors danced before marching into battle. Tribes danced to banish evil spirits and to ask favors of the gods. There were dances to bring rain, dances to celebrate the harvest, dances of birth, puberty, marriage, and death. And there may have been dances that were just for fun.

In one sense, all dances are made similar by use of the human body in motion, but because the body can move in a multitude of ways, dances vary astonishingly from culture to culture. Nevertheless, it is possible to classify dances according to their purpose or function. For example, dances may be divided into three broad categories according to their intent: there are dances performed principally to please the dancers themselves, dances performed to please the gods, and dances performed to please other people. The first category—dances to please the dancers doing them—includes social dancing. It may often be entertaining to watch people in a waltz or the latest pop dance craze. But most such dances are intended to be performed, rather than watched, and many people who are lumbering or graceless can still enjoy themselves enormously on the dance floor. The category of dances to please the gods is that of spiritual, religious, or ceremonial dances. Although such dances may be fascinating to watch, they exist because they are done for some ritualistic purpose.

When the pleasure or edification of onlookers is at least one of the important aspects of a dance, that dance can be said to belong to the category of theatrical dancing. Such dances may not be presented on a stage or in any building that we might recognize as a theatre. Yet if a dance performance in any way emphasizes the distinction between doer and spectator, then it is, at least to some degree, theatrical. Of course, many dances may fit into several categories simultaneously. Certain dances in certain cultures may begin with dancers moving in front of onlookers, only to conclude with performers and spectators all dancing together. And some ceremonial dances may be intended to awe worshipers in a temple as well as to honor the gods in heaven.

This 10th-century A.D. statue of an Indian dancing girl from Rajasthan suggests poses still seen in Indian dance today. *Picture courtesy of the Seattle Art Museum.*

Nevertheless, theatrical dances—dances done by people while other people watch—constitute one of the major forms of dance in cultures around the world, and each great civilization produces its own.

Among the most complex are those of Asia. Like Asian art in general, Asian dance is usually associated with religion and may be contemplative in character. Certain forms of Indian dance exemplify such spiritual dances, for the Hindus believe that the world was created by a dancing god, Lord Shiva. India developed dances containing intricate movements not only for the arms and legs, but for parts of the body often slighted in Western dance, such as the neck, nose, wrists, and eyes.

Some Eastern cultures blended dance with other arts to attain a composite theatrical form. Thus two major styles of Japanese dance, the fastidious Noh and the more robust Kabuki, combine dance with recitation and singing. Similarly, much traditional Chinese theatre makes no firm distinctions among dancing, acting, singing, juggling, and acrobatics.

The most influential of ancient Western civilizations was that of Greece. Believing that dance was divinely inspired, the Greeks allowed the art to play an important part in religion, education, and theatre. Some Greek writers even metaphorically characterized the workings of the universe itself as a cosmic dance. Thus, discussing the order and harmony of the heavenly bodies, the philosopher Plato, in his *Timaeus,* uses choreographic imagery when he speaks of "the choric dances of these stars and their crossings one of another, and the relative reversals and progressions of their orbits."

The Greeks considered dance to be watched over by Terpsichore, one of the nine Muses (goddesses who protected the arts). Hesiod, a poet of the eighth century B.C.E, begins his *Theogony* by praising the Muses who "dance on soft feet about the deep-blue spring" on "the great and holy mount of Helicon." He goes on to say that the Muses were born of the union of Zeus (the ruler of the gods) and Mnemosyne (the spirit of memory) and that they continue to dance on their mount with the Three Graces and Himerus (the spirit of desire).

Two great gods also concerned themselves with dance. Apollo—who, in addition, was the patron of music, poetry, philosophy, and healing—was associated with light: the light of day and, symbolically, the light of the intellect that drives away barbarism. Dionysus was a god of fertility and wine as well as a god of dance. Like wine, his divine powers could induce both cheerful merriment and wildness, and many of his worshipers were known to break loose into riotous dances. Over the centuries, Apollo and Dionysus have come to symbolize two types of art: art notable for its serene majesty and formal balance is often called "Apollonian," whereas art that is emotionally unrestrained or ecstatic is "Dionysiac" (or "Dionysian").

As an art, Greek dance was allied to both poetry and music, and dancers often interpreted poems by means of a complex system of rhythmic body movements known as *cheironomia*. Just as poetry and dance were allied,

so instrumental music was not an autonomous art, as it often is today, but one linked to poetry, song, and movement. The Greeks viewed the union of dance, music, and poetry as symbolic of the harmony of mind and body and, indeed, of civilization itself. At many religious ceremonies everybody danced—the highborn and the lowly, small children and elderly adults—and professionalism tended to be discouraged. Instead, the ideal was

A maenad (or follower of the ecstatic god, Dionysus) plays the krotala, a kind of castanet, in a vase painting by the 6th-century B.C. potter, Andokides. *Courtesy of the Metropolitan Museum of Art, New York.*

the cultivated amateur or well-rounded citizen, rather than the craftsman making a living through a single skill. Consequently, totally professional activities in music and dance were usually left to slaves, freedmen, and foreigners.

MANY GREEK DANCES CAN BE TRACED back to the island of Crete, where a great civilization existed from about 3000 to 1400 B.C.E. Dancing was both a religious rite and an amusement for the Cretans. Among Cretan dances were vigorous male dances involving loud shouts and clanging of weapons that were performed not only to praise military prowess, but also to honor the powers of nature and to frighten evil spirits. Others were religious dances in a circle to invoke the gods, dances in which the participants carried snakes (which were considered sacred), harvest dances, and dances associated with mystic cults.

Crete was conquered by people from mainland Greece known as the Mycenaeans, after their capital, Mycenae, long a major Greek city. It is Mycenaean culture that is celebrated by Homer in the *Iliad,* his epic about the war against Troy (which, by tradition, fell in 1183 B.C.E.). Like many conquerors, the Mycenaeans borrowed from the nations they subdued, and so adopted several Cretan dances. Mycenaean Greece was also swept by waves of dance mania, occasions when, without warning, ordinary people would burst into frenzied movements. The reasons for these outbreaks are unknown, but some historians consider them psychological responses to times of war, pestilence, or privation.

Greece developed distinctive theatrical as well as social and religious dances. When Greek authorities found themselves unable to oppose the wild dances of the followers of Dionysus, they tried to channel the dancers' energies constructively by having them perform rituals at festivals. From such ceremonies came the *dithyramb,* a song-and-dance performance to flute music. Early *dithyrambs* may have been somewhat riotous; Archilochus, writing in the seventh century B.C.E., wryly noted that the imbibing of wine helped one to be an effective *dithyramb* leader. Eventually, *dithyrambs* grew more elevated in tone. According to tradition, Thespis, who led a *dithyrambic* group in the sixth century B.C.E., took a character mentioned in one of the production's songs and assigned it as a role to the leader of the chorus. This bit of impersonation made the *dithyramb* implicitly dramatic, and from it arose the theatrical forms of tragedy and comedy, which flourished in Athens. (The word "tragedy" derives from *tragoidia,* or "goat song," goats being animals sacred to Dionysus.)

The *dithyramb* also continued to exist as an art in itself, so tamed from its tumultuous beginnings that it was a dignified event involving choric songs and dancing. Ten choruses (five of men, five of boys) participated in *dithyrambic* festivals, each chorus of fifty members symbolizing one of the ten tribes of the Athenian people. Awards were given to the best entrants in both the men's and the boys' divisions.

Although much research has been done on the Greek theatre, it is impossible to reconstruct any actual Greek dances. Descriptions of dances survive, and dancers are depicted in sculptures and vase paintings; yet such verbal accounts and pictorial imagery are not necessarily literal depictions of specific dance movements.

However, several types of dances are known to have existed. The vigorous *pyrrhic* dance is said to have been inspired by actions of a soldier in battle such as forward-leaping attacks, withdrawals, and movements to the side to avoid blows. While retaining its formalized offensive and defensive movements, it lost some of its specifically martial aspects as it developed over the years. The *gymnopaedia* resembled the *pyrrhic* dance in vigor, but with movements derived from wrestling rather than warfare. Whereas many Greek dances were performed by only one sex, young men and women danced together in the *hyporchema,* singing choric poems as they moved. All these dances emphasized circular and spiral patterns.

To our eyes, ancient Greek tragedies might appear to be almost semioperatic spectacles: they involved speech, song, chanting, and choreographic movement. The *emmelia,* one of the dances associated with tragedy, may have helped enhance the effect of the theatrical action with stately movements and expressive gestures. Dancing was done by members of a chorus, at first the *dithyrambic* fifty, then twelve, and finally fifteen members. Performances were given in large outdoor amphitheatres. All the participants were male (even though they could be called upon to play women's parts), one of whom acted as leader and was known as the *coryphaeus.* They wore masks and, to facilitate movement, soft slippers.

Greek comedy was often a spectacular blending of song and dance. The dance movement was always lively and sometimes lascivious or obscene. One comic dance form, the *kordax,* was said to involve lewd rotations of the abdomen and buttocks. The *kordax* survived as a solo dance into the era of the Roman Empire.

Dancing formed part of the fancy dinner party entertainment known as the symposium. After a fine meal, the guests at such events were anointed with oil, and garlands (somewhat resembling Hawaiian leis) were placed on their heads and around their necks. Entertainment followed, including music on the lyre and flute and, often, performances by a troupe of professional dancers. At one such party, described by the writer Xenophon in his *Symposium,* the attractions included an acrobatic dance in which a girl juggled twelve hoops, a lyrical dance for a boy, and a love duet that proved so eloquent that the unmarried guests who saw it vowed to get married as soon as possible and the married men rushed home to their wives when it was done.

As ROME CAME TO DOMINATE THE WORLD and the Roman Empire expanded, dance—even in the Greek areas under its domination—became increasingly divorced from poetry, possibly because in the culturally diverse empire it could no longer be taken for granted that everyone in the audience spoke the same language.

A theatrical form that developed in the late days of Greek culture and flourished until the sixth century C.E. in the Roman Empire was what was known as the pantomime. For the Romans, the pantomime was a program, introduced by a plot summary and accompanied by singers and musicians, in which a solo performer portrayed all the characters in a story taken from mythology or history. Often the performer would change costume to indicate the different characters, but the more clever mimes would simply rearrange the folds of their cloaks and convey changes of character entirely through their gestural skills. At times the mimes seem almost to have hypnotized audiences with their dramatic intensity, and women were known to have fainted during performances. Though many of the mimes were dedicated artists, pantomime gradually became both lewd and sensationalistically horrifying. There was a disquietingly violent side to many Roman entertainments. For example, condemned criminals were occasionally forced to dance in an arena until the flammable clothing they wore was set afire and they died in agony.

It is no wonder, then, that such aberrations caused some early Christian moralists to denounce dance. Consequently, Christianity is a religion in which for most of its history dancing has played no regular part in worship services. Traces of the notion that dance is somehow essentially profane still linger in our culture, and choreographic visionaries who have proclaimed the spiritual significance of dance have sometimes been greeted with incomprehension. One of the few dances associated with Christian worship is that of *los seises,* performed by the choirboys who have danced in the cathedral of Seville, Spain, on church holidays since the fifteenth century and perhaps even earlier. No matter what official attitudes toward dance may have been, nothing has ever made people stop dancing.

Not all theologians and philosophers condemned dance. Instead, some criticized it only when it was accompanied by drunkenness or lewdness. Several thinkers even found deep spiritual significance in dance. St. Clement of Alexandria (c. 150–c. 220 C.E.) described pious Christians dancing ecstatically while they prayed. Plotinus (c. 205–270 C.E.), the founder of a philosophical theory called Neoplatonism, believed that everything in the universe is linked to every other thing and that a change in one part of the universe will also affect other parts of it, just as changes in one's limbs may affect states of tension and relaxation throughout one's body— an image that likens the workings of the universe to the movements of a dancer. Another image of unity was devised at the end of the fifth century C.E. by the philosopher known as Dionysius the Pseudo-Areopagite (the name Dionysius should not be confused with that of the Greek god Dionysus). Dionysius envisioned the universe as a great chain of being in which everything was joined to everything else by divine love and moved eternally in a vast choric dance.

DANCE WAS AN IMPORTANT PART OF LIFE in the Middle Ages for aristocrats and common people alike. There was dancing by peasants at street fairs and by noble lords and ladies in castle halls. Dancing was also a part of the entertainments sponsored by the medieval guilds.

Each guild was composed of members of a certain profession and existed to protect workers in that profession, to supervise employment conditions, and to maintain high standards of craftsmanship. Many guilds acquired considerable political power, and some were permitted to hold public celebrations, especially during such feasts as the carnivals that preceded Lent. Several types of dancing were a part of these festivals. During processionals through the streets, guild members might dance with running or skipping steps. These revelers were often fantastically costumed—like the bakers of Strasbourg, who wore ribboned costumes with bells on their feet, blackened their faces, and rushed about carrying hoops adorned with ivy. When the processional stopped for a period of time—at an inn, a private home, or the guildhall itself—there would be social dances. Finally, in the town square, guild members would perform dances specifically associated with the guild that no one else was allowed to do.

Medieval dances included both dances to instrumental music and vocal dances, which were performed to songs sung by spectators or by the dancers themselves. Indoor dances were accompanied by flute, lute, viola da gamba, and other stringed instruments prized for their softness of sound.

Among the festive medieval dances were the *ductia,* a particular favorite of the wealthy, and the *stantipes,* which, because of its complexities, was thought to prevent the thoughts of its performers from straying to vulgar matters. The *estampie* was a stately dance for couples that some scholars believe developed around 1400 into the *basse danse* (or *bassadanze*), a slow-moving dance with low, elegant steps that derived its name from the French *basse* and the Italian *bassa,* both meaning "low."

Two other graceful forms, the *round* and the *carol,* were group dances that featured circular patterns. The fact that the word *carol* survives today to describe a festive Christmas song is a reminder that the medieval *carol* was a danced song during which a musician or group of musicians would sing the verses while onlookers or the dancers themselves answered with the refrain. Thus Jehan Maillart, a fourteenth-century French writer, describes one convivial occasion when, after all "had washed their hands, the carols began. Those ladies who had sweet voices sang loudly; everyone answered them joyfully, anyone who knew how to sing, sang thus."

Many lusty dances were examples of the *moresca,* a form that developed in the twelfth century and enjoyed popularity throughout Europe for several centuries thereafter. A well-known English variant of the *moresca* is the morris dance. The *moresca* featured bizarre movements, and participants wore masks or blackened their faces to make themselves look exotic. Several types of *moresca* existed. One was a solo dance in which the performer capered like a fool or jester. There were also line and circle dances. And some such dances were conceived as mock battles with combatants divided into groups corresponding to opposed armies. Such dances might reflect the actual battles that were taking place between Christians and Moors in Spain, or they might symbolize the triumph of spring over winter or any allegorical struggle between good and evil. Because folk tradition decreed that evil spirits could be banished by noise, bells became a feature of *moresca* costumes.

In the dance of death, death confronts people of all estates before leading them in a dance to the grave. From Dietrich Briesenmeister, *Bilder des Todes. Courtesy of the Dance Collection, The New York Public Library.*

Dancing was a subject beloved by medieval artists. One favorite allegorical theme was the dance of death, which depicted a skeleton leading mortals of every social estate linked together in a dance suggesting the grim democracy of the grave. If such pictures were only artists' fancies, equally strange dances existed in reality. Presumably as the result of some form of mass hysteria, just as in Mycenaean Greece, outbreaks of dance mania might occur, often in the midst of church services when whole congregations felt possessed by an unaccountable urge to cavort. And the dancing at carnivals could turn riotous.

In castles and palaces, dances served as party entertainments. One such entertainment, the *Bal des Ardents* of 1393, nearly claimed the life of Charles VI, the king of France. Charles and several lords decided it might be amusing to dance before the court in a *moresca,* disguising themselves as savages. They were chained to one another and dressed in strange costumes covered with tow and pitch. Apparently their makeup was so successful that no one could identify the revelers, and when the duke of Orléans leaned forward with a torch for a closer look, he accidentally set fire to the dancers' costumes. Luckily the king, who had decided that he would rather chat with a duchess than dance, had slipped his chains. The duchess protected him from the flames by throwing the train of her dress over him. The other dancers died, save for one gentleman who broke the chain and doused himself in a tub of water.

WITH THE COMING OF THE RENAISSANCE, court dance flourished, particularly in Italy. At that time, Italy was not a unified nation but a collection of squabbling states. Their reigning princes continually sought ways to increase their prestige and impress their neighbors. One way to do so was to create a brilliant court life through the encouragement of art and learning. Ostentatious by nature, dance could easily proclaim a court's brilliance and taste. It was in Italy that the first dancing masters appeared, among them Domenico of Piacenza, who around 1400 wrote the first surviving European treatise on dancing; his followers Antonio Cornazano and Guglielmo Ebreo (William the Jew) were often in demand as producers of dances for state occasions. The very word "ballet" is of Italian origin, derived from the verb *ballare,* "to dance."

Italian dance spectacles could be both lavish and curious. A particularly famous example is the "dinner-ballet" that Bergonzio di Botto produced in 1489 at a banquet celebrating the marriage of the duke of Milan. Vaguely reminiscent of a modern nightclub floor show, it consisted of several loosely related scenes, each based on classical mythology, yet in some way appropriate to a particular course of the meal. Jason's Argonauts captured the Golden Fleece (the guests were served roast lamb), Diana went hunting (the guests fell upon a stag), and the fish arrived to dances by sea gods.

Guests at such spectacles loved these entertainments, and the nobles who sponsored them found them effective ways of displaying their culture and munificence. Consequently these courtly displays remained in vogue, and out of them emerged a regal and splendiferous form of theatrical dancing.

Related Readings

An Ancient Greek Dance

And there were young men on it [Achilles' shield] and young girls
   sought for their beauty

with gifts of oxen, dancing, and holding hands at the wrist. These

wore, the maidens long light robes, but the men wore tunics

of finespun work and shining softly, touched with olive oil.

And the girls wore fair garlands on their heads, while the young men

carried golden knives that hung from sword-belts of silver.

And whiles on their understanding feet they would run very lightly,

as when a potter crouching makes trial of his wheel, holding

it close in his hands, to see if it will run smooth. At another

time they would form rows, and run, rows crossing each other.

And around the lovely chorus of dancers stood a great multitude

happily watching, while among the dancers two acrobats

led the measures of song and dance revolving among them.

(Homer, Description of Achilles's shield in *The Iliad,* trans. by Richmond Lattimore. Chicago: University of Chicago Press, 1951; repro 1967, p. 391)

Sappho Watches a Dance

And their feet move

Rhythmically, as tender
feet of Cretan girls
danced once around an

altar of love, crushing
a circle in the soft
smooth flowering grass

(*Sappho,* trans. by Mary Barnard. Berkeley and Los Angeles: University of California Press, 1958; repro 1967, No. 23)

Plutarch Describes Greek Dancing

Cakes were brought in, to be the prize for dancing by the boys. My brother Lamprias was appointed, along with Meniscus the trainer, to be judge, as he gave a convincing performance of the pyrrhic dance and had been thought better at shadow-fighting than any of the boys in the wrestling schools. Many boys now danced with more zest than art: there were two who gained approval, attempting to preserve gracefulness throughout; some of the company demanded that these two should dance phrases alternately.

Thrasybulus inquired the meaning of the word "phrase," and gave Ammonius the opportunity of giving at some length an exposition of the elements of dancing, which he said were three in number: the phrase, the pose, and pointing. "Dancing," he explained, "consists of movements and positions, as melody of its notes and intervals. In the case of dancing the rests are the terminating points of the movements. Now they call the movements 'phrases,' while 'poses' is the name of the representational positions to which the movements lead and in which they end, as when dancers compose their bodies in the attitude of Apollo or Pan or a Bacchant, and then retain that aspect like figures in a picture. The third element, pointing, is something that does not copy the subject-matter, but actually shows it to us. Poetry provides a parallel. Poets employ the proper names of things to indicate or denote them, using the words 'Achilles,' 'Odysseus,' 'earth,' and 'heaven' exactly as they are used by the ordinary man, but employ onomatopoeia and metaphor in their pursuit of imitative representation and vivid suggestion. Thus they say that broken streams 'plash' and 'babble,' and that missiles fly 'longing to take their fill of flesh' . . . Similarly in dancing the pose is imitative of shape and outward appearance. The phrase again is expressive of some emotion or action or potentiality. By pointing they literally indicate objects: the earth, the sky, themselves, or bystanders. If this is done with precision, so to say, and timing, it resembles proper names in poetry when they are uttered with a measure of ornament and smoothness. . . ."

(Plutarch, "Table-Talk," in *Moralia,* Vol. 9, trans. by Edwin L. Minar Jr., F.H. Sandbach, and w.e. Helmbold. London: William Heinemann Ltd., 1919, pp. 289–291, 293)

The Roman Pantomimes

The term "pantomime," which was introduced by the Italian Greeks, is an apt one, and scarcely exaggerates the artist's versatility. . . . It is his profession to show forth human character and passion in all their variety; to depict love and anger, frenzy and grief, each in its due measure. Wondrous art! . . .

Other arts call out only one half of a man's powers—the bodily or the mental: the pantomime combines the two. His performance is as much an intellectual as a physical exercise: there is meaning in his movements; every gesture has its significance; and therein lies his chief excellence. . . .

All professions hold out some object, either of utility or of pleasure: Pantomime is the only one that secures both these objects; now the utility that is combined with pleasure is doubled in value. Who would choose to look on at a couple of young fellows spilling their blood in a boxing match, or wrestling in the dust, when he may see the same subject represented by the pantomime, with the additional advantages of safety and elegance, and with the far greater pleasure to the spectator? The vigorous movements of the pantomime—turn and twist, bend and spring—afford at once a gratifying spectacle to the beholder and a wholesome training to the performer; I maintain that no gymnastic exercise is its equal for beauty and for the uniform development of the physical powers—of agility, suppleness, and elasticity, as of solid strength.

Consider then the universality of this art: it sharpens the wits, it exercises the body, it delights the spectator, it instructs him in the history of bygone days, while eye and ear are held beneath the spell of flute and cymbal and of graceful dance. . . .

But in pantomime, as in rhetoric, there can be (to use a popular phrase) too much of a good thing; a man may exceed the proper bounds of imitation; what should be great may become monstrous, softness may be exaggerated into effeminacy, and the courage of a man into the ferocity of a beast. I remember seeing this exemplified in the case of an actor of repute. In most respects a capable, nay, an admirable performer, some strange fatality ran him aground upon this reef of over enthusiasm. He was acting the madness of Ajax, just after he has been worsted by Odysseus; and so lost control of himself, that one might have been excused for thinking his madness was something more than feigned. . . . the illiterate riff-raff, who knew not good from bad, and had no idea of decency, regarded it as a supreme piece of acting; and the more intelligent part of the audience, realizing how things stood . . . saw only too clearly that it was not Ajax but the pantomime who was mad.

(Lucian, *Works,* trans. by H.W. and F.G. Fowler. Vol. 3, *Of Pantomime.* Oxford: Clarendon Press, 1905, pp. 249–263; also in A.M. Nagler, ed., *A Source Book in Theatrical History.* New York: Dover, 1959, pp. 29–30, 33)

Stanzas from a Vocal Estampie

I

Neither May Day nor the beech tree's leaves nor the song of birds nor gladiolus flowers are pleasing to me, noble and vivacious lady, until

I receive a swift messenger from your fair person to tell me of some new pleasure that love brings me; and may I be joined to you and drawn toward you, perfect lady; and may the jealous one fall stricken before I must leave you. [Refrain:] (And may I be joined . . .)

II
My sweet beloved, for the sake of God, may the jealous one never laugh at my pain, for his jealousy would be very costly if it were to separate two such lovers; for I would never be joyful again, nor would joy be of any benefit to me without you; I would set out on such a road that no one would ever see me again; on that day would I die, worthy lady, that I lost you. (And may I be joined . . .)

III
How shall my lady be lost, or restored to me if she has not yet been mine? For a man or woman is not a lover just by thinking so. But when a suitor is accepted as a lover, the reputation that he gains is greatly enhanced, and the attractive appearance causes much stir; but I have not held you naked nor conquered you in any other sense; I have only desired and believed in you, without any further encouragement. (And may I be joined . . .)

[Sections IV and V are omitted.]

VI
Worthy lady, everyone praises and proclaims your merit which is so pleasing; and whoever would forget you places little value on his life; therefore I worship you, distinguished lady, for I have singled you out as the most pleasing and the best, accomplished in worth, and I have courted you and served you better than Eric did Enide. Lord Engles [the poet's patron] I have constructed and completed the estampida. (And may I be joined . . .)

(Raimbaut de Vaqueiras [c. 1155–1205], "Kalenda Maya," trans. by Robert Taylor, in Timothy J. McGee, *Medieval Instrumental Dances*. Bloomington: Indiana University Press, 1989, p. 51)

A Priest Chides

The man who brings actors and mimes and dancers to his house knows not what a bevy of unclean spirits follow them.

(Alcuin [English priest, eighth century C.E,] in Lincoln Kirstein, *Dance: A Short History of Classical Theatrical Dancing*. New York: G.P. Putnam's Sons, 1935; Anniversary Edition, Princeton, N.J.: Princeton Book Company, Publishers, 1987, p. 61)

The Psalmist Praises

Praise ye the Lord, Praise God in his sanctuary: praise him in the firmament of his power.

Praise him for his mighty acts: praise him according to his excellent greatness.

Praise him with the sound of the trumpet: praise him with the psaltery and harp.

Praise him with the timbrel and dance: praise him with stringed instruments and organs.

Praise him upon the loud cymbals: praise him upon the high sounding cymbals.

Let everything that hath breath praise the Lord. Praise ye the Lord.

(The Bible, Old Testament, King James Version, Psalm 150)

3

Dance at the Royal Courts

ON OCTOBER 15, 1581, AN AUDIENCE OF NOBLES gathered in the Salle Bourbon near the Louvre Palace in Paris to witness what promised to be a most splendid entertainment. The occasion was the marriage of Marguerite de Lorraine, sister of Queen Louise, to the Duc de Joyeuse. The monarch of the time was Henri III, but the important power behind the throne, the one who influenced all political affairs, was the king's mother, Catherine de Medici. Years before she had left her native Italy as the bride of the duke who eventually became Henri II.

Catherine was shrewd, strong-minded, unscrupulous, and autocratic. A force to be reckoned with in politics, she also liked to set styles in manners and the arts. She brought with her from Italy into France the fashion for cosmetics and face powder, and by covering the walls of her Paris mansion with 119 mirrors, she helped create a fashion for large wall mirrors. She also introduced a now-common dinner utensil into France: the fork, at a time when even nobles customarily ate only with their fingers or a knife. A lover of opulence, she wanted to make sure that Marguerite de Lorraine's marriage would be a grand occasion. She sought assistance from one of her valets, a fellow Italian named Baldassarino da Belgiojoso, who was known in France as Balthasar de Beaujoyeulx.

A musician and dancing master, Beaujoyeulx was also what we today would call a choreographer, a maker of dances, and for Catherine he staged an entertainment that surely met her requirements: the *Ballet Comique de la Reine* (originally called *Balet Comique de la Royne)*, which has come to be regarded as the most important early attempt to create an extended

Jacques Patin's engraving of the first scene of the *Ballet Comique de la Reine* shows the Fugitive Gentleman addressing the King in the Salle Bourbon with Pan's grove, right, the golden vault (containing the musicians), left, and, at the rear, Circe's castle and garden. *Courtesy of the Music Division, The New York Public Library.*

choreographic spectacle. Although it was termed a "ballet," it only vaguely resembled anything we now associate with that term.

There was no stage. The action took place on the floor of the hall itself. The audience sat above the performers in galleries along three walls and the royal family on a dais at one end of the room. Despite the word *comique* in its title, the work was not funny, for *comique* in this case derives from *comédie,* the French word that can refer to drama in general. In addition to dances, this ballet contained recitations and songs with music by Lambert de Beaulieu and Jacques Salmon. The plot concerned the attempts of the enchantress Circe to conquer nature with her witchcraft and proclaim herself queen of the seasons. However, the gods vanquish her, and Minerva, goddess of wisdom, pays tribute to a greater queen—the queen of France. Louise, the object of this flattery, actually participated in the production, making an entrance accompanied by court ladies on a moving float adorned with sirens and tritons that spouted water like a fountain. At the conclusion of the ballet—which lasted nearly six hours—symbolic medals were exchanged; the one Queen Louise gave her husband bore the image of a dolphin. Since the royal couple did not have a son and since, in French, *dauphin* can refer both to the sea creature and to an heir apparent, the medal's Latin inscription, *Delphinum ut delphinem rependat,* was a matrimonial pun: "A dolphin is given to receive a dauphin."

In addition to such specifically personal and political references, the *Ballet Comique* contained general moral significance, for Circe represented the base passions of humanity and the divinities who defeated her included not only Minerva but also Pan (symbolizing the power of nature) and Jupiter (the ruler of the gods).

The *Ballet Comique* must have lived up to Catherine's expectations. She certainly wanted the rest of Europe to know about it, for she distributed illustrated descriptions of it across the Continent. It was the most lavish of the theatrical entertainments she loved to produce, but other spectacles at her court had also attracted attention—for example, *Le Ballet des Polonais,* an entertainment presented in honor of the Polish ambassadors in 1573. Beaujoyeulx devised the choreography, which emphasized geometrical patterns, and among the collaborators on the production were the composer Orlando di Lasso and the poet Pierre Ronsard.

Mlle de Chaumont, as Minerva, goddess of wisdom, in the *Ballet Comique de la Reine,* entered in a chariot drawn by a serpent (or monster), typical of the production's elaborate effects. *Courtesy of the Music Division, The New York Public Library.*

Le Ballet Comique and other such works were inspired by theories promulgated by the Académie de Musique et de la Poésie, an organization founded in 1570 by the poet Jean-Antoine de Baïf and the composer Thibault de Courville. They and their followers announced that they wished to revive the poetry, music, and dance of the ancient world. Their actual knowledge of Greek and Roman history might seem inadequate to today's scholars, but they were important for envisioning theatre as a composite art form uniting the separate disciplines of poetry, music, dance, and stage design.

Many plots of Renaissance stage spectacles derived from literary sources and contained spoken or sung verses known as *récits.* Booklets containing their words as well as explanations of the ballet's symbolic content were frequently distributed to the audience.

RENAISSANCE COURT SPECTACLES could often be ornate indeed. Nevertheless, all in a sense were amateur theatricals because they were performed by nobles, rather than professional entertainers. The steps in these ballets differed little from those of the era's ballroom dances; the theatrical form was simply more polished and studied.

Among the sixteenth- and seventeenth-century dances, many are known to us and can be reconstructed from dancing masters' notations and descriptions. One popular dance was the ceremonious pavane, which, in the ballroom, was often coupled with the galliard, a lively dance with leaps and kicking steps. Other dances were the swift courante, which contained running and gliding steps; the volta (or lavolta), in which, assisted by the gentleman, the lady leaped and turned in midair; and the slow-paced sarabande, which some moralists branded lascivious. These and other dances could all be incorporated into ballets. When they were, the female roles were customarily played by men or boys, although women were free to participate in them in the ballroom. Men were assigned jumps and the fancy steps, while the steps for women stressed grace, lightness, and restraint. However, as the Renaissance proceeded, steps grew increasingly intricate and, to facilitate the learning of some of the more complex ones, dancing masters often recommended that their pupils practice them by hanging on to the backs of chairs or to a tightly stretched rope for support. From this custom developed the *barre,* now a standard feature of every ballet classroom.

In addition to teaching ballroom dances and staging ballets, the dancing master was expected to set standards of etiquette and deportment. An example of such a linking of art and manners is found in a charming dance manual of 1588 called *Orchésographie.* Written by Thoinot Arbeau, the pseudonym of a benign, worldly French priest named Jehan Tabourot, *Orchésographie* consists of dialogues between Arbeau and his young pupil Capriol, and discusses several popular dances as well as military marching, flute and drum playing, seemly behavior, and proper grooming. Thus Arbeau warns Capriol, "Spit and blow your nose sparingly, or if needs must turn your head away and use a fair white handkerchief. . . . Be suitably and neatly dressed, your hose well secured and your shoes clean. . . ."

Another important dancing master was Fabritio Caroso, whose *Nobiltà di Dame,* published in 1600, is now considered an invaluable document because it contains examples of completely choreographed dances. Like Arbeau, Caroso offered advice on etiquette and on the various social situations that might arise during the course of a ball, including the problem of "What the Lady is to do if she is *not* invited to dance."

In Arbeau's time dancing, like riding and fencing, was considered one of the arts of a gentleman. So were fine points of behavior, including the seemingly simple act of bowing, which could become intricate both on stage in ballets and offstage in court life. Sometimes various skills were combined, as when it was discovered that horses could be taught to dance. The horse ballet, which enjoyed a certain popularity from the sixteenth century onward, consisted of horses dancing in complicated formations, their trainers serving as both riding masters and dancing masters.

A descendant of these horse ballets is what is known today as *haute école* riding, and among the attractions of Vienna are the white Lipizzaner stallions of the Spanish Riding School, which dance with great refinement in an elegant ballroom built for them in 1729.

Like the *Ballet Comique de la Reine,* many productions were designed for halls in which spectators sat above the action. This led dancing masters to stress geometrical floor patterns with dancers forming figures, such as squares, diamonds, ovals, and triangles. The age delighted in allegory, and symbolical meanings could be assigned to some of these figures. According

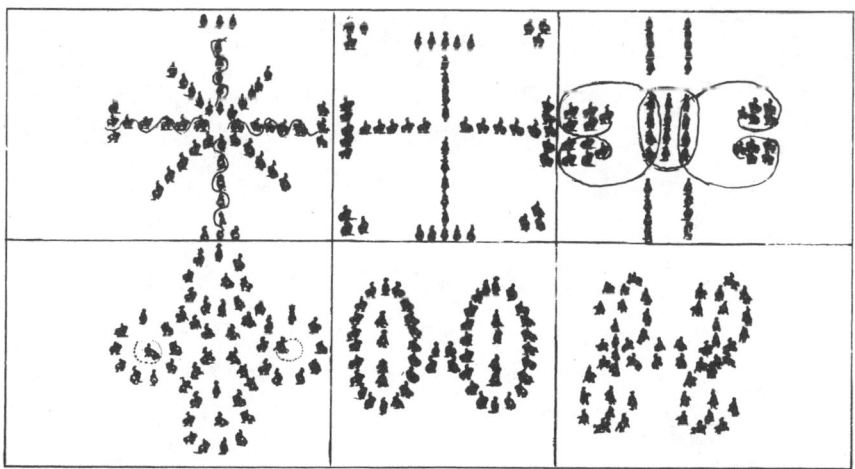

The designs show figures typical of a 1652 horse ballet. *Courtesy of the Dance Collection, The New York Public Library.*

to an account of 1619, triangles symbolize Justice, three circles conjoined mean Truth Known, a square within a square indicates Virtuous Design, and three circles within one another represent Perfect Truth. By means of choreographic patterns, dancers could also form letters of the alphabet or words. Thus, in Sir William Davenant's *Salmacida Spolia,* an English masque of 1640, an ensemble of nymphs spelled out "Anna Regina," a reference to Anne of Denmark, mother of Charles I. The philosopher Francis Bacon scoffed that "Turning dances into figures is a childish curiosity," and sober-sided adults might agree with him. Yet the child in us ever welcomes such curiosities: witness such comparable twentieth-century phenomena as football half-time drills or the precision chorus routines of Busby Berkeley movies.

Dancing may have been an art of the gentleman. Nevertheless, in one community, Seville, Spain—that city where choirboys danced in the cathedral—women achieved considerable importance as choreographers

John Webb's engraving of the final scene of *Salmacida Spolia* (1640) depicts a typical apotheosis of the masques of Inigo Jones. *Courtesy of the Trustees of the Chatsworth Settlement, Devonshire Collection, Chatsworth.*

during the sixteenth and the first two thirds of the seventeenth centuries. Seville celebrated occasions such as religious feasts, royal births, and the arrival of visiting dignitaries with elaborate processions during which dancers marched from the cathedral through the city streets. On their return, they performed both before the cathedral and on specially built stages in public plazas. Their offerings ranged from suites of theatricalized versions of ballroom dances to dramatic works on religious, historical, and mythological themes.

Although all women in these troupes were required to be married, they possessed great artistic freedom. From the 1570s to the 1660s, among those who had careers as choreographers were Leonora Rica, Germana Ortiz, Ana de Medina, Josefa de Cespedes, Juana Valentin de Medina, and Felipa de San Francisca.

DANCING BECAME THE VOGUE at virtually all the courts of Renaissance Europe. England's Queen Elizabeth I loved to dance, and the story has come down to us that every morning she leaped through six or seven galliards as a setting-up exercise. Theatrical spectacles containing dancing were popular in Great Britain from the time of Henry VIII. However, they attained their most elaborate form in the seventeenth-century masques written by Ben Jonson and designed by Inigo Jones. The masque was an aristocratic entertainment in which poetic declamations, songs, and dances—often on serious allegorical themes—were interspersed with contrasting grotesque interludes known as antimasques. At the conclusion, the audience was invited to join with the performers in a dance, and thus theatergoing merged with party giving. More than conviviality was involved in such minglings. The sight of everyone dancing together could be interpreted as an image of social harmony and stability. During the 1630s, Charles I played leading roles in some masques. But in *Salmacida Spolia,* the last of the court masques, he portrayed the king of a troubled realm, a piece of casting that suggested his own political troubles as a monarch.

Although English masques contained many dance sequences, the way their authors stressed literary content over choreography has made them ultimately more important to the history of theatre than to the history of dance. Nevertheless, the masque did exert some influence on the development of dance on the British stage. The grotesque and fantastical dances that occurred in the operas and theatrical spectacles composed by Henry Purcell between 1689 and 1695 can be seen as an outgrowth of the masque tradition. Purcell's opera *Dido and Aeneas* received its premiere in 1689 at a boarding school run by a dancing master, Josias Priest, who choreographed the work. In addition to showing off the singers, it displayed the dancing ability of Priest's pupils. Priest and Purcell collaborated on several subsequent works.

Charles I is seen as Philogenes in this masque. *Courtesy of the Trustees of the Chatsworth Settlement, Devonshire Collection, Chatsworth.*

It was in France that ballet became particularly important. The French looked to Italy because it was the source of so many remarkable developments in art, music, and dance; and as the splendor of the French court increased, Italian artists, composers, and dancing masters sought positions in France. Adopted by the French court as a result of this interest in Italian culture, ballet soon took root and flourished. French aristocrats admired fine manners and made social encounters as intricate as choreography. Dance prospered in such an environment and, consequently, balletic deportment is aristocratic in nature and ballet steps retain French names. Today, ballet remains an art whose skilled practitioners can attain all the airs and graces of French aristocrats, a rank earned through talent and discipline, rather than through mere accident of birth.

Louis XIII danced in court ballets, for which he occasionally also wrote the scenario and the music. As one might expect of a monarch, he often appeared in dignified roles, as when, in 1617, he portrayed the spirit of fire— a cleanser of impurity in the *Ballet Délivrance de Renaud,* a work inspired by Torquato Tasso's epic poem, *Gerusalemme Liberata (Jerusalem Delivered).* The scenario concerned a man's deliverance from an evil sorceress.

The combination of that plot and the king's casting of himself as a cleansing force might have made the audience interpret the action as an allegory, for Louis had just freed himself from various political factions and conspiracies.

Yet the production was not entirely solemn. It contained spectacular magical scenes in which the sorceress conjured up demons in the form of crayfish, tortoises, and snails, all of which were transformed into comic old people. Nor was Louis always sedate as a performer. Indeed, he enjoyed playing comic roles and was particularly fond of portraying women.

A popular form of entertainment in this time was the *ballet à entrée,* a series of independent scenes ranging from the serious to the fantasti cal, linked together by a broad general theme. The episodic construction of these ballets made possible works that could be as simple or as lavish as circumstances required, and they contained roles for a wide variety of character types. Thus, the cast for the *Ballet des Fées de la Fôret de Saint-Germain* of 1625 included roulette players, Spanish dancers, warriors, doctors, and headhunters. The grotesque scenes in such works often called for performers far more agile than even the most well-rehearsed dancing

An *entrée* based on sports in a *ballet de cour* called *Le Ballet des Fées des Fôrets de Saint-Germain* included a dance by players of the game *Balle forcée. Courtesy of the Cabinet des Dessins, Musée du Louvre.*

courtier. Therefore, after 1630, professional entertainers began to be hired, and as choreography grew more demanding the number of professionals increased.

Whereas the clergy in some countries disparaged dancing, in France the Jesuit order encouraged it. Two leading academic schools of seventeenth-century Paris, the Collège d'Harcourt and the Collège de Clermont, were run by the Jesuits, and at both dancing was prominently featured in their annual school plays. A priest, Père Ménéstrier, even became an influential writer on dance in the 1680s.

Several changes in ballet occurred during the seventeenth century. The most important of them was that ballet moved out of ballrooms and halls and into proscenium theatres. The rich scenic possibilities of the proscenium theatre became evident when Cardinal Mazarin, who sponsored Italian opera in Paris, invited Giacomo Torelli, one of the greatest Italian stage designers of the era, to work for him. The proscenium theatre proved to be ideally suited for dance presentations. Because most members of the audience now faced the stage straight-on, choreographers could emphasize individual human figures as well as massed ensembles.

This factor further hastened ballet's professionalization. The proscenium theatre stressed ballet as something to be seen by others, whereas it had been something seen and done by the same people: a performance by courtiers for their fellow courtiers. Now, the proscenium arch helped to separate doer and watcher. At first, that separation was not great. In early proscenium theatres, ramps extending from the stage to the auditorium floor permitted performers and spectators to dance together at the end of the ballet. Furthermore, until well into the eighteenth century, members of the audience were permitted to sit on the stage.

FRENCH COURT BALLET REACHED ITS PEAK under Louis XIV, who reigned from 1643 to 1715. Dance was always part of his life. Even his birth was celebrated by an entertainment called the *Ballet de la Félicité*. Louis began to dance as a boy and Cardinal Mazarin, who supervised his education, was accused of stressing dancing lessons over grammar lessons. Louis first danced in public in 1651 at the age of thirteen, and by the time he was a young man he was appearing several times a week in ballets. He took

Thomas Rowlandson's print of London's King's Theatre shows the wide forestage typical of theatres of the period. *Courtesy of the Dance Collection, The New York Public Library.*

ballet very seriously. Indeed, it was in a ballet that he was able to become the living embodiment of one of his most famous epithets, the "Sun King." Louis was always associated with the sun. With their gilt bronzes and golden curtains and embroideries, his palatial quarters glowed as brightly as the sun. A medal struck at his birth proclaimed him *Orbis Solis Gallici* (The Risen Sun of Gaul). In 1653 he portrayed the Rising Sun in the *Ballet de la Nuit,* a symbolic account of the times of day. During its penultimate episode, thieves in the night try to loot a burning house, but in the conclusion Aurora enters, bringing with her the Rising Sun accompanied by Honor, Grace, Love, Riches, Victory, Fame, and Peace. This was no simple, harmless allegory. Only two years before, a mob had invaded the Palais Royal to protest high taxes and poor living conditions. But since then dissent had been stamped out; France was not to be a burning house: the Rising Sun, the absolute monarch, would reign triumphant—yet his reign would be accompanied by virtue. The *Ballet de la Nuit* gave its audience a moral lesson to ponder.

The self-proclaimed incarnation of *gloire,* Louis tried to make his entire life a theatrical spectacle. Frequent royal visits and processions placed him in full view. Even dining, getting up, and going to bed were ceremonial occasions that others might behold. The course of Louis's day became as regular as the sun, as measured as a dance. Art and life were virtually one and the same for him and his court. No wonder ballet was admired. Its formality must have made it seem the apotheosis of the social structure and the triumph of order. In ballets, courtiers could portray gods and heroes, and offstage they could model themselves on such balletic characters as Apollo or Alexander the Great. It is not surprising that the Greek gods appealed to aristocrats. Not only were these mythological deities larger than life, they were also human in their physical features and endowed with the virtues of courage, strength, elegance, and mental acuity. Although their powers exceeded those of ordinary mortals, they were not so otherworldly as to be beyond a capacity for wit and playfulness. Customarily masked as they

The young Louis XIV represents the sun god, Apollo, in the *Ballet de la Nuit. Courtesy of the Bibliotheque Naionale, Paris.*

danced their roles, courtiers were in a sense playing roles offstage as well, for they displayed to the world artfully designed facades of fine manners. Since court life was artifice, personality was impersonation.

French public life began to resemble a theatrical spectacle. People felt a need to see and to be seen. Architects and city planners rebuilt Paris, making it a city of handsome squares and parks—all of which might be likened to stages on which people could present themselves. City squares—the meeting points of several streets—were also social meeting points, gathering places in which people could assemble. (Today, centuries later, city squares still serve that purpose.) Outside Paris, the gardens of the great royal palace at Versailles had their own imposing avenues and promenades.

Louis XIV chose some of the finest talents of his day to collaborate on ballets. The poet Isaac de Benserade contributed scenarios; Jean Bérain designed lavish scenery and costumes. Through ingenious stage machinery, Bérain could create the illusions of storms, flying gods, and collapsing palaces. His costumes of brocade or velour featured pearls, diamonds, plumes, and gold and silver embroidery. All that glitter was not entirely for ostentation. In candlelit theatres, shiny surfaces—be they jeweled necklaces or mere buttons and shoe buckles—picked up light and helped make figures more visible. So, too, in ballrooms the reflection of candles in wall mirrors helped brighten the space.

Many costumes of the period were inspired by the heroic styles of the Roman Empire, but little scholarly research was involved in designing them and consequently they suggested an antique world of the imagination, rather than any specific historical period. Certainly no ancient Roman ever wore a *tonnelet,* the wide hooped skirt of mid-thigh length that served as the standard costume for male dancers until well into the eighteenth century.

Productions at the court of Louis XIV could be lavish indeed. However, the only surviving notated record of a complete theatrical entertainment of that time is a modest piece: *Le Mariage de la Grosse Cathos (Fat Kate's Marriage),* a comic *ballet-mascarade* of 1688. Somewhat similar to a *ballet à entrée* in form, a *mascarade* was a little work in which songs, dances, and spoken texts were held together by a slender dramatic pretext. *Mascarades* were often performed during masked balls, particularly in the carnival season just before Lent.

Le Mariage concerns a village wedding during which a gargantuan young woman is married off to a country bumpkin. The entire cast was male, and the arias for its obese heroine—who sang as well as danced—are in the baritone range. The complete score by André Danican Philidor *l'aîné* (the elder) and the choreography by Jean Favier, as recorded in notation, were preserved in the royal library. However, whereas the music was easily readable, Favier's personal notation system was considered totally unintelligible until it was deciphered in the 1980s by two American scholars, Carol G. Marsh and Rebecca Harris-Warrick.

MANY MUSICAL SCORES FOR COURT BALLETS were composed by Jean Baptiste Lully, who came to France as a child from his native Florence, where he had been a comic dancer. In Italy, he had also become familiar with commedia dell'arte, a robust, popular form of drama that flourished from the mid-sixteenth century onward. Members of commedia dell' arte troupes had to be versatile, able to act, sing, dance, and play musical instruments. The vigorous, fast-paced commedia shows, featuring character types such as Arlecchino, Pulcinella, Pantalone, Brighella, the meddling Dottore, and the braggart Capitano, greatly influenced French ballet and theatre, particularly French comedy.

Lully entered the service of Louis XIV in 1653. A fine comedian, he was said to be able to make Louis weep with laughter. Although Lully danced in some thirty ballets, his greatest importance was as a composer of elegant, sophisticated music. A ruthless schemer in his private life, he dominated the French musical scene and, because of the power he wielded, he was hated as well as respected. Therefore, it is easy to understand why he once feared that a rival was trying to poison him by mixing arsenic with his tobacco. Although a husband and a father, Lully was also a homosexual whose behavior was considered so scandalous that the king occasionally found it necessary to chide him for his excesses. Lully died in 1687 after a freak accident. He pierced his foot with the staff he used to beat time during concerts and, as a result, a fatal gangrenous abscess developed.

To a modern viewer, theatrical productions of Lully's time might seem hybrids: operas contained dancing, ballets contained songs and poetic recitations. If dance was not regarded as an autonomous art, the mixing of arts could lead to productions of great sumptuousness. For example, *Les Plaisirs de l'Ile Enchantée* of 1664 was a three-day festivity at Versailles that involved ballet, drama, fireworks, mock combats, and banqueting. The mixing of arts also occurred in a lighthearted manner in the *comédie-ballet,* a form developed by Lully and the great comic playwright Molière. Consisting of spoken dialogue interspersed with danced interludes, this theatrical genre can be considered a distant ancestor of the musical comedy. One of its finest examples, Molière's *Le Bourgeois Gentilhomme,* continues to amuse audiences today. Molière's story tells of how gullible, middle-class Monsieur Jourdain tries to ape the aristocracy by taking singing, dancing, and fencing lessons and then is fooled into believing that he has been made an Oriental potentate. Good comedians have loved acting in *Le Bourgeois Gentilhomme* ever since its premiere in 1670, when it was staged with music by Lully, and its balletic finale still provides roles for dancers.

THE FOREMOST DANCING MASTER OF THE ERA was Pierre Beauchamps, teacher of Louis XIV and one of the highest paid of the king's servants. He came from a family of dancing masters and violinists and was distantly related on his father's side to Molière's family. Beauchamps's ballets, like those of many other once-celebrated choreographers, are now forgotten. Yet one can gain a sense of the technique of his time from prints and writings.

Beauchamps stressed some of the fundamentals of ballet, including the five positions of the feet. He would probably be astonished by the amount of turnout today's ballet performers bring to classical steps. Professional dancers are now able to turn out their legs from the hips at a 180-degree angle. In Louis XIV's day, when dancers wore heeled shoes and bulky costumes, the amount of turnout was less. Turnout was first introduced into ballet technique as a theatrical adaptation of the fashionable fencer's stance. Dancing masters discovered that turnout helps the dancer to increase flexibility and balance while permitting the body to open outward toward the audience. Therefore, because of the way it facilitated clarity and visibility of movement, turnout became one of ballet's cardinal principles, although choreographers have always retained the freedom to ignore it in order to achieve special effects—as choreographers in fact did in the seventeenth century when they assigned turned-in movements to grotesque or comic characters.

Louis XIV stopped dancing in ballets in 1670. Perhaps he had noted, and taken to heart, the lines in Racine's play *Britannicus* that criticized a monarch for flaunting himself in public. Racine's specific reference was to Nero, but Louis may have detected a message between those lines. In any case, though only in his thirties, Louis was growing noticeably stout. Yet he continued to love ballet and desired the art to survive. Even before his retirement he took pains to ensure ballet's stability as an art. In 1661 he founded the Académie Royale de Danse, an association of teachers who were given quarters in the Louvre, but who preferred to meet at a nearby inn. Although this organization eventually disbanded, its establishment was a sign that official recognition was being given to dance. In 1669 Louis took a more decisive step: he founded the Académie Royale de Musique, which survives today as the Paris Opéra. Since dancers appeared in its productions from the start, the Paris Opéra Ballet can boast of being the world's oldest ballet company. The Académie's inaugural production, the opera *Pomone,* was staged in 1671 in a converted tennis court. However, managerial quarrels almost caused the Académie to collapse. Lully reorganized it and wielded power there for the rest of his life.

Louis's retirement as a dancer and the opening of the Opéra hastened the development of totally professional dancers. Moreover, although women had occasionally performed in some of the otherwise male-dominated court ballets, it was now possible for women to have careers as dancers at the Opéra.

Among the women to appear on the Opéra stage was one listed in programs as Mlle de La Fontaine. She is said to have made her debut leading three other women in a dance sequence of Lully's *Le Triomphe de l'Amour* in 1681, and this prominent role makes it possible to call her dance history's first prima ballerina. Mlle de La Fontaine continued to dance until 1693, when she apparently retired. Little is known about her dancing or her life. Yet her presence is a sign that the noble amateur, the dancing courtier, was about to bid farewell to the stage.

Related Readings

Beaujoyeulx on the Ballet Comique

In as much, dear Reader, as the title of this book is unprecedented, the word "Comic" having never been applied to a Ballet, nor has any Ballet been published previous to this one, I ask you not to find my usage peculiar.

As for the Ballet, it is a modern invention or is, at least, a revival from such distant antiquity that it may be called modern; being, in truth, no more than the geometrical groupings of people dancing together, accompanied by the varied harmony of several instruments. I confess to you that, merely presented in print, the recitation of a simple Comedy would have had much novelty but little beauty; nor would such an offering be distinguished or worthy of so noble a Queen who desired to present something magnificent and splendid.

Therefore, I bethought myself that to combine the two would be in no way improper; to diversify the music with poetry; to interlace the poetry with music; and most often to intermingle the two, even as the ancients never recited poetry without music and Orpheus played only with verse.

I have, nevertheless, given the first title and honor to the dance, and the second to the story, which I designated "Comic" more for its beautiful, tranquil, and happy conclusion than for the nature of its characters, who are almost all gods and goddesses or other heroic personages.

Thus I enlivened the ballet and made it speak, and made the Comedy sing and play; and, adding some unusual and elaborate decor and embellishments, I may say that I satisfied the eye, the ear, and the intellect with one well-proportioned creation.

I entreat you not to judge this work harshly because of its title or novelty; for my invention, being principally composed of two elements, could not be designated a Ballet without slighting the Comedy clearly evident in the scenes and acts; nor could it be called a Comedy without prejudice to the Ballet which ornaments, enlivens, and completes with harmonious movements the beautiful meaning of the comedy.

(Balthasar de Beaujoyeulx, Introduction to the published libretto of *Balet Comique de la Royne* [1582], trans. by Mary-Jean Cowell, in Selma Jeanne Cohen, ed., *Dance as a Theatre Art, Second Edition.* Princeton, N.J.: Princeton Book Company, Publishers, 1992, pp. 19–20)

Capriol Takes a Dancing Lesson

Capriol: I come to pay you my respects, Monsieur Arbeau. You do not remember me, for it is six or seven years since I left this town of Langres to go to Paris and thence to Orléans. I am an old pupil of yours, to whom you taught computation.

Arbeau: Indeed at first glance I failed to recognize you because you have grown up since then, and I feel sure that you have also broadened your mind by manliness and learning. What do you think of the study of law? I pursued it in bygone days myself.

Capriol: I find it a noble art and necessary in the conduct of affairs, but I regret that while in Orléans I neglected to learn fine manners, an art with which many scholars enriched themselves as an adjunct to their studies. For, on my return, I have found myself in society, where, to put it briefly, I was tongue-tied and awkward, and regarded as little more than a block of wood.

Arbeau: You took consolation in the fact that the learned professors excused this shortcoming in recognition of the learning you had acquired.

Capriol: That is so, but I should like to have acquired skill in dancing during the hours between my serious studies, an accomplishment which would have rendered my company welcome to all.

Arbeau: This will be an easy thing by reading French books in order to sharpen your wit and by learning fencing, dancing and tennis that you may be an agreeable companion alike to ladies and gentlemen.

Capriol: I much enjoyed fencing and tennis and this placed me upon friendly terms with young men. But, without a knowledge of dancing, I could not please the damsels, upon whom, it seems to me, the entire reputation of an eligible young man depends.

Arbeau: You are quite right, as naturally the male and female seek one another and nothing does more to stimulate a man to acts of courtesy, honour and generosity than love. And if you desire to marry you must realize that a mistress is won by the good temper and grace displayed by dancing, because ladies do not like to be present at fencing or tennis, lest a splintered sword or a blow from a tennis ball should cause them injury. . . . And there is more to it than this, for dancing is practiced to reveal whether lovers are in good health and sound of limb, after which they are permitted to kiss their mistresses in order that they may touch and savour one another, thus to ascertain if they are shapely or emit an unpleasant odour as of bad meat. Therefore, from this standpoint, quite apart from the many other advantages to be derived from dancing, it becomes an essential in a well ordered society.

(Thoinot Arbeau [pseudo of Jehan Tabourot], *Orchesography [1588]*, trans. by Mary Stewart Evans. New York: Dover, 1967, pp. 11–13)

The Music Master and the Dancing Master

Mr. Jourdain: And yet I never learned music.

Music Master: You ought to learn, sir, just as you are learning to dance. The two arts are closely allied.

Dancing Master: And develop one's appreciation of beauty.

Mr. Jourdain: What do the quality do? Do they learn music as well?

Music Master: Of course.

Mr. Jourdain: Then I'll learn it. But I don't know how I'm to find time. I already have a fencing master giving me lessons and now I've taken on a teacher of philosophy and he's supposed to be making a start this morning.

Music Master: Well, there is something in philosophy, but music, sir, music—

Dancing Master: And dancing, music and dancing, what more can one need?

Music Master: There's nothing so valuable in the life of the nation as music.

Dancing Master: And nothing so necessary to mankind as dancing.

Music Master: Without music—the country couldn't go on.

Dancing Master: Without dancing—one can achieve nothing at all.

Music Master: All the disorders, all the wars, that we see in the world today, come from not learning music.

Dancing Master: All the troubles of mankind, all the miseries which make up history, the blunders of politicians, the failures of great captains—they all come from not having learned dancing.

Mr. Jourdain: How d'ye make that out?

Music Master: What is war but discord among nations?

Mr. Jourdain: True.

Music Master: If all men studied music wouldn't it be a means of bringing them to harmony and universal peace?

Mr. Jourdain: That seems sound enough.

Dancing Master: And what do we say when a man has committed some mistake in his private life or in public affairs? Don't we say he made a false step?

Mr. Jourdain: We certainly do.

Dancing Master: And making a false step—doesn't that come from not knowing how to dance?

Mr. Jourdain: True enough. You are both in the right.

(Molière [Pseudo of Jean Baptiste Poquelin], *The Miser and Other Plays,* trans. by John Wood. Harmondsworth, Eng.: Penguin Books, 1953, pp.6–7)

4

The Professionalization of Ballet

WITH THE OPENING OF THE PARIS OPÉRA and the emergence of the professional dancer, ballet developed rapidly as an art. Even though the proscenium theatre had replaced the galleried hall, no rigid distinctions were made between theatrical and purely social dances. As in the court theatres of the past, the dances one saw on stage were still likely to be complex variants of the dances one performed for pleasure in the ballroom. The period's most popular ballroom dance, the minuet (or menuet), turned up in ballets. Even in its ballroom form, it possessed a measure of theatricality, for it was intended to be seen as well as done. Each couple danced alone before the eyes of their peers, and was then succeeded by the next couple. The way the lady and gentleman continually moved apart and together again suggested flirtation—always within the bounds of decorum—and made the minuet a dance that could resemble a courtship ritual. Moreover, during the performance of a minuet, dancers could scrutinize one another to determine who had mastered the fine points of deportment, posture, and technique, while flaws in dancing could be taken as signs of flaws in character. Thus Sarah, duchess of Marlborough, once remarked of an acquaintance: "I think Sir S. Garth is the most honest and compassionate, but after the minuets which I have seen him dance . . . I can't help thinking that he may sometimes be in the wrong."

During the early 1700s a new theatrical form, the *opéra-ballet,* came into existence. This form was related to the old *ballet à entrée,* for it consisted of detachable scenes joined by a common theme and utilized singing, dancing, and many of the splendid stage effects made possible by the proscenium theatre. Louis de Cahusac, who wrote scenarios for *opéra-ballets,* tried to define

Kellom Tomlinson's notation for the minuet traces the pattern of this most popular dance. *From Kellom Tomlinson, The Art of Dancing.*

the form by comparing it to painting, likening the *entrées* of *opéra-ballet* to the exquisite miniatures of the painter Jean-Antoine Watteau: *"Opéra-ballet* is a composite spectacle of several different acts, each of which represents a distinct action, with divertissements, songs and dances intermingled. These acts are beautiful Watteaus, spicy miniatures demanding graphic precision, gracefulness of the brush and superior brilliant coloring."

Opéra-ballet reached its height in some of the works of the composer Jean Philippe Rameau who also composed operas that told one single story. A late arriver on the theatrical scene, Rameau was fifty-one when he had his first creation staged at the Paris Opéra. But that work, *Hippolyte et Aricie* (1733), made him famous overnight. One of his best-known *opéra-ballets* is *Les Indes Galantes,* which—complete with a dancing flower garden and an erupting volcano—enjoyed immense popularity both at its Paris premiere in 1735 and when it was revived at the Opéra in 1952. *Les Indes Galantes* exemplified the curiosity about foreign, and particularly exotic, lands and peoples that had begun to develop during the eighteenth century. Each of its scenes, or *entrées,* was a love story that took place in a different corner of the world. The first episode occurred in Turkey, the second was set among the Incas of Peru, the action switched to Persia in the third scene, and the fourth concerned Indians in a North American forest.

The productions of Rameau and his contemporaries could be extremely ornate. But they involved more than frills. Their composers and choreographers were concerned with serious issues and they believed that one way to inspire the mind was first to stimulate the senses. Composers and choreographers alike sought to express the emotions. Characters in eighteenth-century ballets and operas may have been allegorical figures or mythological personages such as the gods and heroes of antiquity, yet through their actions they depicted desires, passions, and feelings known to human beings throughout history. If they seemed larger than life, that was so that the aspect of life they represented would be unmistakable.

Rather than totally immersing themselves in the emotions that they sought to reveal—or "living the part," as we might say today—eighteenth-century dancers took conscious care to shape their steps and gestures to serve as images of states of feeling. Given such pictorial concerns, it is not surprising that many eighteenth-century dancing masters advised their students to study painting. Thus, in his *Theoretical and Practical Treatise on Dancing* of 1779, Gennaro Magri described dancers' stances and movements almost as if they were elements in the composition of a painting: "The true theatrical attitude does not consist of a single and simple gesture

Bernardo Belotto's engraving depicts the final scene of Rameau's *"Les Turcs Généreux"* from *Les Indes Galantes*, in the Vienna production of 1758. *Courtesy of the Dance Collection, The New York Public Library.*

but is a union of several poses, being an accompaniment of the arms, the legs, the head, the eyes, which must express in which emotional state the person is found."

TECHNIQUE DEVELOPED RAPIDLY, and rival factions of ballet goers arose: those who relished increasingly complicated feats of virtuosity and those who favored qualities such as grace, elegance, and nobility.

There were three basic categories of dance styles. The *danse noble* was considered the highest and, as the term itself suggests, the most noble form of dance. An exponent of this style was serious and dignified on stage and was usually cast as a hero from history or mythology. *Demi-caractère* dancing was much livelier and more extroverted. Those who did this type of dancing were technically agile and tended to portray everyday (but not boorish) people or, in mythological works, lesser gods. Dancers who exemplified the *comique* (or *grotesque)* style played comic or rustic roles;

although they were often required to be rough in manner, they could also be genuinely charming.

The eighteenth century saw the rise of the star dancer, and the Paris Opéra Ballet School, which opened in 1713, ensured that well-trained dancers would always be available. Individual dancers achieved fame for their personal style. Claude Balon (sometimes called Jean Ballon) was blessed with good looks and dazzling technique. Louis Dupré was called "le grand Dupré" because of his majestic presence and "the god of the dance" because of the Olympian breadth of his gestures. He continued to dance until he was sixty, his stateliness increasing yearly, although his detractors whispered that this "god" was in danger of becoming a bore.

Giacomo Casanova, the Italian adventurer, libertine, and memoirist, was certainly not impressed when he saw Dupré perform in Paris. Indeed, the experience mystified him for, after taking a few steps and striking some poses, the aging star received thunderous applause. A friend declared that Dupré was exactly the same as he had been forty years earlier—at which the astonished Casanova exclaimed, "What! He never danced differently?" Then the friend, with the zeal of a fan, replied, "He cannot have danced better; for the performance you saw is perfect. Is there anything above perfection? He always does the same things, and we always find it new."

One of Dupré's pupils, Gaetan Vestris, was a member of a dancing family that dominated the Paris Opéra for more than a half-century, from the time of Mme de Pompadour through the French Revolution and into the Napoleonic era. Like Dupré, Gaetan Vestris was nicknamed "god of the dance," and he appears to have inherited his teacher's arrogance as well as his noble bearing. Gaetan passed on his pride to his son, Auguste Vestris, but whereas Gaetan exemplified the *noble* style, Auguste was a *demi-caractère* dancer. Instead of specializing in majestic gestures, he was a virtuoso famed for his jumps and turns. Gaetan once smugly declared of him that "It is through pity of his comrades that my son consents to touch the earth." Like some of his predecessors, he continued to dance past his prime. However, as he grew older his dramatic powers developed and because of his ability to combine virtuosity with expressiveness, he did much to make the old *noble* style obsolete. After his retirement in 1816, Auguste Vestris became one of the most distinguished teachers of the nineteenth century.

Auguste Vestris's virtuosic legerity is implied in this moment from *Les Amans Surpris* (left) compared with the grand style of his father Gaetan Vestris in *Ninette a la Cour* (right). *Courtesy of the Dance Collection, The New York Public Library.*

Women as well as men achieved stardom. In addition to being a brilliantly light, precise dancer with a dramatic flair, Françoise Prévost was a choreographer, her most famous work being *Les Caractères de la Danse.* Created in 1715, this was a suite of solos, each of which showed someone asking a favor of the god of love and doing so in the manner of one of the popular dance forms of the day. During the course of the work, Prévost portrayed male as well as female characters.

Two pupils of Prévost, Marie Anne de Cupis de Camargo and Marie Sallé, were particularly admired; each seems to have developed a different aspect of Prévost's own talents. From the standpoint of the historian, Camargo and Sallé constitute an instructive pair: they exemplify rival artistic viewpoints that continue to exist. These ballerinas were quite unlike, both onstage and off. Camargo was worldly. The toast of Paris at the height of her career, she retired from the Opéra in 1751 with the largest pension ever given a dancer up to that time and lived for the rest of her days surrounded by her beloved pet dogs, cats, parrots, and pigeons in a well-furnished house known for its wine cellar.

Sallé, in contrast, was quiet, reserved, even somewhat secretive about her private life. She was also the century's leading dramatic ballerina and, although she was technically able, "it was not by leaps and frolics that she went to your heart," as the choreographer Jean Georges Noverre wrote of her. Applauded in Paris, she enjoyed an unusual success in London. There she created the dance scenes in several operas by Handel, and thus must be regarded with Prévost as one of history's first female choreographers.

At various times, to heighten the dramatic intensity of a work, Sallé instituted reforms in staging and costuming. She choreographed her own version of *Les Caractères de la Danse,* which she conceived as a love duet, and when she performed it in 1729 she created a sensation, defying convention by dancing without a mask. Even more startling was *Pygmalion,* which she choreographed in London in 1734. In this ballet based on a Greek fable, Sallé portrayed a sculptor's statue that magically comes to life. To look appropriately Grecian, she discarded some of the cumbersome costumes of the day, including the wig and the *panier,* a hooped petticoat that was the female equivalent of the *tonnelet.* Instead she wore a simple, draped muslin robe that made her resemble a marble statue, and her natural hair, without a jewel or ornament, fell loosely to her shoulders. People fought in the streets to obtain tickets for her performances at Covent Garden.

Camargo was a dancer of a totally different sort. A virtuoso famed for her brio, her technical abilities became apparent so early in her career at the Opéra that Prévost, afraid of having a rival, relegated Camargo to the last row of the ensemble. However, one night a male dancer missed his entrance and Camargo leaped forward to complete his solo with verve and assurance. Thereafter she was seldom out of the public eye. Voltaire said that Camargo was the first ballerina to dance like a man, by which he meant that she was the first woman to master the dazzling steps that had previously been associated solely with male dancers. She was particularly celebrated for her *entrechat,* a flashing jumping step in which the feet are repeatedly crossed while in the air. So that audiences could see her *entrechats,* Camargo shortened her skirt by several inches. She was not the first or the only dancer of her time to do so, but because of her fame and brilliance, this costume reform has become particularly associated with her.

Both Camargo and Sallé encouraged costume reforms, but for different reasons. Whereas Camargo wished her technical accomplishments to be visible, Sallé desired to portray specific dramatic characters as convincingly as possible. These two ballerinas have come to exemplify two approaches to the art of dance: Camargo personifying dance as beauty of outward form, Sallé symbolizing dance as an expression of inward feeling.

(Curiously, comparable pairings occur in other periods of dance history: two of the leading ballerinas of the nineteenth century were the ethereal Taglioni and the passionate Elssler, and among the celebrated ballerinas of the early twentieth century were the classical Pavlova and the romantically ardent Karsavina. Both approaches can be valid, and taste often swings like a pendulum from one ideal to another. When the Camargo-dancer's formal perfection starts seeming academically dull or degenerates into meaningless acrobatics, there tends to be new interest in the expressive power of the Sallé-dancer. But should a Sallé-dancer start offering nothing but overwrought gesticulations, then the formal virtues of the Camargo-dancer may once again be treasured.)

The successor to Sallé and Camargo in the affection of Parisians was Barberina Campanini, who was known by the stage name of La Barberina. Trained in Italy, where the schools emphasized speed and agility (as they would for more than a century to come), Barberina delighted audiences with her turns and *entrechats*. Her offstage life was equally lively. She was installed by Frederick the Great as his mistress in Berlin, where he wined and dined her, commissioned artists to paint her portrait, and vociferously applauded her performances. And that, perhaps, was all he did. Frederick was not romantically attracted to the opposite sex and Barberina may have been his mistress in name only—to forestall any scandal that might have been created by the existence of a circle of intimates that was otherwise totally male. All the while, Barberina formed romantic attachments with other young men. Yet at the time of her death in 1799, at the age of seventy-eight, she was the abbess of a convent.

Such a progress from theatre to nunnery was by no means atypical and it suggests much about the period's moral climate. Officially, the Church

Marie Sallé (left) and Marie-Anne de Cupis de Camargo (right), both portrayed by Nicolas Lancret. *(left) Courtesy of the Dance Collection, The New York Public Library. (right) Courtesy of the National Gallery of Art, Washington: Andrew W. Mellon Collection.*

condemned the theatre and refused to marry or bury actors and dancers. At the same time, high-ranking clergymen often hired dancers to entertain at their banquets. A few even took dancers as mistresses. It was widely assumed that female dancers would have well-to-do men as lovers and, because many of these young women came from poor families, it is hardly surprising that they welcomed the jewels, gold, banquets, and other gifts their lovers lavished upon them.

Condemned by conventional moralists, dancers nevertheless seemed to be indispensable as providers of amusement for respectable society. Many dancers were simultaneously carefree and shrewd, living loose lives when young and officially repenting in old age. Under such circumstances, their loose living can even seem an outburst of hearty paganism defying the frowns of pious hypocrites. Occasionally such paganism could take almost riotous forms. Some dancers even participated in erotic shows held at private theatres frequented by courtiers, intellectuals, and clergymen in disguise. One theatre of this sort was on the estate of Marie-Madeleine Guimard, a ballerina known in her heyday for her dramatic stage presence, her extravagance, and her charity to the poor. However, she was to die in 1816 forgotten and penniless, the wife of an impoverished poet.

WITH THE INCREASED POPULARITY OF DANCE in the eighteenth century came a concern for dance notation. Although dancing masters and choreographers have always notated ballets in one way or another, often using their own systems of symbols as memory aids, it was not until the twentieth century that one encounters a general interest in recording movement comparable to the interest that developed in the eighteenth century. Beauchamps had devised a notation system of his own during the seventeenth century and, although he never published it, scholars think it may have had an influence on the notation system that Raoul-Auger Feuillet published in 1700 under the title of *Chorégraphie, ou l'Art de Décrire la Dance*. Feuillet's notation was capable of recording the dances of his time in a manner that was both ingenious and detailed, and it became enormously popular throughout Europe. Professional and amateur dancers alike prided themselves on their ability to read dance notation, and clergymen even complained that too many young ladies were keeping dance manuals, rather than Bibles, on their bedside tables. However, notation declined in popularity as steps in ballets grew more complex and difficult to notate; at the time of the French Revolution, it also seems to have been regarded as one of the aristocratic fashions that had to be abandoned.

As dancers developed the intricacy of ballet technique, innovative choreographers made use of it in their early works. One of the leading choreographers of the early eighteenth century was Guillaume-Louis Pécour, who, at his death in 1729, was described in an obituary as a worthy successor to Beauchamps with "an admirable and versatile genius." He both choreographed ballets for the Opéra and arranged dances for fashionable balls, and he was especially praised for his musicality and inventiveness. Because many of his works were recorded in Feuillet notation and studied by dance lovers in other countries, the French style of dancing spread throughout Europe.

THE MOST SIGNIFICANT NEW FORM OF BALLET to develop in the eighteenth century was the *ballet d'action,* which, unlike the episodic *ballet à entrée,* aimed at dramatic coherence and concision. The early eighteenth century witnessed several experiments in this genre. Responsible for one of them was the duchesse de Maine, who was a wit, an intellectual, a dwarf, and an insomniac. Insomnia made her seek ways to while away her sleepless nights, and her wit and intellect helped her to devise nocturnal entertainments at her chateau at Sceaux. There, one night in 1714, some dancers from the Opéra, including Prévost and Balon, mimed an act of Corneille's *Les Horaces* to music. The experiment was deemed successful, but regarded more as an eccentric lady's latest novelty than as an important new way of making ballets. A more ambitious production was John Weaver's *The Loves of Mars and Venus,* which was staged in London in 1717. This is often cited as the earliest complete ballet to convey its dramatic content entirely through movement, without the use of speech or song, yet it had little immediate impact. Because it appears to have been vaguely similar in style to Sallé's *Pygmalion,* created seventeen years later, there are scholars who believe that Sallé, when young, saw Weaver's ballet in London.

Among the exponents of *ballet d'action* were Jean-Baptiste de Hesse and Franz Hilverding. The former, working in Paris, filled his works with characters drawn from many social classes. Hilverding, a Viennese choreographer who sought to make the entire body expressive, created several works based on love stories from mythology (including those of Orpheus and Eurydice, Venus and Adonis, and Diana and Endymion).

By the mid-eighteenth century, *ballet d'action* had established itself as a major form and its popularity furthered the artistic autonomy of dance. The choreographer acquired considerable creative power, whereas in court ballets or opéra-ballets he might be only one member of a team dominated by a playwright or composer.

(Despite the importance of *ballet d'action* in dance history, one should not rashly assume that everything before it was somehow inferior, or that any dance form that no longer seems significant to us today must therefore have been inherently inconsequential. The *ballet d'action* emphasized unity and drama; the *ballet à entrée* emphasized variety and display.

Throughout dance history, taste has continued to vacillate between a concern for movement for its own beauty and a concern for movement as a revelation of emotional states, and great choreographers can make both concerns seem equally valid.)

The leading advocates of *ballet d'action* were Gaspero Angiolini and Jean Georges Noverre. Personal rivals in their own day, they now seem aesthetic allies when viewed from the perspective of history. A pupil of Hilverding, Angiolini collaborated with the composer Christoph Willibald Gluck in Vienna, staging the dances in the opera *Orfeo ed Euridice* and choreographing the ballet *Don Juan*. Gluck's music for this work is perhaps the best ballet score of the eighteenth century and the story of Don Juan's philandering and eventual damnation rushes along with great excitement, in accordance with Angiolini's belief that ballets should not be overburdened with complicated subplots. Nothing survives of his 1761 choreography, but his scenario is so soundly constructed that choreographers to this day have employed it for their own versions of *Don Juan*.

A caricature pokes fun at Giovanna Baccelli, Gaetan Vestris, and Adelaide Simonet in Noverre's *Jason and Medea*, London, 1781. *Courtesy of the Dance Collection, The New York Public Library.*

Noverre first attracted attention in 1754 for *Les Fêtes Chinoises,* a ballet on Chinese themes created for the Paris Opéra-Comique. Chinese culture was in fashion at the time—pagodas were set up in gardens, and silks and porcelain were in demand—and Noverre's balletic *chinoiserie* seemed so delightfully exotic that the English actor David Garrick invited him to produce it at Drury Lane in London the following year. It was an ill-timed invitation. England and France were on the verge of the Seven Years' War and there was strong anti-French sentiment in London. Though Garrick tried to persuade audiences that Noverre was really Swiss (a half-truth; he was half-Swiss), he nevertheless seemed much too suspiciously French to Londoners, and his ballet occasioned rioting.

Traveling through Europe to stage his ballets, Noverre amused Frederick the Great with comic impersonations of ballerinas and traded naughty stories with Voltaire. In what was probably the high point of his career, he was appointed director of the fine company in Stuttgart. He was also ballet master to companies in Lyons and in Milan, where Angiolini's epistolary polemic against Noverre's concept of *ballet d'action* began. In Vienna, where among his other duties Noverre gave dancing lessons to the young Marie Antoinette, he walked in one day on a rehearsal of Gluck's *Alceste* just as the composer exploded with rage and threw his wig to the ground in despair because he could not get the singers of the chorus to move expressively. To solve the problem, Noverre put the singers in the wings and had dancers mime to the music—an expedient that satisfied both Gluck and the audience.

Noverre continues to be important because of his *Letters on Dancing and Ballets,* a 1760 treatise on dance aesthetics that remains one of the most influential dance books ever published. Here he argues that ballets should be unified works of art in which all aspects of the production contribute to the main theme, that technical display for its own sake should be discouraged, and that such impediments to movement as heeled shoes and bulky skirts should be discarded. Many of Noverre's proposals are directed toward the specific ballet conventions of his time, yet his overall concern for ballet as a unified and coherent art makes his book still relevant. Noverre put his theories into practice in several ballets, including *Jason and Medea,* a ballet based on Greek mythology that caused such a stir following its 1763 premiere that an account of 1780 described it as a *"Ballet Terrible,* ornamented by dancing, suspicion, darkness, pleasure, horror, gaiety, treason, pleasantry, poison, tobacco, danger, *salade,* love, death, assassination, and fireworks."

In their day some of Noverre's ballets were considered fine examples of psychological realism. However, since notions of what is realistic or expressive on stage often change from century to century, action that Noverre's audiences considered realistic might seem stilted to audiences of another time. Moreover, Noverre did not always achieve the goals his *Letters* championed. He could not persuade every dancer with whom he worked to adopt his costume reforms, and while the dramatic power of *Jason and Medea* caused some spectators to faint, other ballet goers accused his choreography of containing too much stately parading about. Mozart, who composed *Les Petits Riens* for him, also charged that Noverre lacked musicality. Nevertheless, because of his high-mindedness and his ability to articulate the theories of the *ballet d'action,* Noverre remains a key figure in ballet history.

Noverre lived to see many of his costume reforms adopted. In the three decades following the French Revolution of 1789, costumes approached his ideals of "light and flowing draperies" and the heeled dancing shoe was replaced by the soft heelless slipper. Not until Isadora Duncan adopted Greek robes at the beginning of the twentieth century would dancers again be so scantily clad. Though corsets and fancy costumes eventually returned during the nineteenth century, the *tonnelet* and *panier* were banished forever.

BY THE TIME OF THE FRENCH REVOLUTION, ballet had begun to attract a wider public and choreographers were experimenting with new subject matter. In addition to ballets based on Greek mythology, which continued to be prized as a source for choreography, there were ballets about ordinary country life. If some of these rustic ballets may have been as fundamentally unrealistic as the little dairy farm that Marie Antoinette built just for herself so that she might indulge her fantasies of playing milkmaid, their existence is nevertheless a sign of changing tastes.

What any of these ballets were really like no one can say, for they were forgotten long ago. Not a step remains of any choreography by Angiolini or Noverre. However, in 1786 Vincenzo Galeotti, an Italian, pupil of

Angiolini, created *The Whims of Cupid and the Ballet Master* in Copenhagen for the Royal Danish Ballet (the Danes continue to dance it to this day). It is the world's oldest surviving complete ballet. As now performed, some of its steps possess technical embellishments that would have been impossible in Galeotti's time; nevertheless, it can serve as a reasonable example of eighteenth-century comic choreography. Best of all, the ballet still seems comic to us. It shows Cupid mischievously mixing up pairs of lovers from several nations and taking delight in these misalliances. Just as *The Whims of Cupid* can easily make dancegoers smile, so it can also make dance historians sigh with relief: the reputations of so many old ballets have to be taken on faith because those ballets have vanished, but here at last is a ballet that was considered charming by its first audiences and proves to be genuinely charming still.

One other comic ballet of the eighteenth century also survives, after a fashion: *La Fille Mal Gardée*. It was staged in Bordeaux in 1789 by Jean Dauberval, a choreographer famous in his time for being both a womanizer and a creator of sweet, witty ballets. One day in the street, Dauberval passed a shop window, where he saw a print of an old woman throwing a hat at a young man fleeing from a cottage while a peasant girl weeps. Dauberval concocted a story around the scene in the print and developed it into a ballet about the way two young lovers thwart the attempts of the girl's crotchety mother to marry her off to a wealthy fool. Dauberval's choreography has been forgotten. But his sunny scenario has never stopped inspiring choreographers.

(A Russian version of *La Fille Mal Gardée* called *Vain Precautions* was popular throughout the nineteenth century. This, in turn, became the basis of a production staged by American Ballet Theatre. Frederick Ashton, England's foremost contemporary choreographer, has choreographed an entirely new production for the Royal Ballet, and his adaptation of a great comic ballet of the eighteenth century has been proclaimed by many critics as one of the great comic ballets of our own time.)

Pierre Gardel, who became ballet master of the Paris Opéra in 1787, held power at that organization until the early nineteenth century. As a choreographer, he believed, along with the proponents of *ballet d'action,* that productions should possess unity and dramatic coherence. However, because he felt that too many examples of *ballet d'action* degenerated into tedious miming, he took care to choose stories that easily adapted themselves to dancing, and he was fond of stage spectacle.

He staged ballets in a variety of genres. *La Dansomanie (1800)* was a comedy about a father so obsessed with dancing that he even requires his daughter's suitors to dance for him in order to win his approval. *Achille à Scyros* (1804), one of Gardel's many mythological creations, told how the mother of Achilles disguises him as a woman to protect him from the dangers of a warrior's life. However, Ulysses arrives, seeking soldiers to fight the Trojans, and the true identity of Achilles is revealed when he shows an interest in military arms rather than finery. This scenario enabled Gardel to devise lyrical dances for women, fiery dances for warriors. Achilles, who was required by the choreography to suggest both masculine and feminine character traits, was portrayed by Louis Duport, a virtuoso said to rival Auguste Vestris.

By the 1820s, some ballet goers had started to call Gardel's works stuffy. Because none of his works has survived and we have no real idea of what they might have been like on stage, this judgment should be regarded with caution. Gardel may very well have had faults. But that adverse criticism may also indicate that balletic tastes were changing. Certainly, for much of his long career, Gardel was admired by audiences and critics alike.

INFLUENCED BY A RENEWED INTEREST in the passionate dramas of Shakespeare, Romantic poets such as Lord Byron and Sir Walter Scott, and painters and sculptors such as Jacques Louis David, Jean Auguste Dominique Ingres, Antonio Canova, and Bertel Thorvaldsen, many choreographers in addition to Gardel began to create heroic ballets during the late eighteenth and early nineteenth centuries. In Italy, where ballet was popular and the standard of teaching was high, the leading exponent of this genre was Salvatore Viganò, an Italian choreographer who was also the nephew of the composer Luigi Boccherini. Viganò's ballets, which he termed *coreodrammi*, were on a grand scale, and titles such as *Richard Coeur de Lion, Joan of Arc, Otello,* and *Coriolanus* suggest the sort of subjects he favored. What made these ballets particularly exciting was their dramatic momentum: instead of alternating mime scenes with dancing, as some choreographers did, Viganò blended them in passages of continually developing expressive movement and often contrasted statuesque groupings inspired by classical sculpture with sweeping ensembles. Viganò's opponents claimed that he relied too heavily on mimetic movement and that his works contained too little real dancing.

Because similar charges are occasionally raised against dramatic ballets throughout dance history, this objection is worth examining. Sometimes it is justified, as when a ballet consists of virtually nothing but agitated gestures that presumably are intended to express much, but that in reality manage to convey little. In such cases, movement is vainly trying to do the work of speech. Yet there are times when those who argue that a dramatic ballet is deficient in dancing are merely revealing their own preference for decorative or abstract movement; considered on its own terms, the dramatic dance may be both genuinely expressive and eloquent. Moreover, in recent years, experimental choreographers have refused to make rigid distinctions between "dance" and "nondance" movement and, when seen in this light, certain aspects of Viganò's practice and the critical arguments for and against it may seem surprisingly contemporary.

Alessandro Sanquirico's monumental designs for *Gli Strelizzi* (1809) epitomize Salvatore Viganò's heroic dance-dramas. *Courtesy of the Board of Trustees of the Victoria and Albert Museum, London.*

So, too, are the implications of Viganò's use of music. Although Beethoven composed *The Creatures of Prometheus* for him, Viganò occasionally composed his own music for his ballets and, like other choreographers of his time, also assembled scores that were medleys of themes by several composers. These medleys were put together to fit the dance, just as medleys were assembled to accompany the action of silent films. Because of this, some theorists might find Viganò musically weak. But others—those for whom movement alone is the paramount ingredient in a dance production—could claim him as spiritually akin to those early modem dancers who deliberately kept their musical accompaniments spare so that the focus of a production would always be the stage action.

Audiences in Viganò's time may have welcomed medleys of tunes by various composers. Living long before the invention of the radio, the phonograph, or the tape recorder, they had only limited opportunities to hear music. Consequently, a score that was a medley might have been a way to make people better acquainted with these themes. Some scores of this type contained orchestral versions of well-known songs or operatic arias; knowing the original words to these songs helped viewers follow the ballet's gestural action because the songs were placed so that their lyrics would be relevant to the dramatic situation being expressed. Such potpourri scores continued to be assembled on occasion throughout the nineteenth century.

Though his theories continue to interest us, Viganò's choreography has not survived. Like Noverre and Angiolini, he must have possessed real gifts. He once declared, "It is not enough to please the eye; I wish to engage the heart." And, for his devoted admirers, he did just that. Among those admirers was the novelist Stendhal, who proclaimed Viganò "the Shakespeare of the dance," an honor that Garrick had earlier bestowed upon Noverre.

Charles Didelot was also concerned with dramatic expression. This French choreographer, who was born in Stockholm, staged ballets throughout Europe, notably in St. Petersburg, where he helped influence the course of Russian ballet. Like Viganò, he often based poses and groupings on paintings and sculpture, and he, too, was praised by a great writer. The Russian poet Pushkin declared that there was more poetry in Didelot's

choreography than in all French literature of the
period, a compliment Didelot returned by
basing a ballet on Pushkin's *The Prisoner
of the Caucasus*. Didelot was also fascinated by innovations in stagecraft.
He once put mirrors on a stage
so that the audience
could see the same
dancer moving from
several angles. By his
advocacy of tights, he
contributed to the simpli-
fication of costuming. And
in 1796, in *Flore et Zéphyre*,
which became his most celebrated
ballet, he devised a remarkable system of
rigging that permitted dancers to be
raised aloft and suspended
on wires, giving the
illusion of flight. The
effect was spectacu-
lar and so frequently
imitated that zeph-
yrs and nymphs were
soon flying on wires
across the stages of
Europe.

Adelaide Mersy and Giovanni Rousset in Charles
Didelot's *Flore et Zéphyre* suggest the choreographer's
aerial style. *Courtesy of the Dance Collection, The New
York Public Library.*

Again by means of wires, Didelot could lower a ballerina to the ground
so that she appeared to be poised on tiptoe. Eventually, ballerinas would
discover how to balance on their toes without the assistance of wires—a
discovery that inaugurated a whole new era of ballet history and profoundly
affected the development of the art.

Related Readings

In Praise of Notation

Long was the dancing art unfixed and free;
Hence lost in error and uncertainty:
No precepts did it mind, or rules obey,
But ev'ry master taught a different way:
Hence, ere each new-born dance was fully tried,
The lovely product, ev'n in blooming, died:
Thro' various hands in wild confusion tossed,
Its steps were altered, and its beauties lost:
Till Feuillet at length, great name! arose,
And did the dance in characters compose:
Each lovely grace by certain marks he taught,
And ev'ry step in lasting volumes wrote.
Hence o'er the world this pleasing art shall spread,
And ev'ry dance in ev'ry clime be read;
By distant masters shall each step be seen,
Tho' mountains rise and oceans roar between.
Hence with her sister-arts shall dancing claim
An equal right to universal fame,
And Isaac's* rigadoon shall last as long
As Raphael's painting, or as Virgil's song.

(Soame Jenyns, *The Art of Dancing* [1729], ed. by Anne Cottis. London: Dance Books Ltd., 1978, p. 31)

---

*   A famous dancing master of the day who called himself Mr. Isaac.

Prévost's Caractères

Courante: An elderly lover, mocked by a young coquette, asks Amour to let him "believe himself loved."

Menuet: A child of twelve, already feeling a thousand confusions of love, asks Amour to keep her mother asleep as she awaits her lover.

Bourrée: A shepherdess in love begs Amour to open the eyes of a shepherd who disdains her charms.

Chaconne: A fop requests neither hearts nor favors from Amour, but only the reputation of good fortune in love.

Sarabande: A deceived lover complains to Amour and asks advice.

Gigue: A mad young thing, sweeping up all hearts that come her way, asks Amour for a loving shepherd who will never tire of dancing with her.

Rigaudon: A fool assures Amour that "without sighing or languishing he has his choice of beauties" in view of his money.

Passepied: An abandoned lover requests Amour to give her strength to feign indifference in the hope that coolness will inflame her flighty lover.

Gavotte: A woman who has caused her lover to flee cries to Amour and asks only for his prompt return.

Loure: A lover, disciple of Bacchus, asks Amour to let him go on drinking, since wine often induces love.

Musette: A woman who is perfectly content in love has no favors to ask of Amour and thus renders homage to him.

(The characters and dance forms of Françoise Prévost's *Les Caractères de la Danse*. From the program notes for a performance by Concert Royal and the New York Baroque Dance Company, Florence Gould Hall, New York, N.Y., September 23 and 25, 1988)

Weaver's Emotional Gestures

SCENE II

After a Simphony of Flutes, etc., the Scene opens and discovers Venus in her Dressing-Room at her Toilet, attended by the Graces, who are employ'd in dressing her. . . .

Enter to Venus, Vulcan: They perform a Dance together; in which Vulcan expresses his Admiration; Jealousie; Anger; and Despite; and Venus shows Neglect; Coquetry; Contempt; and Disdain.

This last Dance being altogether of the Pantomimic kind; it is necessary that the Spectator should know some of the most particular Gestures made use of therein; and what Passions, or Affections, they discover; represent; or express.

Admiration. Admiration is discover'd by the raising up of the right Hand, the Palm turn'd upwards, the Fingers clos'd; and in one Motion the Wrist turn'd round and Fingers spread; the Body reclining, and Eyes fix'd on the Object; but when it rises to

Astonishment. Both hands are thrown up towards the Skies; the Eyes also lifted up, and the Body cast backwards.

Jealousy. Jealousy will appear by the Arms suspended, or a particular pointing the middle Finger to the Eye; by an irresolute movement throughout the Scene, and a Thoughtfulness of Countenance.

Upbraiding. The Arms thrown forwards; the Palm of the Hands turn'd outward; the Fingers open, and the Elbows turn'd inward to the Breast; shew Upbraiding and Despite.

Anger. The left Hand struck suddenly with the right; and sometimes against the Breast; denotes Anger.

Threats. Threatening is express'd by raising the Hand, and shaking the bended Fist; knitting the Brow; biting the Nails, and catching back the Breath.

Power. The Arm, with impetuous Agitation, directed forwards to the Person, with an awful Look, implies Authority. Impatience. Impatience is seen by the smiting of the Thigh, or Breast with the Hand.

Indignation. When it rises to Anguish, and Indignation, it is express'd by applying the Hand passionately to the Forehead; or by stepping back the right foot, leaning the Body quite backward, the Arms extended, Palms clos'd, and Hands thrown quite back; the Head cast back, and Eyes fix'd upwards.

These are some of the Actions made use of by Vulcan; those by Venus are as follows: Coquetry. Coquetry will be seen in the affected Airs, given her self throughout the whole Dance.

Neglect. Neglect will appear in the scornful turning the Neck; the flirting outward the back of the right hand, with a Turn of the Wrist.

Contempt. Contempt is express'd by scornful Smiles; forbidding Looks; tossing of the Head; filliping of the Fingers; and avoiding the Object.

Distaste. The left Hand thrust forth with the Palm turn'd backward; the left Shoulder rais'd, and the Head bearing towards the Right, denotes an Abhorrence, and Distaste.

Detestation. When both the turn'd-out Palms are so bent to the left Side, and the Head still more projected from the Object; it becomes a more passionate Form of Detestation, as being a redoubled Action.

(John Weaver, from the libretto for *The Loves of Mars and Venus [1717]*, in Selma Jeanne Cohen, ed., *Dance as a Theatre Art, Second Edition*. Princeton, N.J.: Princeton Book Company, Publishers, 1992, pp. 54–55)

Noverre on Balletic Reform

Dancing needs only a fine model, a man of genius, and ballets will change their character. Let this restorer of the true dance appear, this reformer of bad taste and of the vicious customs that have impoverished the art; but he must appear in the capital. If he would persuade, let him open the eyes of our young dancers and say to them:— "Children of Terpsichore, renounce *cabrioles*, *entrechats* and over-complicated steps; abandon grimaces to study sentiments, artless graces and expression; study how to make your gestures noble, never forget that it is the life-blood of your dancing; put judgment and sense into your *pas de deux*; let will-power order their course and good taste preside over all situations; away with those lifeless masks but feeble copies of nature; they hide your features, they stifle, so to speak, your emotions and thus deprive you of your most important means of expression; take off those enormous wigs and those gigantic head-dresses which destroy the true proportions of the body; discard the use of those stiff and cumbersome hoops which detract from the beauties of execution, which disfigure the elegance of your attitudes and mar the beauties of contour which the bust should exhibit in its different positions.

"Renounce that slavish routine which keeps your art in its infancy; examine everything relative to the development of your talents; be original; form a style for yourselves based on your private studies; if you must copy, imitate nature, it is a noble model and never misleads those who follow it.

"As for you young men who aspire to be *maîtres de ballet*. . . . Learn the difficult art of selection. Never undertake great enterprises without first making a careful plan; commit your thoughts to paper; read them a hundred times over; divide your drama into scenes; let each one be interesting and lead in proper sequence, without hindrance or superfluities, to a well-planned climax; carefully eschew all tedious incidents, they hold up the action and spoil its effect. Remember that *tableaux* and groups provide the most delightful moments in a ballet.

"Make your *corps de ballet* dance, but, when it does so, let each member of it express an emotion or contribute to form a picture; let them mime while dancing so that the sentiments with which they are imbued may cause their appearance to be changed at every moment. If their gestures and features be constantly in harmony with their feelings, they will be expressive accordingly and give life to the representation. . . . Bring love as well as enthusiasm to your art. To be successful in theatrical representations, the heart must be touched, the soul moved and the imagination inflamed."

(Jean Georges Noverre, *Letters on Dancing and Ballets* [1760], trans. by Cyril W. Beaumont. Brooklyn, N.Y.: Dance Horizons, 1966, pp. 29–30)

Stendhal on Viganò

There is a genius alive today, and dwelling here in Naples; yet his art is despised and ill-considered—Viganò, the creator of *gli Zingari* (the *Gypsies*). The good folk of Naples were convinced that he was having a joke at their expense. . . . There was one episode in particular, where the dancers moved to an accompaniment of timpani, which shocked the poor Neapolitans to the very depths of their being; they were convinced that the whole thing was a deliberate hoax; and indeed yesterday, among the guests of Princess Belmonte, I met a young captain who would fret and storm himself into a very frenzy at the mere mention of Viganò. . . . It was Noverre (so I am told) who discovered the *sensual* element in dancing; Viganò has widened its horizon of *expression* at every point. Yet this same unerring instinct for his art impelled him further, and led him to disclose the ultimate secret of the ballet, which is that ballet is *par excellence* the art of the *romantic*. The loftiest heights to which the spoken drama may attain have long since been scaled by Shakespeare; but *il Noce di Benevente* is not merely a feast of delight for the entranced imagination, but explores a realm of fancy unknown to *Imogen* in her *Cave,* or to the *melancholy Jaques* in the *Forest of Arden.* So vivid is the joy, so captivating the originality of it, that the soul, transported, knows no release from ecstasy from curtain-rise to curtain-fall—full five-and-seventy minutes. . . .

His imagination has about it a certain *Shakespearian* quality—yet the very name of Shakespeare, I suspect, would mean nothing to him. Painting and music alike have a share in his genius. Frequently, when he cannot lay hands on a melody ready-fashioned to express his meaning, he will compose his own. I would be the last to deny that his *Prometée* is not entirely free from absurdities; yet, ten years after, the memory of it lives on as fresh as ever, and my mind is still astonished at its power. A further and most original characteristic of Viganò's genius is his *patience.* He will stand on the stage at *la Scala,* surrounded by eighty dancers, with a band of ten musicians in the orchestra-pit at his feet, there to spend a whole morning composing and implacably rehearsing, over and over again, ten bars of choreography which seem to him to fall short of final perfection. There is no stranger sight in all the world. . . .

(Stendhal [pseudo of Henri Beyle], *Rome, Naples and Florence,* trans. by Richard N. Cae. New York: Braziller, 1959, pp. 366–370)

5

The Sunshine and Moonlight
of Romantic Ballet

THE PREMIERE OF GIACOMO MEYERBEER'S *Robert le Diable* at the Paris Opéra in 1831 came close to being one calamity after another. So much kept going wrong on stage. The leading tenor accidentally plummeted through a trapdoor. Another singer barely escaped being struck by a falling gaslight. A dance episode in this opera began with the ballerina poised upon a tomb and the choreography required her to glance soulfully upward. What she saw as she did so on this particular occasion was no celestial vision, but a piece of scenery that had come loose from the flies and was hurtling toward her. If she had not jumped aside in the nick of time, she might have been seriously injured.

In spite of these catastrophes, *Robert le Diable* was a tremendous success, thanks to Meyerbeer's powerful operatic music and to a ballet sequence so unusual as to be almost unprecedented. This episode was set in a ruined cloister where ghosts of lapsed nuns rose from their tombs to dance by the light of the moon. The sight of flickering moonbeams—a lighting effect created by suspended gas jets—Gothic ruins, and dancing phantoms caused audiences to shiver with delight, and even though a few critics thought Filippo Taglioni's choreography for the episode confused in design, it was effective nonetheless. Equally remarkable was the choreographer's daughter, the ballerina Marie Taglioni, who seemed to float across the stage as if she truly were the spectre her role called upon her to portray. Nothing quite like this had ever been seen before, and the "Ballet

The Ballet of the Nuns in *Robert le Diable* (1831), choreographed by Filippo Taglioni and designed by Pierre Ciceri, brought Romanticism into ballet. *Courtesy of the Bibliothèque de l'Opera, Paris.*

of the Nuns" from *Robert le Diable* is the first choreographic triumph of the artistic movement known as Romanticism.

The heyday of Romanticism in the ballet extends from the 1830s to the 1850s, although aspects of Romanticism can be found in ballets as late as the 1870s. Romanticism developed in a time of social upheaval. Visionary radical ideas were in the air, yet people retained bitter memories of the excesses of the French Revolution and of Napoleon's defeat. Moreover, a new middle class, which had grown prosperous through commerce and industry, was gaining power, and this class had started to patronize performances of drama, opera, and ballet. The rise of the middle class was accompanied by a wave of materialism, prudishness, and hypocrisy which, a few years before the premiere of *Robert le Diable,* had led the Opéra's management to require all its *danseuses* to lengthen their skirts, lest the sight of naked flesh arouse the male spectators.

Rebelling against both stultifying moral convictions and outworn artistic forms, young artists began to praise feeling and passion. The turbulence of Romanticism can be noted in the poems of Lord Byron and Victor Hugo, the paintings of Eugene Delacroix, and the music of Hector Berlioz and Franz Liszt. Two important elements of Romantic art profoundly affected the development of ballet: a fascination with the colorful or even exotic aspects of this world and a pining after the nonrational or supernatural. French choreographers often utilized themes from folklore and set their ballets in foreign lands—Spain, Italy, or Egypt. The Industrial Revolution may have helped generate this interest in faraway places and curious customs. If, thanks to such inventions as the railroad, improved methods of transportation made it easier to visit remote corners of the world, industrialism threatened their unspoiled charm. In its blending of realism and fantasy, Romantic ballet could be both a danced travelogue and an escape into a dream world.

In much Romantic art one senses a melancholy yearning. The Romantics were painfully aware of the gulf that can exist between aspiration and actuality. Commenting on this, the twentieth-century choreographer George Balanchine has written, "To be Romantic about something is to see what you are and to wish for something entirely different. This requires magic." Many ballets of the Romantic era were filled with magic. Sprites and elves figured in some of the ballets, but these supernatural beings were not necessarily treated only as quaint figures out of legend; they could also symbolize irrational psychic forces. Given the preoccupations of the Romantics, it is not surprising that ballets about such phenomena as madness, sleepwalking, and opium dreams also became popular. Ballets were even compared with dreams on occasion. Thus Théophile Gautier, the French poet and novelist who was also a major nineteenth-century dance critic, wrote:

> Nothing resembles a dream more than a ballet, and it is this which explains the singular pleasure that one receives from these apparently frivolous representations. One enjoys, while awake, the phenomenon that nocturnal fantasy traces on the canvas of sleep: an entire world of chimeras moves before you.

Certain works of this era could give psychologists and sociologists much to ponder. For example, by depicting harem wives led in a rebellion against male oppressors and by having the Spirit of Womankind disguised as a slave, Filippo Taglioni's *The Revolt in the Harem* of 1833 may be the world's first ballet about the emancipation of women. Other thematically provocative works are *Gemma,* concerning an evil hypnotist's attempts to seduce a young woman, and *La Volière,* which tells how a woman who has been unhappy in love raises her sister in complete ignorance of the male sex. When a man finally appears, she tells the girl that he is a bird and must be caged. Both of these dramatically curious works were choreographed by women: *Gemma* by Fanny Cerrito and *La Volière* by Therese Elssler.

Not only did balletic plots stress magic, the theatre itself became a magical place thanks to new developments in stagecraft. The introduction of gaslighting made possible contrasts between brightness and gloom on stage. It also allowed the houselights to be lowered during operas and ballets whereas, previously, performances took place with the houselights up. The darkened auditorium combined with the flickering gaslight on stage, which enhanced the ghostliness of nocturnal landscapes, did much to create a sense of theatrical enchantment. Designers delighted in scenic surprises. In the past, it had been the custom at the Paris Opéra not to lower the curtain between the scenes of an opera or a ballet. However, by lowering the curtain, scenic wonders could be prepared out of sight and then unveiled before the eyes of astonished spectators—as those who attended the premiere of Gioacchino Rossini's *William Tell* in 1829 discovered as the curtain rose and fell upon settings representing Swiss villages and Alpine landscapes.

The wonders of stagecraft did more than enhance works about the supernatural, for many ballets were staged that had nothing to do with elves or sylphs. Nevertheless, we today tend to remember the ones involving mystery and fantasy.

The choreographic possibilities of such Romantic subject matter, which were hinted at in the cloister scene of *Robert le Diable,* were fully explored in *La Sylphide,* a two-act ballet choreographed by Filippo Taglioni for his daughter Marie in 1832 to music by Jean Madeleine Schneitzhoeffer. The scenario was devised by Adolphe Nourrit, the leading tenor of the Paris Opéra at the time; it was Nourrit who had sung the title role in *Robert le Diable.*

La Sylphide tells how James, a young Scotsman, becomes enamored of a Sylphide—a spirit of the air—on the day of his wedding. So entranced is he by this ethereal creature that he deserts his human fiancée to run off to the woods with the Sylphide. A witch gives him a scarf that she claims will magically tie the Sylphide to him forever. Unaware that the witch seeks to do evil and that the scarf is cursed, he binds the Sylphide with it, whereupon her wings fall off and she dies. This story of a love between a mortal and a spirit is quintessentially Romantic, and Taglioni united the two main aspects of balletic Romanticism—the earthy and the fantastical—by filling the first act with vigorous ensembles based on Scottish folk dances and the second act with airy dances for the Sylphide and her attendant sprites. *La Sylphide* is also Romantic in the treatment of its scenario's themes. Thus it expresses Romantic yearning for the unattainable, here personified by the Sylphide. By pursuing this embodiment of the ideal, James separates himself from the human community. But the very moment he grasps and binds her, he loses her forever; by definition an ideal is something that is always beyond one's grasp. At the ballet's end he is overcome by despair, having lost both the human and the spirit world.

La Sylphide gave Marie Taglioni the most celebrated role of her career. So convincing was she as the Sylphide that audiences adored her and scores of other dancers tried to emulate her, which forwarded a tendency to idealize and idolize women in ballet. Nourrit had adapted his scenario for *La Sylphide* from *Trilby,* a novel by Charles Nodier. However, in *Trilby* it is a *male* spirit who seeks to lure a young Scottish woman. No wonder, then, that when Nodier saw Taglioni as the Sylphide, he exclaimed, "I never dreamed of such a wraith!" The sexual reversal of the leading roles in *La Sylphide* is a sign of the rising influence of the ballerina.

Costuming did much to make women look striking on stage. Taglioni's illusion of airiness was certainly enhanced by her costume. It had a tight bodice and a bell-shaped skirt made of masses of billowing material that reached almost to the ankle. Instead of revealing the dancer's figure, as the light draperies of the previous era had done, this so-called "Romantic tutu" concealed it, making the ballerina's bare neck and shoulders the only signs of real flesh and blood. Though dancers later shortened this costume—thereby devising the "classical tutu," which displayed the whole

The Queensland Ballet with Luke Schaufuss and Sarah Thompson James at the London Coliseum in Bournonville's *La Sylphide. Photograph courtesy Vibrant Pictures / Alamy Stock Photo.*

leg—it was the Romantic tutu that decisively succeeded in associating ballerinas with supernatural visions.

FILIPPO TAGLIONI's *La Sylphide* VANISHED from the stage generations ago (the contemporary French teacher and dance historian Pierre Lacotte has attempted a conjectural reconstruction of it). Marie and Filippo Taglioni belonged to one of the dancing families that greatly influenced European ballet. Filippo's brother Salvatore directed the ballet company at Teatro San Carlo in Naples and founded its important ballet school, which produced dancers who achieved fame in many countries. Marie's brother Paul was a successful dancer and choreographer, sometimes partnering Marie until his wife Amalia Galster became his regular partner. Their daughter Marie grew up to be a dancer billed as Marie Taglioni "the younger." Comparable dancing dynasties flourished in other nations, including France, Russia, and Denmark, from which comes a version of *La Sylphide* as authentically Romantic as Taglioni's original production.

IN 1836, IN COPENHAGEN, the Danish choreographer August Bournonville created his own *La Sylphide,* to new music by Herman Severin Løvenskjold, starring the young ballerina Lucile Grahn. This *Sylphide* remains in the repertoire of the Royal Danish Ballet and has also been produced by many other European and American companies.

The son of Antoine Bournonville, the Royal Danish Ballet's director, August Bournonville, was sent to Paris for advanced training with Auguste Vestris. After appearing at the Paris Opéra, he returned to his native Copenhagen. Except for sporadic interruptions, he spent the rest of his life there as dancer, choreographer, and teacher, and he succeeded his father as director of the Royal Danish Ballet. One of the interruptions in his Danish career was indirectly caused by Grahn, a ballerina he had initially encouraged. When Grahn was dismissed in 1839 in a contractual dispute, her fans insisted that she be rehired. At a performance in 1841, they hissed Bournonville during the course of a ballet in which he had cast himself in the leading male role. Angered, Bournonville stopped dancing, turned toward the royal box, and asked King Christian VIII, "What is Your Majesty's command?" "Go on," said the king. The performance resumed. But the next day the king banished Bournonville for six months. By involving King Christian in a petty quarrel, Bournonville had offended the monarch's dignity and consequently was guilty of *lèse majesté.* However, his exile proved fruitful, for Bournonville visited Italy, where he gathered source material for some of his sunniest choreography.

As preserved by the Danes, the extant Bournonville ballets constitute the only surviving body of works by any choreographer of the Romantic era. Some, like *La Sylphide* and *A Folk Tale* (which was adapted from Danish legends), reflect Romantic interest in the supernatural. Others derive from Romantic curiosity about foreign lands, such as Italy *(Napoli)* and Flanders *(The Kermesse in Bruges).* Still others are topical: *Far from Denmark* was inspired by a Danish vessel's voyage around the world, and *Konservatoriet* contains an affectionate depiction of ballet classes in Paris in the days of Vestris.

Many of Bournonville's ballets are tender and lighthearted, but virtually all contain reflections on human nature. Bournonville heartily agreed with the statement about the nature and purpose of the theatrical arts

In August Bournonville's *A Folk Tale,* the Elf Maidens, who symbolize the dangerous lure of the supernatural, drive Junker Ove, the work's hero, into a frenzy. *Courtesy of the Teatermuseet, Copenhagen.*

that is still inscribed above the proscenium arch of the Royal Theatre in Copenhagen: *"EI BLOT TIL LYST"*—Not for Pleasure Alone. Bournonville utilized Romantic themes in an idiosyncratic manner. At a time when many artists were fascinated by excesses of passion, Bournonville extolled balance and harmony, and he was always concerned with human happiness and humane behavior. Aware of the dark powers of the psyche, he tried to make light out of darkness. Although *La Sylphide,* which had a scenario borrowed from another choreographer, came to a melancholy conclusion, Bournonville preferred to resolve his works happily. A typical example of his balletic dramaturgy and his attitude toward passion is *The Guards on Amager,* a comedy in which a wife learns that she has an amorously errant husband; to teach him a lesson, she disguises herself at a masked ball, lets him flirt with her, then reveals her true identity. The marriage is eventually saved and calamity is avoided. Yet even as he celebrates the triumph of domesticity, Bournonville implies that, if it is not to grow stale, a marriage must retain some sense of adventure.

Bournonville's choreography is characterized by light, fleet footwork, intricate steps in which one leg is beaten against the other in the air *(beats),* and that bounciness that ballet teachers term *ballon.* Some of these qualities may be the result of Bournonville's attempts to hide his own defects in performance. Wishing to disguise his brittle way of landing from jumps, he composed sequences in which landings were followed not by sustained poses—which would give the audience time to scrutinize him for faults—but by immediate takeoffs into other movements. The resultant Bournonville style emphasizes speed and elevation in its steps for men, sweetness and charm in its steps for women.

Bournonville wrote essays on ballet technique, and his followers preserved his pedagogical methods in a series of six set classes, one for each day of the week (except Sunday). As taught by his most fanatical disciples, they never varied from year to year. Paradoxically, Romanticism may have stressed irrational and spontaneous behavior, but the mastery of a structured and rational training method was needed to portray such behavior on stage. Ballet's technical vocabulary was constantly expanding, and the need for fine teaching became apparent.

ONE INFLUENTIAL TEACHER WAS CARLO BLASIS, who in 1837 was appointed director of the Royal Academy of Dance at La Scala in Milan. As a result of his teaching skill, Milanese dancers were famed for their prowess and dancers from many nations studied with him. What is perhaps more important, Blasis taught teachers who, in turn, taught other teachers, thereby codifying classical ballet. Though Romantic choreography could be ebullient, Blasis's teaching was sober. He loved to hold up examples of ancient or neoclassic art as models of noble deportment and made Giovanni da Bologna's bronze statue of the god Mercury the prototype for the position known as *attitude* (in which the dancer stands on one leg, the other raised behind him with bent knee).

In addition to maintaining high standards in the classroom, Blasis wrote books about dance training. *The Code of Terpischore, Notes Upon Dancing,* and other works express his theories of dance technique and offer students advice on finding a good teacher and developing their bodies properly. Blasis's teaching methods serve as reminders that ballet is a conservative art, in the best sense of that term: choreographers may make bold experiments on stage, while teachers continue to uphold the great traditions in the classroom.

Of all technical innovations in ballet, none has had more far-reaching effects for good and for ill as dancing *en pointe,* toe dancing. So closely is toe dancing linked to ballet in the popular imagination that many people are surprised to learn that it is a relatively recent invention. Virtuosos such as Camargo and La Barberina never knew of it. Until the beginning of the nineteenth century neither did any other ballerina. Just who did invent *pointe* work—and when—remains a mystery. Letting dancers dangle from wires as in *Flore et Zéphyre* certainly helped them hover momentarily on their toes when they reached the ground. And it is believed that around 1820 the dancers Geneviève Gosselin, Amalia Brugnoli, and Avdotia Istomina may have danced *en pointe* without the aid of wires.

The illustrations of *entrechats* and *temps d'elevation* in Carlo Blasis's *Traité Elementaire* exemplify his codification of ballet technique.

To dance *en pointe,* today's ballerina wears shoes that have the toes reinforced by layers of glue between layers of material. The Romantic ballerina, in contrast, wore slippers with merely a bit of wadding inserted and a little darning outside to improve the grip on the floor. She danced with no other support—as any well-schooled dancer should still be able to do. The reinforced toe is no magic gimmick; it is merely an aid to dancing. The real secret of toe dancing lies not in the shoe, but in the ballerina's properly trained body.

Because of her magical stage personality, Camargo alone remains forever associated with the costume reform of the shortened skirt; just so Marie Taglioni has come to epitomize the ballerina *en pointe* because of the way she amazed audiences with her ability to skim across the stage on her toes in an otherworldly fashion. (From its first use onward, *pointe* dancing has been associated with women, although there is no anatomical reason why it cannot be done by men; in fact, some contemporary choreographers have occasionally put men *en pointe* in eccentric or fantastical roles, and several all-male ballet companies have required their members to be experts in dancing *en pointe*.) Taglioni's ethereality was a result of the training she received from her father. He urged her to remove all traces of the carnal from her dancing, and consequently her style was sometimes called chaste. But it was not totally so for, like all the great ballet stars of the time, she was adept at character as well as classical dancing and her Spanish dancing was almost as famous as her Sylphide. Her father's classes to build

The ethereal Marie Taglioni in *La Sylphide* created a vogue for supernatural heroines *Courtesy of the Dance Collection, The New York Public Library.*

The earthier Fanny Elssler portrayed a Spanish dancer who played castanets in the cachucha from *Le Diable Boiteux. Courtesy of the Dance Colletion, The New York Public Library.*

strength were so grueling that by a lesson's end she was ready to faint and had to be undressed, sponged, and dressed again before she regained full consciousness. Curiously, such rigor, far from causing her to despise dancing, only increased her desire for perfection.

She became a ballerina who seemed the very incarnation of a sylph, and wherever she appeared audiences thronged to see her. She was frequently on tour, her travels even bringing her to Russia. There, something happened to her that was as odd as any incident in a ballet. One day, while out in the countryside, Taglioni's carriage was halted by bandits. Since she had jewels with her, she naturally enough was terrified. What did the bandit chief want—money? diamonds? No, he only wished to see the great Taglioni dance. Rugs were spread on the road, two violinists traveling with her tuned their instruments, and Taglioni gave an impromptu recital. The bandit chief must have liked it; although he kept the rugs as souvenirs, he let Taglioni and her entourage go free with all their belongings.

THE AUSTRIAN BALLERINA FANNY ELSSLER was considered the greatest of Taglioni's contemporaries. Dr. Louis Véron, who became director of the Paris Opéra in 1831, was shrewd enough to realize that to present both

Taglioni and Elssler would be a triumph for his ballet company. However, when word of Elssler's talents reached him, she was performing in London in programs with her sister Therese, and neither dancer wished to leave England. Therefore, to demonstrate what Parisian hospitality was like and what a devoted Parisian impresario could do for dancers, Dr. Véron hosted a lavish dinner for the Elssler sisters at a London hotel. At dessert time, the chef placed on the table a silver salver heaped with precious jewels and this salver was passed along with the fruit basket. The Elssler sisters' eyes widened with astonishment as the jewelry drew near. They were tactful enough to choose only two of the more modest pieces for themselves, but Dr. Véron's point was not lost on them and they signed an Opéra contract.

What resulted was a sort of Camargo-Sallé rivalry between Marie Taglioni and Fanny Elssler. Théophile Gautier termed Taglioni a "Christian" and Elssler a "pagan" dancer; in contrast to the famously cool and spiritual Taglioni, Elssler danced with special warmth and passion. Among Elssler's specialties were sparkling solos inspired by folk dances. She delighted Parisians in 1836 when, in Jean Coralli's *Le Diable Boiteux,* she performed the "Cachucha," a Spanish dance in which, as she played castanets, she twisted and turned with bewitching gestures that some viewers found voluptuous. Prudes may have been shocked by the solo, yet audiences kept coming back to see it, and its success inspired many imitations, including one by Camille Leroux, a French dancer and equestrienne who performed a cachucha balanced on a padded saddle while her horse galloped around a ring. Another of Elssler's folk-dance solos was the "Cracovienne" in Joseph Mazilier's *La Gypsy* of 1839. Here she wore boots with steel spurs, and their merry clinking suggested "castanets on the heels" to Gautier.

The most widely traveled ballet star of her time, Elssler made guest appearances throughout Europe and was the first major ballerina to visit the New World, where her performances were received with wild enthusiasm. In Havana she was surprised when an admirer gave her a cigar box as a present; when she opened it, she discovered that all the "cigars" were made of solid gold. In Washington, D.C., Congress adjourned on the day of one of her performances. Her enthusiastic fans christened such diverse commodities as boots, horses, boats, stockings, garters, corsets, shawls, parasols, fans, shoe polish, shaving soap, and champagne after her. The New England intellectuals also fell under her spell. At one Boston performance, Margaret Fuller remarked to Ralph Waldo Emerson, "Ralph, this is poetry." "No," he replied, "it is religion." Nathaniel Hawthorne seems to have agreed, for he hung a picture of Elssler on his wall between portraits of Ignatius Loyola and Francis Xavier. Elssler's most devoted fans did even stranger things. Some drank champagne from her slipper. Others presented her with a cross made from the wood of George Washington's bier. And Elssler was not the only ballerina to receive such adulation: once, Taglioni's fans in St. Petersburg cooked and ate a pair of her ballet slippers at dinner.

A TOUCH OF HYSTERIA ACCOMPANIED THE CULT of the ballerina; ballet, for some audiences, was almost a mania. If, in earlier times, ballet was a male art, now it was dominated by charismatic women and some devotees candidly admitted that they attended performances to ogle the ladies of the ensemble.

The Paris Opéra's management was fully aware of the power of feminine charms. Visitors were allowed to go backstage and mingle with dancers in the *foyer de la danse,* a large room next to the stage where the ballet company warmed up. One box in the theatre quickly acquired the nickname of the *loge infernale,* for there sat fashionable men-about-town whose interest in ballet was something other than purely aesthetic.

As in the eighteenth century, prominent men took dancers as mistresses although, according to the conventions of respectable morality, they were obliged to pretend that this was not so. Baron Haussmann, the city planner who rebuilt Paris, was the lover of the dancer Francine Cellier. To avoid attracting attention, he had her dress like his daughter when they went out driving together. Nevertheless, Mme Haussmann eventually learned of the affair and left him, taking their real daughter with her.

Scandals abounded, and the worldly Dr. Véron once observed, "Thucydides has written that the most virtuous woman is she of whom the least is spoken. The ladies of the Opéra are those of whom the most is spoken." Certainly, gossips had much to chatter about in the case of Caroline Forster and Elina Roland, two dancers of the Paris Opéra who brought a lawsuit for defamation of character against a journalist. He had written that these young women were such close friends that they not only danced in the same company, but also shared the same house and, occasionally, the same bed. The most notorious nineteenth-century dancer was not associated with the Opéra. This was the Irish-born woman who toured the world performing Spanish dances under the stage name of Lola Montez. Her private affairs proved more remarkable than her attempts at dancing, and she reached the summit of her career when she became the mistress of Ludwig I of Bavaria.

But not all dancers led scandalous lives. Although few possessed much formal education, many were quite intelligent and some were genuinely learned. Among the dancers of the Paris Opéra Ballet were several who had taught themselves foreign languages and who had read the classics; one wrote a treatise on theology, another was a political expert, still another knew a great deal about medicine. In any case, life for them all was more than champagne parties. Life meant hard work and long hours, usually for little pay. No wonder the attentions of wealthy male admirers could be welcome.

A dancer's life could also be perilous. The major peril—the menace of all gaslit theatres—was fire. Tutus were dangerously flammable and many instances are recorded of dancers dying in horrible stage accidents. Thus, during a performance of *The Revolt in the Harem,* Clara Webster, of London's Drury Lane Theatre, bumped against an oil burner. Her tutu caught fire and she ran hysterically about the stage, costume ablaze, until a stagehand stopped her long enough to put out the flames. But she was already fatally burned and died two days later. Emma Livry's fate was even more terrible. A protégée of Marie Taglioni, who choreographed *Le Papillon* especially to show off her abilities, Livry touched a lamp while rehearsing at the Opéra, and her dress was enveloped in flames. Unlike Webster, Livry lingered on through eight months of agony before she died. Looking back on the accident, it now seems ironically prophetic that in one scene of *Le Papillon* the heroine, who has been magically transformed into a butterfly, is attracted by a torch that shrivels her wings. It also seems ironic that, shortly before the accident, the Opéra's management ordered dancers to dip their costumes into a fireproofing solution. Livry refused, complaining that the treatment would make her tutus look dingy.

ROMANTIC BALLET REACHED ITS HEIGHT IN 1841 with the premiere of *Giselle* at the Paris Opéra. A ballet still loved the world over, *Giselle* came about through a distinguished artistic collaboration. Its score was by Adolphe

Adam, a popular composer of opera and ballet who is best remembered today for the Christmas carol known in English as "O Holy Night." The scenario, based on a legend recorded by the poet Heinrich Heine, was by Théophile Gautier and the experienced professional librettist Jules-Henry Vernoy de Saint-Georges.

In some ways, *Giselle* resembles *La Sylphide*. Both are in two acts, each act exemplifying one of the dual aspects of Romanticism: its sunlit side in the first act, its moonlit side in the second. *Giselle's* first act is set in a Rhineland village during a vintage festival. Giselle, a charming yet frail young peasant, is in love with a handsome, but mysterious, young man. When she learns that he is really Albrecht, Count of Silesia, and that he is already affianced to a noblewoman, her mind gives way. She tries to commit suicide, then swoons and falls dead. The second act is set beside her tomb in the depths of a forest. Every night, at the stroke of midnight, this glade becomes the domain of the Wilis, the ghosts of women who have died unhappy in love and who are doomed for all eternity to lead perfidious men to destruction (the word "wili" derives from a Slavic word for "vampire"). Giselle's ghost is summoned from the tomb by Myrtha, Queen of the Wilis, and when the repentant Albrecht comes to place flowers on Giselle's grave, Myrtha orders her to dance him to death. But Giselle's love for him prevails and she shields him until the first rays of dawn drive the Wilis away.

Giselle was created to show off a new ballerina, Carlotta Grisi. Announcements for the production listed Jean Coralli as choreographer, and Coralli was widely respected as a fine craftsman. Yet everyone knew that a second and even more gifted choreographer was also collaborating on the ballet. This was Jules Perrot, Grisi's lover. Together, Coralli and Perrot produced a masterpiece. Tautly constructed, *Giselle* is also enormously varied in its dramatic action and dances. Hearty peasant dances in the first act are contrasted with the eerie dances for the Wilis in the second, and the challenging solo roles include those of Albrecht, the playboy nobleman who is morally transformed by love and repentance; Myrtha, the beautiful, but cruel, Queen of the Wilis; and Hilarion, the gruff gamekeeper, who first discovers that Albrecht is a nobleman. The title role—one of the most coveted in ballet—requires its interpreter to be both a fine technician and a convincing actress as she progresses from innocence to madness in the first act; then, when she reappears as a ghost in the second act, she must seem light as air. Conceptions of the part have differed widely over the years. In the Romantic period alone, Grisi was sweetly melancholy as Giselle, while Elssler was said to have been dramatically intense.

The choreography of Perrot can be cited as an example of how easily ballets may vanish into oblivion. Perrot was universally regarded as a fine choreographer during his lifetime. Nevertheless, the only work by him that survives today is *Giselle,* a collaboration with someone else. Like Bournonville, Perrot studied with Vestris and was a distinguished dancer, winning acclaim even at a time when male dancing was growing unfashionable. However, his features were so plain and his proportions were so odd that Vestris advised him to learn how to move rapidly and brilliantly so that the audience would not have time to get a close look at him.

As a choreographer, Perrot was praised for his ability to give individual attention to everyone from the stars down to the last member of the ensemble. A man of liberal views, he could create believable characters from all social classes. His ballets were said to be swift in their action, and their episodes united mime and dance so that every movement assumed dramatic significance. His mass movement was favorably compared with the paintings of the great Romantic artist, Delacroix. He produced some of his best ballets between 1843 and 1848 in London, where he worked at Her Majesty's Theatre which, under Benjamin Lumley's management, briefly rivaled the Paris Opéra as a dance center. The theatre's stars included Grisi, Elssler, and the flamboyant Cerrito. It was here that Perrot choreographed two notable, but very different, ballets. *Esmeralda* (1844) was an ambitious adaptation of Victor Hugo's novel, *Notre Dame de Paris* (or *The Hunchback of Notre Dame,* as it is known in English). Judging from reviews, it was a masterpiece of gestural detail.

The other of these acclaimed ballets, the *Pas de Quatre* of 1845, was only a trifle. Yet it was a remarkable one. Lumley came up with a bright idea: why not have four great ballerinas—Taglioni, Cerrito, Grisi, and Grahn—dance together in the same ballet? As the London *Times* observed, such a meeting of possibly temperamental ballerinas threatened "a collision that the most carefully managed railroad could hardly hope to equal." To Perrot fell the task of devising choreography that would make each of these

Alfred Chalon portrayed Carlotta Grisi, Marie Taglioni, Lucile Grahn, and Fanny Cerrito in the most famous pose of the *Pas de Quatre* (London, 1845). *Courtesy of the Dance Collection, The New York Public Library.*

stars shine, without any one of them eclipsing the others. To everyone's delight, rehearsals progressed smoothly until one day a distraught Perrot rushed into Lumley's office saying that the ballet could never be performed because the ballerinas had started squabbling over the order of their solos. On the assumption that the final solo was the place of honor, the three other ballerinas had ceded it to Taglioni as a gesture of respect to this artist who had so profoundly influenced ballet style. But who would precede Taglioni in the penultimate solo? Ah, that was the question! And the ballerinas were quarreling over it that very moment. What could be done?

Lumley pondered a while, then came up with a devilishly clever solution: he ordered Perrot to tell the dancers that they would appear on stage in order of age—with the eldest last. When the ballerinas heard this, suddenly no one wished to be last, and rehearsals proceeded in peace. *Pas de Quatre* soon became the talk of London. Queen Victoria and Prince Albert even attended one of its performances. (The concept of *Pas de Quatre* has not lost its appeal: in the twentieth century, Anton Dolin and Keith Lester have made attempts to reconstruct *Pas de Quatre* with new choreography in the Romantic style, and many twentieth-century ballerinas have danced the roles of their illustrious predecessors.)

CERRITO'S HUSBAND WAS ARTHUR SAINT-LÉON, who, in 1870, the year of his death, choreographed the period's last great ballet, *Coppélia, or The Girl with the Enamel Eyes*. With a delightful score by Leo Delibes that includes the first balletic use of the Hungarian folk dance known as the czardas, *Coppélia* treats Romantic yearning in a lighthearted way. Its comic plot gets under way when Swanilda discovers that Frantz, the young man she loves, has been paying court to Coppélia, the mysteriously aloof daughter of an eccentric old inventor, Dr. Coppélius. Swanilda sneaks into Coppélius's house and discovers that the supposed "daughter" is only a mechanical doll. When she hears Coppélius return, she hides in the doll's alcove. But she is not the only intruder in Coppélius's workshop that night: Frantz arrives to see Coppélia, whereupon Dr. Coppélius drugs him and conceives of the demented scheme of bringing Coppélia to life by transferring Frantz's life-force into the doll. Unknown to Coppélius, Swanilda has changed places with the doll and when she pretends to come to life, she mischievously upsets the workshop. Finally, Coppélius realizes that he has been fooled and Frantz learns that his beloved was only an automaton.

Whereas another choreographer might have turned such a story into a macabre, gloomy ballet about the perils of infatuation, Saint-Léon made *Coppélia* a comedy, and young Giuseppina Bozzacchi was enchanting as

Swanilda. But that moment of triumph was followed by calamity. The Franco-Prussian War broke out. Paris was besieged. The Opéra closed. Food grew so scarce that Parisians had to eat their pet dogs and cats, and some were forced to dine on sewer rats. Saint-Léon died of exhaustion and Bozzacchi died of a fever on her seventeenth birthday.

THE OPÉRA REOPENED IN 1871, and in 1875 it moved into the palatial building that remains its present home. It is a grand theatre and a great tradition is preserved there. However, by the end of the nineteenth century a measure of creative excitement had gone out of French ballet. The Opéra Ballet School continued to train fine dancers and pleasant new works were still produced. Moreover, when Carlotta Zambelli made her debut at the Paris Opéra in 1894, the company acquired yet another great ballerina. Though Italian-born, Zambelli seemed a truly Parisian dancer because of her elegance and sophistication, and she reigned at the Opéra until 1930, when she retired to become head of the Opéra Ballet School.

During the late nineteenth century, one could also note a disturbing tendency to regard ballet as no more than light entertainment. Symptoms of this decline had long been visible. For example, in *Coppélia,* Frantz was portrayed not by a man, but by the shapely Eugénie Fiocre, who looked particularly attractive *en travesti* (in male attire). The role continued to be assigned to a woman at the Opéra until the mid-1950s. Similarly, in several other ballets the leading male role was given to a woman. Consequently, male dancing was ignored and ballet itself became a display of lovely ladies in charming costumes. But male dancing was not totally ignored and male soloists continued to be applauded. Degas's paintings of dancers date from this time, a time when ballet was pretty, but not always artistically significant.

Although successful ballet companies were established throughout Europe, some cities witnessed a similar artistic decline. As early as the 1850s, Benjamin Lumley was disturbed to find that his audience seemed to be demanding, "We only want legs, not brains." Many talented dancers had difficulty finding creative companies with which to work. Thus, once she left her native Denmark, the charming Adeline Genée spent much of her career dancing in English music halls.

Massed dancers representing the forces of progress overcome the powers of darkness in Luigi Manzotti's *Excelsior* (1881). *Courtesy of the Museo Teatrale alla Scala, Milan.*

Italian ballet schools continued to produce prodigious technicians that were often in demand as guest stars. Italian choreography tended to be grandiose, sometimes peculiarly so. Yet, although Italian audiences were famous for adoring opera, they also took ballet seriously and it may be significant that whereas in Paris ballets were often inserted into operas, in Italy they followed operas as separate entities. Luigi Manzotti, the leading Italian choreographer of the late nineteenth century, favored lavish extravaganzas. His *Sport* choreographically celebrated the pleasures of skating, fishing, boating, horse racing, and big-game hunting, while his *Amor* concerned the creation of the world, the persecution of the early Christians, and the fall of Rome; the cast included 200 dancers, 250 extras, 18 horses, 2 elephants, and an ox. A patriot passionately devoted to the cause of Italian nationalism and a choreographer fond of moving large masses of people, Manzotti could be called the Cecil B. De Mille of his day; his spectacles, like those of the great film director, extolled moral and social ideals and at the same time provided audiences with action packed entertainment and glimpses of lovely legs. Manzotti's greatest success was his *Excelsior* in 1881.

Exemplifying the era's faith in science and progress, this tribute to human ingenuity contained scenes showing the invention of the steamboat, the electrical experiments of Alessandro Volta in his laboratory, the operations of the Washington Telegraph Office, and the building of the Brooklyn Bridge, the Suez Canal, and the tunnel through Mount Cenis. The last episode, a "Festival of Nations," culminated in an "Apotheosis of Light and Peace." *Excelsior* must have been amazing to behold. Yet one wonders if it could be taken seriously.

By the century's end, although ballet could be found throughout Europe, western Europe had been superseded by Russia as ballet's creative center.

Related Readings

Taglioni in La Sylphide

Taglioni's Sylph is one of the most ideal things I have seen in the way of dancing and plastique. Here it was not a matter of admiring school and technique, this *pas* or that *pas,* this pose or that pose; it was the figure of a living and breathing Greek goddess that was here revealed to show the present generation that such forms and attitudes as we admired in antiquity could have flesh and blood and were not derived merely from the realm of fantasy.

I can never forget her as she looked when the curtain rose on *La Sylphide.* I have seen various dancers perform this part at different theatres, one in this, another in that artificial attitude. Taglioni, however, simply *posed* by the chair (in which her lover was sleeping), gazing at him intently, with one arm leaning on the arm of the chair. This scene has remained engraved in my memory. There she stood, like a fine, transparent marble statue, whose first movement surprised one as much as if a real marble statue had actually begun to stir. What is it that makes a human being wondrously beautiful and graceful? It is well known that Taglioni did not possess perfect beauty of form: her arms were thin and entirely too long, and not a single one of her limbs might have been said to be perfectly beautiful. What was it, then? It was, once again, the ideal of Beauty that radiated from the depths of the soul into this body, animated it, lifted it with such power that something marvelous took place before our eyes as we saw the invisible made visible.

(Johanne Luise Heiberg, "Memories of Taglioni and Elssler," trans. by Patricia McAndrew, *Dance Chronicle* 4(1), 1981, 15)

Johanne Luise Heiberg (1812–1890) was the greatest Danish actress of the nineteenth century.

Bournonville on the Mission of Ballet

The Dance is an art because it demands vocation, knowledge and ability (skill). *It is a fine art* because it strives for an ideal, not only of *plastic* beauty but also of *lyric* and *dramatic* expressiveness.

The beauty to which the Dance ought to aspire is not determined by vague principles of taste and pleasure, but is founded on the immutable laws of Nature.

It is the mission of Art in general, and the theatre in particular (whether its direction be comic or tragic) to elevate the mind, strengthen the spirit and refresh the senses.

Consequently, the Dance should above all beware of indulging a blasé public's fondness for effects which are as harmful to taste and morals as they are alien to true art.

Joy is a strength; *intoxication,* a weakness. *The beautiful* always retains the freshness of novelty. *The astonishing* soon grows tiresome.

The Dance can, with the aid of music, rise to the heights of *Poetry.* However, through an excess of acrobatics, it can equally degenerate into *buffoonery.* So-called "difficult" feats can be executed by countless adepts, but the appearance of *ease* is achieved only by the chosen few; for it is the height of ingenuity to know how to conceal the mechanism through a *harmonious calm,* which is the only real grace.

To maintain this natural grace during the most fatiguing movements is the main task of the art of Dance; and such virtuosity cannot be acquired without appropriate exercises, designed to develop the natural aptitudes and to eliminate the flaws and imperfections which everyone—even the greatest talent—is obliged to combat.

(August Bournonville, *Études Chorégraphiques* [1861], trans. by Ulla Skow. Copenhagen: Rhodos, 1983, p. 19)

Blasis on Dance Training

Success or failure in all studies chiefly depends on the manner in which they are commenced. Your first attention must be therefore directed to the choice of a master, with whom you may run no hazard of being led astray. All professors have not issued from good schools, and few have distinguished themselves in the art which they pretend to teach. Many there are of ordinary abilities, who, far from increasing the number of good dancers, are daily diminishing it, and whose defective mode of instruction imparts a variety of vicious habits, which the pupil afterwards finds extremely difficult, nay sometimes, impossible to eradicate. Neither follow the precepts of simple unpracticed theorists, utterly incapable of demonstrating clearly the true principles of the art: nor be guided by the imaginary schemes of innovating speculators, who, whilst they think themselves contributing to ameliorate the elementary rules of dancing, are gradually working its destruction.

Carefully shun the baneful lessons of such preceptors; and seek to place yourself under the direction of an experienced master, whose knowledge and talent will serve as true guides to perfection. . . .

Nothing is of greater importance in dancing than frequent practice; to masters even it is necessary, to students indispensable. No other art demands a stricter attention in this particular; without it, he that has made himself perfect cannot long remain so; he soon loses part of what has cost him so much labour to acquire, his equilibrium becomes less steady, his springs less elastic, and he at length finds, that through a remission of diligence, he has much to do over again. This is not the case with music and singing; a good ear, a fine voice, are usually sufficient, with a few years of moderate study, to conquer all difficulties. Nor does painting require such intense application, both from learners and professors, as dancing, which, like all other bodily exercises, cannot be acquired and retained without the utmost study and assiduity. Remain not, therefore, twenty-four hours without practicing. . . .

Particularly attend to the carriage of your body and arms. Let their motions be easy, graceful, and always in accordance with those of the legs. Display your form with taste and elegance; but beware of affectation. In the *leçon* and *exercices* pay an equal regard to both legs, lest the execution of the one surpass that of the other. I have seen many dance with one leg only; these I compare to painters that can draw figures but on one side. Dancers and painters of such limited talent are certainly not to be considered as good artists.

Take especial care to acquire perpendicularity and an exact equilibrium. In your performance be correct, and very precise; in your steps, brilliant and light; in every attitude, natural and elegant. A good dancer ought always to serve as a model to the sculptor and painter.

(Carlo Blasis, *The Code of Terpsichore* [1828], trans. by R. Barton. New York: Dance Horizons, 1975, pp. 49–52)

Fanny Elssler in the Cachucha

She comes forward in her pink satin *basquine** trimmed with wide flounces of black lace; her skirt, weighted at the hem, fits tightly over the hips; her slender waist boldly arches and causes the diamond ornament on her bodice to glitter; her leg, smooth as marble, gleams through the frail mesh of her silk stocking; and her little foot at rest seems but to await the signal of the music. How charming she is with her big comb, the rose behind her ear, her lustrous eyes and her sparkling smile! At the tips of her rosy fingers quiver ebony castanets. Now she darts forward; the castanets begin their sonorous chatter. With her hand she seems to shake down great clusters of rhythm. How she twists, how she bends! What fire! What voluptuousness! What precision! Her swooning arms toss about her drooping head, her body curves backwards, her white shoulders almost graze the ground. What a charming gesture! Would you not say that in that hand which seems to skim the dazzling barrier of the footlights, she gathers up all the desires and all the enthusiasm of the spectators?

---

*   A richly ornamented petticoat.

(Théophile Gautier, from *Les Beautés de l'Opéra* [1845], trans. by Cyril W. Beaumont, in his *The Romantic Ballet*. Repr. New York: Dance Horizons, 1972, p. 15)

Backstage at the Paris Opéra

It is in the green room that the soloists rehearse the mime sequences; but the rehearsals for the corps de ballet can take place only on stage. These ballet rehearsals in no way resemble those for the operas. One hears nothing but constant noise, chattering, uproar, and bursts of laughter. The ballet master in charge of the whole group continuously carries a great stick, but his ever more frantic floor pounding can barely restore order. It is one of the most amusing scenes imaginable, and worthy of the brush of a painter with a sense of humor. Luxury and poverty hold hands. Next to poor girls in rags and broken-down shoes there flower the richest and most elegant costumes. Diamonds and precious gems—rubies, sapphires, and emeralds—flash next to glass trinkets and paste. During the rehearsal the dancers all hang their headgear on props or scenery set up on stage. Near the tired hats, faded of color and grimy of ribbon, are displayed by contrast the most stylish ones, fitted with clean ribbons and trimmed with flowers, lace, and feathers. However little claim a corps girl may have to becoming a soloist and however humble her position, she, like a ballerina, owns a dancing dress, bloomers falling to just below the knee, white silk tights, white or pink pointe shoes, and a trim little bodice, elegantly cut, in white pique. The one came in a carriage, the other in sandals; but a spirit of camaraderie pervades their little world. She who is penniless does not grovel; she who is possessed of luxury is not arrogant. . . .

Everywhere one looks there are people nibbling on candies and cake. Some read novels . . . while some of the small children make fun of a mime scene that has just been rehearsed. Do not disturb this beautiful, preoccupied young person who is avoiding your gaze. She is passionately poring over a letter which the theatre concierge just gave her. It concerns matters of the utmost gravity; it is a love letter. Some of the dancers are running; others are stretched out on the floor. There is nothing more cheerful, diversified, and picturesque than the encampment of dancers. In such a pagan temple, sacrifices are offered to Venus, Love, Fortune, and Terpsichore.

The initial rehearsals of a ballet are done with a rather sorry orchestra—a first and second violin—and, be it night or day, there is only the glow of one or two Argand lamps to illumine the entire stage and house. The ballet master and the composer very carefully indicate the timing for the choreography and the mime. The rehearsals sometimes go on for as long as two or three hours, which does not stop either corps girl or ballerina from punctually taking class and even from staying on her feet at night throughout the entire performance.

(Louis Véron, "Confessions of an Opera Director," Part II, trans. by Victoria Huckenpahler, *Dance Chronicle* 7(2), 1984, 217–218)

6

The Imperial Russian Ballet

ECAUSE BALLET IS AN ART OF MOVEMENT that comes fully alive only when it is presented on stage and because the eloquence of dancing lies in the eloquence of motion itself, balletic plots should not be judged as if they were novels or short stories. Dramatic situations that can seem odd or unsatisfying from a literary standpoint can sometimes be quite convincing when treated choreographically. Here, for example, is the plot of one popular nineteenth-century ballet.

The curtain rises on an Egyptian landscape. An English lord and his comic servant, John Bull, who are on safari in Africa, huddle for shelter inside a pyramid during a sandstorm. There, the nobleman is offered some opium and, after a few puffs on the pipe, finds himself whisked back into the distant past. He has been transformed into Ta-Hor, a handsome young man of ancient Egypt who saves Aspicia, the pharaoh's daughter, from a lion. Although the two young people promptly fall in love, Aspicia is already betrothed to the Nubian king. When the king pursues them along the Nile and tries to seize Aspicia, she jumps into the water.

The scene changes to the bottom of the river. The Spirit of the Nile summons all the great rivers of the world into his presence so that they may dance before the beautiful Aspicia. Then he restores her to dry land. She tells her father how rudely the Nubian king had treated her and is therefore granted permission to marry Ta-Hor. But suddenly the opium dream comes to an end. Ta-Hor is a Victorian gentleman again, back in the nineteenth century. And the final curtain falls.

This is the plot of *The Daughter of Pharaoh,* choreographed by Marius Petipa in St. Petersburg in 1862. Although it may sound ludicrous when summarized in such a fashion, the ballet was enormously popular and was danced for decades. Ballerinas coveted the role of Aspicia and sophisticates considered *The Daughter of Pharaoh* a treasure of Russian ballet.

Like western European ballet, Russian ballet can be traced back to productions of the seventeenth and eighteenth centuries that combined dance with speech and song. Ballet was imported into Russia during the country's first period of Westernization when many European fashions, including dancing, were widely imitated. Several foreign ballet masters were invited to Russia, and one of them, the French-born Jean Baptiste Landé, founded the St. Petersburg Ballet School in 1738. However, dance did not receive official patronage until 1766 when Catherine II established the Directorate of the Imperial Theatres, which had jurisdiction over opera, drama, and ballet. Patronage was extended in 1806 to Moscow. Filippo Beccari had organized a dancing school at the Moscow Orphanage in 1764 and its students performed at the Petrovsky Theatre, a predecessor of the Bolshoi, until 1784, when the orphanage school was taken over by the Petrovsky's management.

Russian choreographers began to develop—one of the earliest was Ivan Valberkh, who specialized in melodramas, including anti-Napoleonic works inspired by Napoleon's Russian invasion of 1812—but the most influential during the nineteenth century were foreign. Charles Didelot came to St. Petersburg in 1801, expecting to stay only a short time, but, except for one brief interruption, he remained until his death in 1837 and did much to raise the standards of Russian dancing. Jules Perrot created ballets in St. Petersburg in the 1840s and 1850s and he, in turn, was followed by Arthur Saint-Léon. Although Saint-Léon's ballets were criticized for not being dramatically cohesive, they were filled with exuberant dancing and one of his works, *The Little Humpbacked Horse,* was an ambitious attempt to make choreographic use of Russian folklore. Blasis taught in Moscow from 1861 to 1864. And far from Paris as Russia was, international stars, such as Taglioni, Elssler, and Grisi, loved to dance there because of the warm response they received. The most important of the foreign choreographers was Marius Petipa, who was invited to be a *premier danseur* in St. Petersburg in 1847. Like Didelot, he assumed his stay would be brief; instead, he was associated with the Imperial Theatres for almost sixty years and became the virtual dictator of Russian ballet.

Ballet in nineteenth-century Russia grew rapidly in popularity. The dance scene there was unlike that of any other country in the world. There were several privately run companies, but the most prestigious of the ballet troupes were those attached to the state-supported theatres. The directors of these companies were personally appointed by the tsar, and all the dancers were, in a sense, Imperial servants. The tsar and his family often attended rehearsals and distributed prizes at ballet school graduations. In the theatre, the men in the audience always remained standing until the tsar entered his box and, out of respect, after the performance they remained in their places until he had departed. Curtain calls were arranged according to a strict pattern: first, the ballerina bowed to the tsar's box, then to that of the theatre director, and finally to the general public.

If dancers were morally suspect in western Europe, Imperial patronage made dancing a respectable career for both men and women in Russia. Dancing provided women with job security and the opportunity to lead an independent life. Male students at the state ballet schools were considered the equals of students at military or naval academies and had similar uniforms. But whereas naval cadets had an anchor and would-be army officers crossed sabers as insignias on their collars, the ballet student's insignia was Apollo's lyre.

By the mid-nineteenth century there were state-supported companies in both Moscow and St. Petersburg. In Moscow, performances took place at the Bolshoi (which means "big") Theatre; in St. Petersburg, at both the Bolshoi and the Mariinsky (often rendered into English as Maryinsky) Theatres until the former was declared structurally unsafe and all performances were confined to the Mariinsky. (Originally named for a Russian empress, it was called the Kirov Theatre, after a Soviet hero, until its name was restored, just as St. Petersburg was until recently Leningrad.) The Moscow and St. Petersburg companies were rivals—as they still are—and each had its partisans: the fans of the St. Petersburg ballet accused Moscow dancers of being crudely flamboyant, while Muscovites considered the St. Petersburg troupe too coldly academic.

Under Petipa's guidance, ballet flourished in St. Petersburg, a city celebrated for its elegance. There, Italian architects built Baroque palaces in formal gardens and the city's imposing avenues reminded some visitors of

Rome. But this was a Rome that was icebound for months beneath the frosty gleam of the Northern Lights. With its chandeliers and its color scheme of gold, white, and peacock blue, the Mariinsky was a handsome theatre, beloved by its patrons. In certain ways it resembled a private club, since most of the seats were reserved for nobles, diplomats, bankers, and prominent merchants. Some devotees virtually made ballet going an addiction and never missed a performance. These fans were called the balletomanes and they were walking ballet encyclopedias, for they knew all the facts and figures about every dancer's career. However, because their taste tended to be conservative, they often exerted a retrograde influence.

MARIUS PETIPA WAS BORN IN MARSEILLES to a family of itinerant dancers, touring and performing wherever work could be found. The rough-and-tumble conditions of life "on the road" taught the Petipas to be resourceful. Once, in Antwerp, they found that they had been booked into a theatre where all the stage lamps had been broken during a recent revolution. Unwilling to cancel their performance, they placed potatoes at strategic places on the stage, stuck candles into them, and went on with the show. Later, Petipa danced in several major cities, including Paris. There, however, he was overshadowed by his brother, Lucien, who had been the first Albrecht in *Giselle.* Determined to have a successful career of his own, Marius moved to Russia and prospered.

In addition to dancing, he served as a choreographic assistant to both Perrot and Saint-Léon. His first great success as an independent choreographer was *The Daughter of Pharaoh,* which came about when the ballerina Carolina Rosati unexpectedly demanded a new ballet for herself. Rehearsal time was limited. Nevertheless, Petipa accepted the challenge and staged his five-hour extravaganza in less than six weeks. By doing so, he proved himself a choreographer worth watching and, with the departure of Saint-Léon in 1869, he was placed in full charge of the St. Petersburg ballet.

Portraits of Petipa in his mature years depict him as a courtly gentleman with medals pinned to his chest. So impressive does he look that one could easily think him not a ballet master, but a diplomat. Indeed, in a sense, he had to be something of a diplomat—a theatrical diplomat capable of pleasing the public and the government bureaucracy without totally compromising his

Following tradition, Anna Pavlova wore a conventional tutu with Egytian designs when she portrayed an ancient princess in *The Daughter of the Pharaoh*, partnered by Mikhail Mordkin in 1906. *Courtesy of the Pavlova Museum, London.*

artistic integrity. In this respect, he recalls certain film directors who can combine genius with commercial shrewdness. Because of this combination of qualities, Petipa's ballets are often not easy to assess. Some were unabashedly sentimental, with many sequences that could be called trite: in one scene of *The Blue Dahlia* a ballerina with a sprinkling can waters a bed of flowers and all the flowers turn into dancing girls; *The Magic Pills* contains a scene in which dancers are costumed as playing cards and dominoes. Moreover, Petipa's compositional procedures were often formula-ridden. He worked at home, inventing groupings by using figures resembling chessmen, and he liked to have dances "on reserve" that he could automatically insert into any ballet requiring an extra number, no matter what that ballet's ostensible theme might be. Occasionally, he had assistants choreograph scenes for him that he either was not interested in or had no time to devise himself. And although he collaborated splendidly with important composers such as Tchaikovsky and Glazunov, he was also happy to work with minor composers such as Cesare Pugni and Leon Minkus, who could grind out rhythmically lilting and eminently danceable, but not always distinguished, tunes by the dozen. And whether he was collaborating with a Tchaikovsky or a Minkus, he often gave his composers meticulously detailed specifications about what sort of music he desired.

The costumes for Petipa's ballets might well seem strange today. Minor characters wore costumes reflecting the work's historical period or geographic locale. But the costumes for the stars were much more conventionalized. For example, Aspicia in *The Daughter of Pharaoh* wore a classical tutu with a lotus pattern on it, the sole indication that she was supposed to be an Egyptian. Similarly, the ballerina in a work about Spain would also wear a tutu; only a rose in her hair revealed that she played a Spaniard. A star often appeared wearing her favorite jewels on stage, even when cast in the role of a slave. Nevertheless, despite the peculiarities of his stagings, Petipa ranks with Bournonville and Perrot as one of the choreographic geniuses of the nineteenth century.

To appreciate that genius, one must accept the way Petipa structured his ballets. He liked to stretch out a narrative over three or four acts, even when the story could be told more concisely. Near the end of the ballet occurred what was termed a *divertissement,* a sparkling suite of dances that in no way advanced the plot, but was inserted into the ballet—as the term suggests—simply to divert. It was usually not difficult to find a pretext for the *divertissement:* the dancers might represent guests at a wedding or visitors to a castle. Yet the connection between the *divertissement* and the plot could at times be tenuous. Also near the end of the ballet, convention prescribed a *grand pas de deux* for the ballerina and *premier danseur,* and this duet was almost always constructed according to a strict form. In many instances, the duet began with an imposing entrance for the stars (the *entrée).* This was always followed by a stately section (the *adagio)* for both performers that emphasized lyrical and sustained movements. Next came solos (called "variations"): the first, for the cavalier; the second, for the ballerina. Finally, in the coda, the stars were reunited in quick, flashing steps. The *pas de deux* form could seem stereotyped, yet it permitted effective displays of contrasting types of movement. No wonder, then, that choreographers remain fond of it even today.

Petipa deliberately used many styles of movement in his ballets and labels existed for several of them. Classical dancing emphasized the balletic vocabulary at its purest and was usually reserved for a work's hero and heroine or for dancers representing fairies or spirits. Character (or *caractère)* dance derived from folk forms, such as the mazurka, czardas, or tarantella; in addition, the term served also to describe movement intended to depict certain occupations, social classes, or personal idiosyncrasies and eccentricities. *Demi-caractère* dance spiced classicism with touches of character dance. Comic and soubrette roles—for example, Swanilda in *Coppélia*—were often *demi-caractère.*

The ballets of Petipa's time also contained long passages of mime gestures that helped to tell the story. Nineteenth-century choreographers took mime seriously and tended to consider it equal in importance to the dancing. (Even though many choreographers today make little use of mime, any contemporary dancer who wishes to excel in the nineteenth-century classics in their most authentic form must be an expressive mime, as well as a brilliant technician.) At least two kinds of mime existed. One involved a heightening and choreographic stylization of realistic gesture. Petipa made use of this sort of mime. But he also used a mime that was in its way as codified a sign language as the sign language for the deaf. The meanings of some of the gestures in this language were obvious: hand on heart meant love, shaking fists meant anger. Others were more cryptic: to circle one's face with one's hands indicated that the person to whom one referred was beautiful. And still other gestures seem purely arbitrary: to circle one's hands around each other above one's head symbolized dance.

Panoramic in nature, Petipa's ballets were filled with mime, classical dance, character dance, *demi-caractère* dance, lyrical dance, dramatic dance, and *divertissements.* If some ballet goers of today might consider these long and leisurely multi-act works lacking in unity, they certainly had variety; so many different kinds of things happened in them that the best of them never turned monotonous. Regarding ballet as a visual spectacle, Petipa replaced the softness of Romantic style with a gemlike sharpness; his ballets were conceived as treats for the eyes. And because many are brilliant indeed, their anachronisms do not matter. Just as no one seriously objects to the fact that Shakespeare's Antony and Cleopatra speak blank verse—a poetic form the ancient Egyptians never knew—so no one really blames Petipa for making ancient Egyptian princesses wear tutus. Instead of worrying about archaeological accuracy, Petipa concentrated on purely choreographic effects, many of which remain impressive.

One such occurs in the "Kingdom of the Shades" episode from *La Bayadère*, a ballet of 1877 set in the India of the rajahs. In this scene, a young man journeys to the land of the dead in search of his beloved. The ghosts of dead maidens enter one by one, identically dressed and performing identical steps. The first of the spectres steps forward and raises and extends one leg in a straight line behind her, then lowers her leg from the *arabesque* (as this pose is called), steps forward again, and sustains another *arabesque*. As she does so, another spectre enters behind her, and behind that spectre is still another. They all progress slowly forward in a snaking line, performing the same sequence of steps over and over. By the time thirty or more dancers have entered, these choreographic repetitions may have transported the viewer into a state of mystic calm.

The plots of Petipa's ballets ranged from the florid drama of *The Daughter of Pharaoh* to the light comedy of *Don Quixote*. The woebegone old knight of the Cervantes novel on which the ballet is loosely based is only a minor character and most of the action is devoted to romantic intrigues involving two high-spirited young people. In some ballets the plot served only as a thread on which Petipa could string a necklace of glittering dances. Thus, no one has ever been much interested in *Raymonda's* story about how a Crusader saves the heroine from a villainous Saracen. What makes *Raymonda* still popular are its dances that blend classicism with Hungarian national dances. In a work such as this, Petipa so emphasized the purely kinetic, as distinct from the dramatic, qualities of dance that narrative and dancing become almost separate entities. Later, daring choreographers would make the separation complete. But that would not occur until the next century.

Many critics, historians, and dancegoers would agree that *The Sleeping Beauty* is Petipa's most opulent surviving work. Ivan Vsevolozhsky, director of the Imperial Theatres, devised the scenario and, on the basis of it, Petipa gave his composer, Tchaikovsky, detailed instructions about the type of music he wished, virtually measure by measure for the entire duration of the ballet. Instead of feeling thwarted by these specifications, Tchaikovsky regarded them as challenges and composed one of ballet's greatest scores. But when the tsar heard it at a dress rehearsal before its premiere in 1890, his only comment was a polite, but unenthusiastic, "Very nice." Tchaikovsky was hurt by that remark. However, it soon became clear to ballet goers that *The Sleeping Beauty* was a masterpiece.

Regarded as the basis for a play, the ballet's scenario might be judged long-winded, for not enough seems to happen in its acts. In the prologue, a wicked fairy curses the newborn Princess Aurora by saying she will one day prick her finger on a spinning needle and die. But the Lilac Fairy, one of Aurora's fairy godmothers, modifies this curse so that, instead of dying, Aurora will sink into a sleep. The prophecy is fulfilled in the first act when, on her twentieth birthday, Aurora injures herself while playing with a spindle. The second act takes place a century later: the Lilac Fairy shows a prince a vision of the slumbering Aurora and leads him to her palace where he awakens her with a kiss. And the last act is Aurora's wedding.

A play could easily say twice as much in half the time. But ballet is not a verbal art; instead, it makes its effects entirely through movement, and the movement Petipa created for *The Sleeping Beauty* is both visually beautiful and rich in thematic significance. Its many regal processions could be considered a glorification of monarchy—a tribute the tsar took for granted. But those of us who live in an age without tsars can also appreciate the way the choreography celebrates dignity, graciousness, and fine manners—qualities worth valuing in any society. Moreover, the ballet depicts the growth of a woman. Aurora is first seen as an innocent girl at her birthday party, during which she is courted by four cavaliers in the so-called "Rose Adagio," in which she must maintain difficult balances without wavering while her suitors present her with roses. The sequence is more than a test of technique; it is a ceremony of courtship in which Aurora is made an object of adoration. Later, when the prince beholds her in the vision scene, she becomes his ideal. Finally, awakened from her sleep, she is a fully human woman.

It is not only the dances for Aurora that make *The Sleeping Beauty* memorable. The prologue contains sparkling variations for each of the fairies at Aurora's christening. There is a celebrated waltz in the birthday-party scene. The prince's vision of Aurora includes beautiful choreographic patterns for an ensemble of spirits. And the final *divertissement,* in which many fairytale characters—including Red Riding Hood and Puss in Boots—come to the wedding, culminates in two contrasting *pas de deux:* a swiftly fluttering and notoriously difficult one for a bluebird and an enchanted princess, and a majestic one for Aurora and the prince.

Petipa's ballets were demanding, and the Imperial School assembled a distinguished faculty to train young dancers. The notable teachers included Pavel Gerdt, the noblest of Russian male dancers; Christian Johannsen, a pupil of Bournonville, whose class was rightly dubbed "the class of perfection"; and Enrico Cecchetti, a virtuoso Italian dancer whose classes emphasized the brilliance associated with the Italian schools. The resultant Russian classical style was therefore an amalgam of elements from the French, Danish, and Italian traditions. The presence of several guest ballerinas from Italy also acted as an incentive to Russian dancers. Virginia Zucchi, the first of the guests, was admired for her expressive dramatic power; others—including Pierina Legnani and Carlotta Brianza (the first Princess Aurora)—were dazzling technicians.

OF PETIPA'S CHOREOGRAPHIC ASSISTANTS, the Russian-born Lev Ivanov was surely the most enigmatic and talented. Ivanov was, by all accounts, a charming man. Yet he was also introspective, slightly lackadaisical, and possibly a bit too fond of drink. And he was never able to escape from Petipa's shadow. At the Mariinsky he occasionally choreographed scenes for which Petipa took credit. No one knows how good a choreographer he might have been had he been more assertive, but there is no question that he possessed genius because he choreographed *The Nutcracker* and parts of *Swan Lake.*

The Nutcracker was to have choreography by Petipa and, just as he had done for *The Sleeping Beauty,* he sent Tchaikovsky the musical specifications for this fantasy about a little girl's Christmas Eve dream journey to the realm of the Sugar Plum Fairy. Then Petipa fell ill and Ivanov choreographed the first production, in 1892, of a ballet which, in one form or another, has become a beloved holiday tradition.

The Sleeping Beauty, it tells a simple story. Yet *The Nutcracker* is by no means entirely frivolous. The first act, a Christmas party, is a celebration of friendship and family life, while the second act—the little girl's dream—is a flight of fancy that testifies to the power of the imagination.

Swan Lake, Tchaikovsky's earliest ballet, was the last to achieve success. Initially produced by Moscow's Bolshoi Ballet in 1877, it apparently had

Alla Osipenko portrays Odette in *Swan Lake* with St. Petersburg's Kirov Ballet. *From Alexander Demidov, The Russian Ballet: Past and Present.*

unremarkable choreography by Julius Reisinger and the seriousness of its music confused some ballet fans, who pronounced it "too Wagnerian." A later version by Joseph Hansen attracted little more interest. However, following the success of *The Sleeping Beauty* and *The Nutcracker,* there was talk of an entirely new production in St. Petersburg. Then Tchaikovsky died in 1893. For a memorial concert the following year, Ivanov choreographed the second act of *Swan Lake,* and the complete ballet was staged in 1895 with the first and third acts by Petipa and the second and fourth by Ivanov.

Unlike some of the Mariinsky's leisurely, panoramic works, *Swan Lake* is dramatically concise as it tells how Prince Siegfried, on a hunting trip, encounters the beautiful Odette, queen of the swans, who has fallen under an evil sorcerer's spell. Only if a man remains faithful to her can this spell be broken. Siegfried swears his allegiance to her, but at a ball he meets Odile, the sorcerer's daughter, who has disguised herself as Odette. Deceived by

Pierina Legnani, the exciting technician who created Odette-Odile in the Ivanov-Petipa *Swan Lake*, is seen in poses from Marius Petipa's *Cinderella*. *Courtesy of the Museo Teatrale alla Scala, Milan.*

appearances, Siegfried pledges to marry her. Stagings of the ballet differ from this point onward: in the original, Odette and Siegfried plunge into the lake and are united in the afterworld; in some, Siegfried battles the sorcerer and emerges victorious. In either case, love triumphs over deception.

Both Ivanov and Petipa contributed memorable sequences to the ballet. Ivanov's lakeside scenes are tender and lyrical. Petipa's most famous contribution is the "*Black Swan Pas de Deux*," during which Odile tries to convince Siegfried that she is Odette by dazzling his eyes. The roles of Odette and Odile, usually performed by the same dancer, can be considered a sort of Jekyll-Hyde challenge for the ballerina, Odette representing goodness, Odile an incarnation of evil. The climax of the *pas de deux* is a series of thirty-two whipping turns, called *fouettés,* by which Odile tries to entice Siegfried. The *fouetté* was a speciality of Pierina Legnani, the first Odette-Odile. Earlier, she had amazed St. Petersburg audiences with her *fouettés* in Petipa's *Cinderella* and, realizing that the *fouettés* could be dramatically effective as a way of bewitching Siegfried in *Swan Lake,* Petipa incorporated them into the role of Odile.

Russian dancers tried to imitate Legnani's *fouettés,* but for a long time were unable to do so. The secret of the turns was one Legnani had learned in Italian studios, and she was not eager to share it. Eventually, however, a Russian ballerina, Mathilde Kschessinska, discovered that to spin rapidly without losing one's balance, one had to keep a visible fixed point before one's eyes. (Dancers call this "spotting.") By making her own fixed point the shiny medals on the chest of a baron who always sat in the same seat, Kschessinska was able to whirl away—and prove that Russian dancers could equal any foreign guest in dexterity. Kschessinska plays a part in Russian political, as well as balletic, history. Mistress of Tsar Nicholas II before his accession to the throne, she later married his cousin, the Grand Duke André. And it was from the balcony of Kschessinska's house that Lenin delivered his first speech after he came to power.

By THE EARLY TWENTIETH CENTURY, Russian ballet was the finest in the world, at least when judged from the standpoint of technique and training. Nevertheless, some observers felt that productions were becoming hidebound and stale. Reformers arose to meet the challenge. One, Alexander Gorsky, who had been trained in St. Petersburg, went to Moscow in 1898 to work with the Bolshoi Ballet. The theatrical realism he encountered in the productions of Konstantin Stanislavsky's Moscow Art Theatre impressed him deeply and led him to revise the Petipa repertoire. He broke up Petipa's ensemble patterns, which he considered rigid, and introduced additional realistic stage business. It is difficult for non-Russians to appraise Gorsky. He certainly revitalized the Bolshoi, but for some Western audiences his restagings of Petipa seem to be filled with bothersome tinkering: if they are no longer completely authentic Petipa, neither are they radically different enough to be judged as totally new conceptions.

Another, and more important, reformer, Michel Fokine, also came out of St. Petersburg. He was more interested in creating new works than in restaging old. Early in his career, Fokine concluded that ballets should be artistically unified, that outworn conventions should be discarded, and that choreographers should seek to be expressive at every moment in their productions. By formulating these theories, he was restating the ideas of Noverre in terms appropriate for his own time. The reactionaries were horrified, and the management of the Mariinsky often proved uncooperative. Thus, in 1907, when Fokine wished dancers to be barefoot in *Eunice,* a ballet about ancient Rome, theatre officials protested, and the dancers had to wear tights with toes painted on them. However, the previous year, after a performance of Fokine's *The Vine,* Petipa, the elder statesman of Russian ballet, sent the young man a note that began, *"Cher Camarade,"* and concluded, "You will be a great ballet master."

Petipa was right. Intelligent and inquisitive, Fokine came to know the artistically progressive members of the St. Petersburg intelligentsia. Among them was Sergei Diaghilev, who, though he had edited an influential art magazine and had organized art exhibitions, still felt that he had not found his proper niche in life. Soon Diaghilev would be the director of a ballet company, Fokine would be his principal choreographer, and their innovations would change the course of ballet history.

Related Readings

Balletomania in St. Petersburg

There had been a period when, by the majority of the public, the ballet was regarded with scepticism and the lovers of it thought eccentrics. Now, no longer the Cinderella of the stage, the ballet had become fashionable. A competition for seats, for the right to be a subscriber, well proved the interest it aroused. To obtain a seat, a petition to the Chancery of the Imperial Theatres had to be filed; the chance of success was so small that big premiums were constantly offered by advertisement to the original holders of the stalls. The subscribers held tenaciously to their prerogative. No outsider could ever penetrate into their first row of stalls without a Sesame, a favour of a *balletomane* friend. Even then, a new face would be looked upon as an intrusion and eyed suspiciously by the neighbours. The seats were handed down from father to son, the name of *balletomane,* once given in derision, was becoming almost an hereditary dignity. . . .

A very knowledgeable, exacting, dogmatic and conservative public, *balletomanes* were capable of high enthusiasm. They were conservative in the extreme. A new venture, the slightest variation from the old canons was heresy to them; an occasional modification of a step an irreverence as well as a disappointment. There were some favourite steps eagerly awaited. One could feel from the stage how the whole audience stiffened in breathless expectation of a favourite passage. The passage well executed, the whole theatre burst out clapping in measure to the music. Artistic reputations were made and undone by casual remarks of the leaders of the stalls. A foreign celebrity, in a series of performances, displayed a sound virtuosity. She was round-shouldered. "A flying turkey," drawled Skalkovsky. His remark had been caught and repeated all round. They were a tyrannical public, those *balletomanes,* and pig-headed to a degree; if once they pronounced a dancer lacking some quality, no amount of evidence to the contrary would dispel the prejudice. They classified and ticketed the dancers as graceful, dramatic, lyrical, and did not encourage any attempt to develop qualities beyond those originally assigned. But they were enthusiastic. . . .

Less pontifical, but hardly of smaller importance, were the lesser *balletomanes,* the pit and the gallery. They also crowned and dethroned. Erudition and the terminology of the ballet they may have lacked, but in spontaneity of admiration, in fantastical transports of young enthusiasm they far outstripped their colleagues of the stalls. While the stalls preserved a certain decorum, the gallery spared not their throats. Long after the stalls had emptied and the lights gone down in the auditorium, the gallery raved. The safety curtain crept down, dust sheets were brought in; the gallery still shouted. A last rite was to be performed yet—waiting at the stage door. Manifestations at the stage door varied in proportion to the popularity of each artist. They ranged from silence to delirious enthusiasm.

(Tamara Karsavina, *Theatre Street.* London: Constable, 1948, pp. 125–127)

The Imperial Ballet School

Behind the Imperial Alexandre Theatre stretched the wide but short Theatre Street, leading to the Tchernichev Bridge. This yellow-and-white ensemble in St. Petersburg Empire style was one of the finest in the capital. In Theatre Street there were none but official buildings. Starting from the Alexandre Theatre on the right was the Ministry, where the Lord Chamberlain exercised his functions; on the left the whole street was filled by the magnificent Imperial Theatre School, whose walls were decorated with reliefs.

The Alexandre Theatre's façade, its roof surmounted by three bronze horses, faced the Nevsky Prospect. Theatre Street was always very quiet. At most a coach carrying future dancers to rehearsals or performances sometimes passed through the large gateway. Even for such a short journey, at all times of the year, the School's pupils only went out in these vast, old-fashioned vehicles, hermetically sealed, which never ceased to excite the curiosity of passers-by anxious to catch a glimpse of the pretty faces hidden behind the windows.

Every autumn, after a medical inspection and a strict test of their dancing aptitudes, children aged from nine to eleven were admitted to the School whose full strength was sixty to seventy girls and forty to fifty boys, all bound by the boarding school's rules.

When they had finished their studies at the Ballet School, the pupils of both sexes, now seventeen to eighteen years old, passed into the Imperial Theatre Company where they remained for twenty years, after which they could either retire, safe with a pension, or be re-engaged by contract. The Ballet School taught not only ballet but also general subjects, like an ordinary school. . . .

The girls lived on the first floor of the School, the boys on the second. Each floor consisted of huge dormitories and rehearsal rooms with high ceilings and enormous windows. The first floor also contained the little School theatre, very well arranged, with only a few rows of seats. This was where the graduation performances took place. . . .

(Mathilde Kschessinska, *Dancing in Petersburg*, trans. by Arnold L. Haskell. Garden City, N.Y.: Doubleday, 1961, pp. 22–24)

The Magic of the Mariinsky

I can still remember my enthusiasm when one day (I was eight years old) I heard that we were to celebrate Christmas by going to see a performance at the Mariinsky Theatre.

I had never yet been to the theatre, and I plied my mother with questions in order to find out what kind of show it was that we were going to see. She replied by telling me the story of the Sleeping Beauty—a favorite of mine among all fairy tales, and one which she had already told me countless times.

When we started for the Mariinsky Theatre, the snow was brightly shining in the reflected light of street lamps and shop windows. Our sleigh was noiselessly speeding along the hard surface, and I felt unspeakably happy, seated beside my mother, her arm tenderly enclosing my waist. "You are going to enter fairyland," said she, as we were being whirled across the darkness toward the theatre, that mysterious unknown.

The music of the *Sleeping Beauty* is by our great Tchaikovsky. As soon as the orchestra began to play, I became very grave and attentive, eagerly listening, moved for the first time in my life by the call of Beauty. But when the curtain rose, displaying the golden hall of a wonderful palace, I could not withhold a shout of delight. And I remember hiding my face in my hands when the old hag appeared on the stage in her car driven by rats.

In the second act a swarm of youths and maidens appeared, and danced a most delightful waltz.

"How would you like to dance thus?" asked my mother with a smile.

"Oh," I replied, "I should prefer to dance as the pretty lady does who plays the part of the Princess. One day I shall be the Princess, and dance upon the stage of this very theatre."

My mother muttered that I was her silly little dear, and never suspected that I had just discovered the idea that was to guide me throughout my life.

(Anna Pavlova, "Anna Pavlova: Pages of My Life," trans. by Sebastian Voirol, in Paul Magriel, ed., *Nijinsky, Pavlova, Duncan* [Part two: Pavlova]. New York: Da Capo, 1977, pp. 1–2)

*Petipa's Instructions to Tchaikovsky**

At the rise of the curtain the stage is empty. The hunters' horns are heard. It is Prince Desiré's huntsmen, hunting wolves and lynx among the pine trees. The hunters and their ladies enter the scene, intending to rest and eat on the green grass. The Prince appears almost immediately with his tutor Gallifron and some noblemen from his father's Court. The Prince and his companions are served with food.

(1) The hunting horns are heard. The music of the hunt, which changes into the motif of rest—must be very short. . . . Gallifron urges his pupil to join in with his companions and particularly to become acquainted with the ladies, because he must select a bride from amongst the courtiers of his kingdom. . . .

(4) Gallifron, seizing the opportunity, compels the girls—the Royal courtiers—to pass before them.

(4) (Gallifron, seizing the opportunity, another motif. 16 bars before the dance begins.)

About 24 bars for each dance of these ladies.

(5) 24 bars. Dance of the Duchesses. Noble and proud.

(6) 24 bars. Dance of the Baronesses. Haughty and finicky.

(7) 24 bars. Dance of the Countesses. Coquettish and amusing.

(8) 24 bars. Dance of the playful Marquesses. They carry little darts, with which they tease the other ladies and their cavaliers.

(9) One of the marquesses proposes to dance a Farandole, because some of the local peasants can dance it. Farandole for Coda, from 48–64 bars, the heavy tempo of a mazurka. . . .

---

*The excerpts are taken from the second-act "Vision Scene" of *The Sleeping Beauty*. The numbers indicate the ballet's musical sequences or dramatic incidents. When a number is repeated, it first refers to the dramatic action, then specifically to the music for that action. Passages printed as "conversations" refer to mime scenes.

(11) . . . as the hunt dies away, on the river appears a mother-of-pearl boat, adorned with gold and precious jewels. In it stands the Lilac Fairy, who is also Prince Desiré's godmother. The Prince bows before the good Fairy, who graciously tells him to rise and asks him with whom he is in love.

"You are not in love with anyone?" she asks him.

"No," answers the Prince. "The noble ladies of my country cannot capture my heart and I prefer to remain single than marry a suitable Court lady."

"If this is so," answers the Fairy, "I will show you your future bride, the most beautiful, the most charming and the wisest Princess in the whole world. . . ."

(11) (Only as the hunt dies away, on the river appears the mother-of-pearl boat. Fantastic poetical music. Grand music from 48–64 bars.)

(12) The Lilac Fairy waves her wand over the rock, which opens and discloses Aurora, with her sleeping friends. At a new wave of the Fairy's wand Aurora awakens and runs on the stage with her friends. The rays of the setting sun bathe her in a rose-coloured light.

(12) (At a new wave of the Fairy's wand, Aurora awakens and runs on to the stage. A tender and happy adagio. A little coquettish adagio. Variation for Aurora and a small Coda. For the Coda the music must be muted 2/4, like in [Mendelssohn's] "A Midsummer Night's Dream.")

(Marius Petipa, "The Sleeping Beauty," trans. by Joan Lawson, in Selma Jeanne Cohen, *Dance as a Theatre Art, Second Edition*. Princeton, N.J.: Princeton Book Company, Publishers, 1992, pp. 99–100)

7

Balletic Astonishments

ASTONISH ME, JEAN."

So ballet director Sergei Diaghilev once ordered the young artist and writer Jean Cocteau. That piece of advice reveals much about both Diaghilev's temperament and twentieth-century art in general. Modern artists have loved to astonish. If their attempts to do so can occasionally degenerate

In this Royal Ballet (London) performance of Fokine's exotic *The Firebird*, Mara Galeazzi is the Firebird. The ballet is based on Russian folk tales, for which Igor Stravinsky wrote his first ballet score. *Photograph by Robbie Jack/ Corbis via Getty Images.*

into strident efforts to jolt blasé sophisticates, the creative energy of modern art at its best has dared to be the enemy of complacency.

It was Diaghilev who made classical ballet a modern art. He was not a dancer, a choreographer, or a composer. Nevertheless, as a company director he was blessed with intelligence, willpower, and above all taste. Diaghilev's Ballets Russes, which flourished from 1909 to 1929, danced to new music by Stravinsky (whose career he launched with *Firebird*), Prokofiev, Ravel, Debussy, Richard Strauss, Satie, Falla, Milhaud, and Poulenc; and Diaghilev commissioned decor from artists such as Picasso, Matisse, Bakst, Benois, Derain, Braque, Utrillo, Miró, Tchelitchev, de Chirico, and Rouault. Furthermore, Diaghilev proclaimed the value—even the necessity—of imaginative choreography by encouraging five of the most important ballet choreographers of the century: Michel Fokine, Vaslav Nijinsky, Léonide Massine, Bronislava Nijinska, and George Balanchine.

Having previously arranged art shows and opera presentations in Russia, Diaghilev was encouraged by his friend Alexander Benois to introduce Russian ballet to western Europe. During the first of Diaghilev's Parisian seasons, in 1909, dance performances alternated with operas, and the featured dancers, who came from both St. Petersburg and Moscow, included Anna Pavlova, Tamara Karsavina, Yekaterina Geltzer, Vera Koralli, Vaslav Nijinsky, Mikhail Mordkin, and Adolph Bolm. At first, Diaghilev and his associates regarded the ballet troupe not as a permanent company, but as a showcase for dancers on leave from the established theatres. But as Diaghilev's Ballets Russes achieved artistic success, it grew increasingly independent until it became a completely autonomous company.

A shrewd showman, Diaghilev did his best to make his company's Paris debut memorable. He completely redecorated and refurbished the large but shabby Théâtre du Châtelet. Not simply content to make the building look fresh, he sent free tickets for the opening performance to the most beautiful actresses in Paris and seated them all in the first row of the balcony. However, the real impact of that opening night, May 19, 1909, had more to do with art than with publicity stunts. When the curtain fell on hordes of warriors leaping ferociously in the Polovetsian dances from Borodin's *Prince Igor,* an ecstatic audience ran down the aisles and tore off the orchestra rail in an attempt to embrace the dancers.

THE POLOVETSIAN DANCES—and all of Diaghilev's other early triumphs—
were choreographed by Fokine. At the Mariinsky, where he had tried to
institute his choreographic reforms, Fokine had had to contend with bureaucratic red tape and the incomprehension of conservative balletomanes. But
the Diaghilev company provided him with the opportunity to stage the
ballets he desired. French ballet goers who were starting to find the Paris
Opéra Ballet's productions anemic were amazed at the vigor and exoticism
of Fokine's creations. *Firebird,* set to Stravinsky's first ballet score, was based
on old Russian fairy tales. *Schéhérazade* was an Arabian Nights story about
marital infidelity that culminated in an orgy in a seraglio. Audiences found
it so shockingly passionate that it stirred up a major scandal. Léon Bakst's
extravagant setting was considered an orgy in itself, and it prompted fashion
designers and interior decorators to banish drabness from their designs in
favor of bright colors. The equally exotic *Cléopâtre* contained an unforget-
table entrance for the fabled queen of Egypt: she was carried on stage in a
sarcophagus, wrapped in veils like a mummy; when the veils were removed,
there stood Cleopatra in all her glory. Fokine returned to Russian folklore
in *Petrouchka,* which, set to one of Stravinsky's most famous scores, told the
pathetic tale of a puppet who comes to life during a winter carnival, only
to prove unlucky in love. More than a fantasy, *Petrouchka* proved unusually
eloquent. Fokine made his title character so poignant that, for some viewers,
this doll symbolized downtrodden, suffering humanity. Fokine also brilliantly contrasted the massed movements of the carnival revelers with solo
passages for Petrouchka and two other dolls: a pretty but empty-headed
Ballerina and the crude Moor who is Petrouchka's rival for her affections.

Fokine's ballets were important for several reasons. For one thing, they
were compact. Although Fokine admired Petipa's choreography, he thought
that, at its worst, the evening-long ballet that Petipa made popular was a
hodgepodge, lacking unity or even coherence. An advocate of tightly organized works that would present unified artistic images, he established the
one-act ballet as the choreographic norm in western Europe and America. For Fokine, there was no such thing as a single all-purpose balletic
style. Rather, he believed that each work must be choreographed in a style
uniquely appropriate to its story, setting, or theme. Even though some of

his ballets may have been exotic, most of them nevertheless concerned adult emotions. Whereas such a ballet as *The Sleeping Beauty,* though beautiful, can also seem slightly cool, Fokine's works were hot-blooded in comparison. They contained fine parts for men as well as for women, and Fokine elevated male roles—which at the Paris Opéra were still sometimes danced by women—until they were equal in importance to those for the ballerinas.

Analyzing the multi-act ballets of the nineteenth century, Fokine realized that they often contained both highly dramatic passages and dance sequences that existed primarily to display the beauty of motion itself. Fokine separated these two types of dance. Although he devoted most of his career to dramatic dance, he also created a few plotless, or abstract, ballets in which he demonstrated that movement could exist free of narrative structure. The most beloved of these works is *Les Sylphides,* a suite of ethereal dances to various pieces by Chopin. Because the women in the ensemble wear white tutus in the Romantic style associated with Taglioni, *Les Sylphides* is both a pioneer of the contemporary abstract ballet and a tribute to the Romantic era of *La Sylphide.* By proving that a dramatic situation is not necessary as a pretext for dancing, Fokine did more than make it possible for choreographers to produce plotless works; he also freed choreographers interested in dance-drama from the need to pad their ballets with *divertissements:* if drama is what such choreographers wish, they can make every moment of their works as dramatic as possible.

Even though he was responsible for the company's early successes, Fokine soon left the Ballets Russes, for his professional relations with Diaghilev had become increasingly strained. A lover of novelty, Diaghilev could grow tired of the dancers, artists, and choreographers he had encouraged. Moreover, Diaghilev did not always separate his artistic from his personal life. He did little to conceal his homosexuality—in fact he once jokingly chided some male colleagues for having "a morbid interest in women"—and he became infatuated with one of his company's stars, Vaslav Nijinsky.

OFFSTAGE, NIJINSKY APPEARED TO BE A SLIGHTLY THICKSET and diffident young man. But on stage he was electrifying. And he possessed the ability to look different in each role he played. Thus his Petrouchka resembled a lumpy straw-stuffed doll; his Favorite Slave in *Schéhérazade* caused critics to compare him with both a serpent and a panther. In more conventionally classical roles he was blessed with an elevation that Fokine used magnificently in *Spectre de la Rose,* in which Nijinsky portrayed the spirit of the rose that a young woman has brought home after her first ball. Appearing before her and dancing for and with her like a waking dream, he leaves by soaring out her bedroom window in the most celebrated leap in all ballet. Cocteau noted the often paradoxical aspects of Nijinsky's stage personality when he called the great dancer "vigorous beyond anything human and feline to a disquieting degree. He upsets all the laws of equilibrium, and seems constantly to be a figure painted on the ceiling; he reclines nonchalantly in mid-air, defies heaven in a thousand different ways, and his dancing is like some lovely poem written all in capitals."

In his revolutionary *L'Après-midi d'un Faune* (1912), Vaslav Nijinsky modeled his movements after Greek vase paintings. *From Comoedia Illustré, 1912. Photograph probably by Waléry.*

Not content for him to be merely the foremost male star of the Ballets Russes, Diaghilev also encouraged Nijinsky as a choreographer, and this threat of rivalry hurt Fokine deeply. A slow worker who labored endlessly over details, Nijinsky nevertheless managed to choreograph several ballets, each of them controversial. The only one that has survived in the standard repertoire is *L'Après-Midi d'un Faune (Afternoon of a Faun),* to a piece by Debussy, which created a stir at its premiere in 1912 because of its alleged obscenity. In its most provocative scene, a nymph escapes from an amorous faun, dropping her scarf in her haste. He then slowly lies down upon it with gestures which, to some viewers, hinted at masturbation and fetishism. Quite apart from its morality or immorality, Nijinsky's choreography was striking to behold: in contrast to Debussy's lush, flowing music, the choreography emphasized contrasts between curves and straight lines and angles; movements were turned in; and poses recalled ancient Greek friezes and vase paintings.

Over the years, dancers may have exaggerated the choreography's angularities. In 1990, when dancers of the Juilliard School in New York City performed a revival of *Faune* based upon Nijinsky's own notation system, as deciphered by Ann Hutchinson Guest and Claudia Jeschke, the choreography proved rich in flowing as well as abrupt movements. However, the resulting contrasts between lyricism and angularity still made the ballet visually striking. Since then, this version of *Faune,* based on the notation, has been staged by many companies.

Nijinsky used a commissioned score by Debussy in 1913 when he choreographed *Jeux,* which depicted a flirtation among three tennis players. This ballet was notable for possessing a contemporary setting and it proved that, far from being suitable only for legendary or historical subjects, ballet could deal with aspects of modern life. *Jeux* might have had more impact if it had not been overshadowed by another Nijinsky premiere that same season, *Le Sacre du Printemps (The Rite of Spring),* which occasioned one of the most notorious riots in theatrical history. As soon as the first notes of Stravinsky's score were played, boos and catcalls were heard. Fistfights broke out between Stravinsky's champions and opponents and the pandemonium inside the Théâtre des Champs-Elysées became so great that the dancers could not always hear the music. Although it was the score's rhythmic and harmonic strangeness that caused most of the commotion, the choreography was equally unconventional. The ballet concerned rites of a prehistoric tribe and reached its climax when a Chosen Maiden danced herself to death to propitiate the gods. Although its setting was ancient Russia, the ballet managed to suggest that strange, primordial psychic forces may be buried within anyone. Like many works created for Diaghilev, *Le Sacre du Printemps* demonstrated that ballet could incorporate nonclassical, or even violently anticlassical, movement without destroying its traditional foundations; *Le Sacre* thereby attested to both the soundness of ballet's traditions and the art's capacity for change.

IN 1987 THE JOFFREY BALLET OFFERED a hypothetical reconstruction of *Le Sacre* made, on the basis of meticulous research, by Millicent Hodson and Kenneth Archer. If it is impossible to say how exactly it duplicated the original production, it was nevertheless theatrically convincing. The vivid colors in the costumes and scenery—originally designed by Nicholas Roerich, who was a folklorist as well as a painter—made it understandable why the tribe depicted in the ballet thought it worthwhile to sacrifice a human being to ensure the rebirth of spring and its brightness out of the gloom of winter. The choreography emphasized contrapuntal line dances, circle dances, solemn rituals, and athletic contests, and it culminated in an explosive sacrificial dance during which the victim appeared to be trying to jump her way to join the sun god in the sky.

Nijinsky would probably have continued to choreograph for the Ballets Russes if he had not chosen to marry in 1913, whereupon Diaghilev dismissed him. Nijinsky was later rehired, but he was no longer Diaghilev's favorite. His behavior started to grow increasingly erratic. He missed performances, developed a fear of falling through trapdoors, and accused other dancers of trying to attack him. At last, it was evident that he was mentally ill, and in 1917 his stage career came to an end.

DIAGHILEV'S NEXT PROTÉGÉ WAS LÉONIDE MASSINE, who became a fine character dancer and an extraordinarily inventive choreographer. Massine's ballets were often witty, sophisticated, and filled with quirky gestures. His *Pulcinella,* with music by Stravinsky and settings by Picasso, paid tribute to the commedia dell'arte. *The Three-Cornered Hat,* also designed by Picasso, told how a miller's wife saved herself from the unwanted attentions of a haughty governor; it therefore could be interpreted as a parable of freedom. *La Boutique Fantasque* was a comedy on the ever-popular theme of dolls coming to life.

With Massine's choreography, the Ballets Russes underwent a change. Diaghilev's first seasons, when Fokine's ballets were emphasized, impressed Western audiences with their Russian exoticism. But Diaghilev

Léonide Massine, shown here with Tamara Toumanova, based *The Three-Cornered Hat*, designed by Picasso, on Spanish dance. *Courtesy of the Dance Collection, The New York Public Library.*

was not content to remain a purveyor of the picturesque, particularly after World War I and the Russian Revolution separated his company from its homeland. Cosmopolitan in taste and interested in modern art, he turned to Cubist and Surrealist painters for stage designs and to experimental composers for music. Conservative historians occasionally deplore these developments. It is true that Diaghilev could be guilty of faddism, but it was surely admirable for him to be interested in the art of his time and to believe that ballet could be as innovative as painting or music. From

World War I onward, Diaghilev's Ballets Russes was decidedly international in outlook; at least, it was so in most respects. However, the personnel remained largely Russian, and when dancers from other countries were hired they were expected to adopt Slavic names. Among Diaghilev's later stars were Alicia Markova, Anton Dolin, and Lydia Sokolova. Despite their names, all three were British. (Such changing of names may have inadvertently exerted a detrimental influence on ballet in England and America. It encouraged audiences to regard the art as inherently Russian, and attempts to organize American or English companies were initially greeted with derision by some ballet fans.)

A typical example of Diaghilev's modernism was *Parade,* of 1917. Massine choreographed sideshow entertainers at a Parisian street fair. The managers of the entertainers wore as costumes enormous skyscraper-like Cubist constructions designed by Picasso. The flickering gestures in a solo for a little American girl were inspired by silent movies, and sounds of typewriters and steamship whistles were incorporated into Satie's score. *Parade* helped usher in the nervous excitement of the Jazz Age. When revived by various companies in the 1970s, Massine's choreography looked as insouciant as ever.

Nathalia Goncharova's designs for *Les Noces* suggest the architectural grandeur of Bronislava Nijinska's choreography. *From Boris Kochno, Diaghilev et les Ballets Russes. Courtesy of the Dance Collection, The New York Public Library.*

Balanchine's *Prodigal Son* continues to be danced by companies around the world. A recent production shows Carlos Acosta with the Royal Ballet (London). *Photograph by Robbie Jack/Corbis via Getty Images.*

THROUGHOUT THE 1920S, DIAGHILEV PRODUCED several cheeky and topical works that came to be dubbed "choreographic cocktails." Among them were two comedies about the Riviera smart set, *Les Biches* and *Le Train Bleu,* both choreographed by Bronislava Nijinska, Nijinsky's sister and a distinguished choreographer in her own right. Nijinska became the resident choreographer of the Ballets Russes after Diaghilev quarreled with Massine. Although she was a fine satirist, Nijinska's enduring masterpiece is surely *Les Noces,* to Stravinsky's ballet-cantata about a Russian peasant wedding. In this eminently serious work, Nijinska filled the stage with monumental architectural groupings of dancers to convey the awesomeness of religious sacraments and the natural cycle of growth and regeneration.

Diaghilev's last choreographic discovery was George Balanchine. Trained at the Mariinsky, Balanchine was touring western Europe with a small group of Soviet dancers when Diaghilev hired him in 1924. Of his ten productions for the Ballets Russes, two survive. *The Prodigal Son,* to a score by Prokofiev and with designs by Rouault, retells the biblical parable in an Expressionist manner. Among the strangest scenes are those concerning the prodigal's dissipation. They include an almost serpentine dance for the siren who attempts to seduce him, and dances for a group of revelers which, far from being merry, look almost mechanical, as if Balanchine were trying to show how compulsive and debilitating debauchery can be. In contrast, *Apollo,* to a serene score by Stravinsky, shows the birth of the Greek god and his encounters with three muses. During the course of the ballet, the young god grows from gawkiness into nobility and learns to be worthy of his own divinity.

WHATEVER CHOREOGRAPHER'S STYLE may have been emphasized at any given moment of its existence, the Ballets Russes was always dominated by its director. It was Diaghilev's company, just as court ballets belonged to monarchs. Indeed, with his monocle and the white streak in his hair that earned him the nickname of "Chinchilla," Diaghilev resembled a monarch. However, unlike many monarchs, he did not have a fortune at his disposal. Diaghilev may have mounted lavish productions, yet he was not personally wealthy. His company was constantly threatened with bankruptcy and he had to spend much of his time seeking out benefactors. As a result, he grew crafty and tenacious, and when Cocteau described him as having "the face of a bulldog and the smile of a baby crocodile," he may have been saying as much about Diaghilev's personality as his physiognomy.

A man of contradictions, Diaghilev, for all his cultivation, was superstitious, given to pondering omens and trembling at black cats. A hypochondriac, he would wipe his hands after touching a doorknob in an attempt to get rid of any germs he may have acquired. And, although he was a diabetic, he loved chocolates and champagne. A gypsy fortune-teller's prediction that he would die on the water made him reluctant to take sea voyages. In a sense, the gypsy's prophecy came true: he died in 1929 in Venice, the city of canals.

The Ballets Russes died with him. However, Diaghilev left a legacy: a conception of ballet as a perfect blending of choreography, dancing, music, and decor that remains a noble ideal. Furthermore, Diaghilev proved that, far from being a trivial diversion, ballet could be serious and eloquent. Although it is always possible for people to dislike ballet, after Diaghilev it is no longer possible to argue—as some people once did—that ballet cannot be a major art.

DIAGHILEV'S COMPANY WAS CERTAINLY the most significant ballet company of the early twentieth century, but it was not the only one of merit. There was, for example, Les Ballets Suédois, which from 1920 to 1925 modeled itself on Diaghilev's avant-gardism. Officially Swedish, its spiritual home was the Parisian art world, and the productions of its choreographer, Jean Börlin, were collaborations with artists such as Léger, Picabia, and de Chirico and composers such as Milhaud, Honegger, and Satie. Because Börlin's ballets have not survived, it is now difficult to determine how distinguished a choreographer he was. Yet he surely possessed enough skill to produce lively and often daring stage spectacles.

At various times during the 1920s and 1930s, Ida Rubinstein, who had portrayed the leader of the unfaithful wives in the premiere of *Schéhérazade,* organized companies of her own, commissioning new choreography from Nijinska, Fokine, Massine, and the German modern dancer Kurt Jooss to scores by Stravinsky, Honegger, Ravel, and other composers. A statuesquely beautiful woman with considerable mimetic powers, Rubinstein also had an attractive speaking voice and some of her creations required her to recite as well as move. Unfortunately, although she was admired as a mime and possessed great stage presence, Rubinstein was considered by some critics to be technically limited,

Important though Börlin and Rubinstein were, the most famous ballet company of the early twentieth century—other than Diaghilev's Ballets Russes—was the itinerant troupe directed by Anna Pavlova. For thousands of people around the world, the name Pavlova was synonymous with "ballerina." Born into a poor family, Pavlova studied at the Imperial Ballet School in St. Petersburg and was accepted into the Mariinsky Ballet. She also appeared briefly with Diaghilev's company where, in a manner akin to that in which Camargo and Sallé, and Taglioni and Elssler, were compared, Pavlova was compared and contrasted with Tamara Karsavina. Audiences applauded Karsavina for her dramatic passion and Pavlova for her classical grace. However, Pavlova and Diaghilev were temperamentally and artistically at odds, and after she broke with the Ballets Russes in 1910 she founded her own company.

Whereas Diaghilev's productions were collaborative endeavors, Pavlova glorified the individual artist. Her company was a good one, yet it had no other leading female stars and Pavlova often replaced her male partners. She also once admitted that she liked to hire English dancers because she found them docile. Very much a grand lady in manner, Pavlova tried to look as glamorous in the street as she did on stage. She combined this love of glamour with an awesome capacity for hard work. For her, dancing was almost a compulsion. As if trying to satisfy some demand that gnawed at her psyche, Pavlova toured incessantly. Between 1910 and 1925 her company traveled a total of 300,000 miles and gave nearly 4,000 performances. Nevertheless, it is possible to wonder how much lasting happiness her success brought Pavlova. She once wrote in an autobiographical statement that when she was a child, she thought "that success spelled happiness. I was wrong. Happiness is like a butterfly which appears and delights us for one brief moment, but soon flits away."

However happy or unhappy she may have been, Pavlova brought happiness to adoring audiences everywhere and inspired many young people to become dancers. Among them was Frederick Ashton, who saw her when he was a child, fell in love with ballet as a result, and grew up to become one of England's greatest choreographers. Remembering Pavlova's performances, Ashton says, "Her personality was of such power and vibrancy that on her first entrance on to the stage she sent an electric shock throughout the audience."

Pavlova could defy all customary standards of artistry: her taste tended to be conservative and after hearing Stravinsky's music for *Firebird,* which Fokine had originally planned to choreograph for her, she pronounced it rubbish and refused to dance to it, yet she had no qualms about dancing a coquettish gavotte to the ditty known in English as "The Glow-Worm." She had technical faults as well, including limited turnout. However, none of this mattered because she so completely immersed herself in her roles that what she danced was not as important as the way in which she danced it; she managed to transcend both her personal limitations and those of her material.

One of the few large-scale masterpieces that she retained in her repertoire was *Giselle,* and she gave a memorable interpretation of its title role. But she was most famous for unabashedly sentimental vignettes in which she portrayed frail, vulnerable birds, insects, and plants. Among the best known of these sketches were *The Dragonfly* and *The California Poppy*. According to Ashton, such brief pieces, far from seeming insignificant, were little jewels, for "more emotion was distilled into these items than one might get from a complete ballet." The most celebrated of Pavlova's miniatures was *The Swan* (often referred to as *The Dying Swan)*, a solo choreographed for her by Fokine. Based on a few gliding and fluttering movements, it was technically simple. Yet Pavlova could reduce audiences to tears with it, for she invested her swan with the poignancy of all mortality. *The Swan* also came to symbolize Pavlova's own mortality. She came down with pneumonia in The Hague in 1931, and on her deathbed she was heard to murmur, "Prepare my swan costume." She died shortly thereafter. The following night her company played its scheduled performance in Brussels. When the time came for *The Swan,* the curtain opened on an empty stage and the audience rose in tribute.

Whatever artistic differences may have prevented them from collaborating, both Diaghilev and Pavlova believed that the art of theatrical dance was rooted in classical ballet. Diaghilev may have loved experimentation, but he also respected the classics and in 1921 he presented a complete *Sleeping Beauty*, lavishly designed by Bakst; and Pavlova's trifles were always couched in the purest classicism. However, even as Diaghilev and Pavlova were winning new audiences to ballet, other dancers arose to champion ways of moving that had little to do with classical precepts. They became the pioneers of what is now known as modern dance, and through their efforts and those of great ballet choreographers and company directors, the twentieth century saw the triumph of two major forms of theatrical dance.

Related Readings

Fokine's Five Principles

Not to form combinations of ready-made and established dance-steps, but to create in each case a new form corresponding to the subject, the most expressive form possible for the representation of the period and the character of the nation represented—that is the first rule of the new ballet.

The second rule is that dancing and mimetic gesture have no meaning in a ballet unless they serve as an expression of its dramatic action, and they must not be used as a mere divertissement or entertainment, having no connection with the scheme of the whole ballet.

The third rule is that the new ballet admits the use of conventional gesture only where it is required by the style of the ballet, and in all other cases endeavours to replace gestures of the hands by mimetic of the whole body. Man can be and should be expressive from head to foot.

The fourth rule is the expressiveness of groups and of ensemble dancing. In the older ballet the dancers were ranged in groups only for the purpose of ornament, and the ballet master was not concerned with the expression of any sentiment in groups of characters or in ensemble dances. The new ballet, on the other hand, in developing the principle of expressiveness, advances from the expressiveness of the face to the expressiveness of the whole body, and from the expressiveness of the individual body to the expressiveness of a group of bodies and the expressiveness of the combined dancing of a crowd.

The fifth rule is the alliance of dancing with other arts. The new ballet, refusing to be the slave either of music or of scenic decoration, and recognizing the alliance of the arts only on the condition of complete equality, allows perfect freedom both to the scenic artist and to the musician. In contradistinction to the older ballet it does not demand "ballet music" of the composer as an accompaniment to dancing; it accepts music of every kind, provided only that it is good and expressive. It does not demand of the scenic artist that he should array the ballerinas in short skirts and pink slippers. It does not impose any specific "ballet" conditions on the composer or the decorative artist, but gives complete liberty to their creative powers.

These are the chief rules of the new ballet.

(Michel Fokine, "Letter to *The Times,* July 6th, 1914: The Five Principles," in Cyril W. Beaumont, *Michel Fokine and His Ballets.* London: C. W. Beaumont, 1945, pp. 145–147)

Le Sacre du Printemps

As he had in *Faune,* Nijinsky in *Sacre* took the ensemble as a whole and in his choreographic composition manipulated the artists as one unit. In

Nijinsky's choreography the symmetrical arrangements and repeated patterns of the *corps de ballet* no longer existed. . . .

. . . the theme of *Sacre,* depicting the primitiveness of the pagan rituals in Russia in the pre-Christian era, excluded the possibility of such orderly formations and the invariable preservation of symmetrical patterns in choreographic composition.

The men in *Sacre* are primitive. There is something almost bestial in their appearance. Their legs and feet are turned inwards, their fists clenched, their heads held down between hunched shoulders; their walk, on slightly bent knees, is heavy as they laboriously straggle up a winding trail, stamping in the rough, hilly terrain.

The women in *Sacre* are also primitive, but in their countenances one already perceives the awakening of an awareness of beauty. Still, their postures and movements are uncouth and clumsy as they gather in clusters on the tops of small hillocks and come down together to meet in the middle of the stage and form a large crowd.

Nijinsky's creation of a novel structure in the choreography and his innovative movements and poses demanded an exactness of execution to the minutest detail. All this was strange and unfamiliar to the artists brought up in the traditions of the old classical ballet. . . .

Sometimes when they were so tired and exhausted by the long rehearsals they refused altogether to work with Nijinsky. One must possess a strong conviction in his truth and a strong willpower to be able to proceed and work in such a hostile and negative atmosphere. . . .

I remember one particular incident during the early rehearsals in Monte Carlo. Nijinsky demonstrated a *pas-mouvement* in the choreography to the musical count of 5/4. During his huge leap he counted 5 (3 + 2). On count 1, high in the air, he bent one leg at the knee and stretched his right arm above his head, on count 2 he bent his body towards the left, on count 3 he bent his body towards the right, then on count 1, still high in the air, he stretched his body upwards again and then finally came down lowering his arm on count 2, graphically rendering each note of the uneven measure.

Nijinsky worked in this manner on each measure, accenting the beats for the artists, and would not proceed in his composition until he obtained from each artist the exact execution. This took considerable time and created the impression that Nijinsky himself was proceeding at a slow pace in creating his composition. This was far from the truth, as could be seen when Vaslav worked with those few artists who understood him and with whom the work went fast.

(Bronislava Nijinska, *Early Memoirs,* trans. and ed. by Irina Nijinska and Jean Rawlinson. New York: Holt, Rinehart and Winston, 1981, pp. 459–460)

Diaghilev and Parade

Parade was the invention of the young French poet Jean Cocteau and it introduced the painter Picasso and the composer Erik Satie to the ballet-going public. Diaghilev always liked to feel he was in touch with all that was new in music and painting. Sharper than most people to spot good quality in the work of young artists, he needed, nevertheless, someone to keep him informed

When Sergei Diaghilev commissioned Pablo Picasso to design Leonide Massine's *Parade* (1917), elements of Cubism were introduced into ballet, as seen in the set design below, while the Chinese Conjurer's costume reflects Oriental influences. *Courtesy of the Dance Collection, The New York Public Library.*

of what was going on in the studios of Paris. This function Jean Cocteau was delighted to fulfill, as Boris Kochno did later.

Parade combined several novelties. Cubism was already ten years old, but *Parade* introduced it to the theatre public. . . . *Parade* was the first ballet to take its theme from the popular entertainments of the present day—the first of many to deal with the circus and the music-hall. *Parade* discovered America. . . .

The scene of *Parade* was outside a booth on a fairground, in front of which performers came out to give a sample of their turns and lure the public inside. These turns—two acrobats on a tight-rope, a dancing horse, a Chinese conjurer, and a child prodigy in the form of an American girl who cranked up a car, used a typewriter, and imitated Charlie Chaplin were punctuated by the altercations of rival managers, one American and one French. In lieu of costumes the managers wore eight-foot-high structures in wood and *papier-mâché*—cubist compositions by Picasso—in which sky-scrapers, human features and fragments of clothing contrived to suggest their personalities, their backgrounds and their ruthless nature. These two monsters conversed partly in gesture, waving a stick, a contract, a pipe or a megaphone, partly percussively beating a tattoo with their feet. In this extraordinary way they conveyed a vivid picture of a business conference.

Into Satie's tuneful, jazzy score, which was a sort of crystallised popular music, Cocteau insisted on introducing the naturalistic sounds of shooting, of ships' sirens and of typewriters: those noises were intended to give mental prods to the public and to supply a third dimension, in the way that cubist painters used fragments of real newspaper as reminders of everyday triviality in their visions of a serene and ordered other-world.

Parade was so delightful that I am sure it would be a favourite if it could be done today.

(Lydia Sokolova, *Dancing for Diaghilev*. New York: Macmillan, 1961, pp.102–104)

8

The Rise of American Ballet

AMERICANS HAVE ALWAYS LOVED DANCE, both as a theatrical and as a participatory art. Despite occasional protests by strict religious groups, social dances were performed in the Colonies and after the Revolution in the new Republic. Eventually, Americans took up dancing as a theatrical career and welcomed professional dancers from overseas.

Many French émigrés—dancers and musicians among them—came to the United States at the end of the eighteenth century. Some of the dancers made a point of boasting that they had studied with Pierre Gardel and Gaetan Vestris. Whatever the truth of their claims may have been, they did much to enrich American culture and make French music, dance, and clothing fashions popular.

The United States may have been a democracy. Nevertheless, just as if they were Renaissance courtiers, young Americans from cultivated families were expected to be able to dance. Dance even became a part of the curriculum of the military cadets at West Point in 1817; their teacher, Pierre Thomas, also served as their fencing master.

Like the other theatrical arts, dance occasionally had to defend itself against charges of frivolity. It is no wonder, then, that when the New Theatre of Philadelphia opened in 1793, a motto above the proscenium arch declared that the building was intended "for useful mirth or salutary woe"—a sentiment remarkably similar to the one associated with the Royal Theatre in Copenhagen.

The eighteenth century produced at least one important American dancer: John Durang, a nimble artist famous for the deftness of his hornpipe. Once, in 1791, he danced this specialty with thirteen eggs placed on stage near his feet, without treading upon or breaking any of them.

Four American ballet stars were acclaimed in the nineteenth century: Mary Ann Lee, Julia Turnbull, Augusta Maywood, and George Washington Smith. Maywood appeared successfully at the Paris Opéra and Smith, the first American Albrecht in *Giselle,* was considered proficient enough to dance with Fanny Elssler, who was only one of several foreign ballerinas who toured America.

BALLET BECAME A POPULAR FORM OF ENTERTAINMENT. After the Civil War, there was a vogue for elaborate theatrical productions involving ballet. *The Black Crook* (1866), the first and best known of these, was lavishly designed, told a fantastic story about a pact with the devil, and included ballet episodes led by Marie Bonfanti and Rita Sangalli, two much-admired Italian ballerinas. The success of *The Black Crook* prompted a host of imitations and sequels across the country. For the touring versions of such productions, a ballet master would simply go out on the road to audition and train dancers in the next town in which the show was to appear. Since he had only a short time to drill his ensemble, and since the dancers he selected were often children of poor immigrants who, to make ends meet, had to work in factories or shops during the day, it is not surprising that the choreography usually emphasized elementary steps and clear, simple patterns.

In extravaganzas of this sort, plot was usually of minimal importance and served largely to permit spectacular scenic and choreographic effects. An anonymous journalist of 1866 termed the plot of one work "only an attenuated thread whereon were strung, like so many clothespins, or pins with no clothes to speak of, the limbs of . . . ballet girls." By present-day standards, however, some of these "ballet girls" might seem overdressed. Indeed, their costumes were often deliberately padded so as to enlarge the leg and create the soft plump look fashionable in the middle of the nineteenth century.

Among the leading creators of spectacles were the Hungarian-born Kiralfy Brothers—Bolossy and Imre, who came to America in 1869 and became famous for their elaborate stagings. Working together at first and then, after their split in 1886, on their own, they devised productions that literally involved casts of thousands and that included animals as well as humans. A typical example of their choice of subject matter was Bolossy Kiralfy's *King Solomon, or the Destruction of Jerusalem,* a success of 1891. Their choreography featured geometrical patterns and showed off sumptuous costumes. In many ways, their works were akin to those made popular by Manzotti in Italy.

Although there was much ballet to be seen in America during the nineteenth century, it never developed as a serious art until well into the twentieth century. The spectacles of the nineteenth century were considered aesthetically insubstantial by sophisticated theatergoers, and even some of ballet's serious admirers considered it to be, by its very nature, a foreign art that could never put down roots in the United States.

Because of the lack of permanent American companies, there was little sustained creative development. Standards of dance training also varied alarmingly from city to city. Some unscrupulous teachers put tiny children *en pointe,* which threatened them with serious physical injury, and certain dancing schools did little more than teach acrobatic tricks to showgirls seeking jobs in Broadway musicals. Fortunately, there were also serious, talented, and dedicated teachers who dreamed of a time when there would be a real American ballet.

ALTHOUGH COMPANIES WITH SERIOUS REPERTOIRES may not have existed, ballet dancers were often popular in the musical theatre. One such star was Bessie Clayton, a pupil of George Washington Smith, who in 1894 married Julian Mitchell, Broadway's highest paid choreographer in the early years of the twentieth century and the director-choreographer for the first seven years of the *Ziegfeld Follies,* the enormously successful series of revues that began in 1907. A blonde, blue-eyed, elfin dancer, Clayton reminded some viewers of Adeline Genée and, like that Danish ballerina, she spent most of her career in musicals and vaudeville productions. During the height of her fame, from 1895 to 1915, Clayton charmed audiences with a number of specialty dances, including a version of the cakewalk performed in ballet slippers that emphasized both *pointe* steps and, during the traditional cakewalk strut, deep backbends.

As the twentieth century progressed, ballet dancing in Broadway shows was often eclipsed by tap dancing and by the ballroom dance teams that had been formed after Vernon and Irene Castle achieved enormous popularity through their appearances in Irving Berlin's show, *Watch Your Step,* in 1914. Nevertheless, one of the greatest musical comedy stars of the 1920s was another ballet-trained dancer, Marilyn Miller, who captivated audiences in productions such as *Sally* (1920), *Sunny* (1925), and *Rosalie* (1928). No other female dance star was as popular on Broadway until Gwen Verdon appeared on the scene in the 1950s.

One of the leading Broadway choreographers of the 1920s and 1930s was Albertina Rasch, an Austrian dancer trained at the Imperial Ballet School in Vienna who opened her own ballet school in New York in 1923. Rasch organized highly disciplined groups of six to twenty women who could be hired out as units to dance in musical comedies, revues, or "prologs," the fancy stage shows that preceded the motion pictures in the more grandiose movie palaces. If Rasch's ballet numbers were seldom more than light entertainment, they were skillfully assembled and Rasch, who was fascinated with American culture, incorporated jazz movements into some of her works. In 1929 she choreographed a complete ballet to Gershwin's "An American in Paris" for *Show Girl,* a musical starring Ruby Keeler and Jimmy Durante that also featured Harriet Hoctor, a ballet dancer who, like Bessie Clayton before her, was famous for her backbends.

As for serious ballet attractions, in the early twentieth century, America saw performances by Anna Pavlova, Mikhail Mordkin, and the Diaghilev Ballet. After World War I and the Russian Revolution, many Russian dancers—among them Fokine, Mordkin, and Bolm—settled in the United States and from 1927 to 1930 Léonide Massine created dances for the spectacular stage shows at New York City's Roxy Theatre.

Some of the Europeans who settled here began to champion their American pupils. For example, in the 1920s and 1930s Fokine put together a technically able company composed of his best New York students. In his choreography, however, it could be argued that Fokine never fully adjusted to the New World: his *Thunder Bird,* although based on Aztec mythology, used music by several Russian composers, including Alexander Borodin and Mikhail Glinka.

In contrast, America appears to have stimulated the choreographic and organizational abilities of Adolph Bolm. He staged many successful ballets in Chicago, including *Krazy Kat* (1920), which was based on a popular comic strip of the time. Chicago in the 1920s was also the home of the Pavley-Oukrainsky Ballet, a touring group headed by Andreas Pavley and Serge Oukrainsky. The presence of such choreographers in Chicago helped to make that city an important ballet capital from World War I to the outbreak of World War II. American-born choreographers began to work in Chicago, including Ruth Page, a pupil of Bolm, and Bentley Stone and Walter Camryn, who established a respected school.

After moving to California, Bolm was appointed ballet master of the San Francisco Opera and in 1933 he founded the company that survives today as the San Francisco Ballet. In 1937, when Willam Christensen took over as director, the company began its long and fruitful association with the Christensens, three dancing brothers from Utah. For many years, Harold Christensen headed the company's school. When Willam left San Francisco to found a ballet department at the University of Utah in 1951, Lew Christensen took over the San Francisco Ballet. In 1973 he appointed Michael Smuin as codirector, and in 1985 Helgi Tomasson became director. In Utah, Willam Christensen's activities at the university led to the establishment of a professional company, Ballet West.

Philadelphia also had its heyday as a ballet center. It was there that Catherine and Dorothie Littlefield established a company—variously known as the Philadelphia Ballet and the Littlefield Ballet—that flourished during the 1930s. By dancing in Paris, Brussels, and London in 1937, it became the first American ballet company to tour Europe.

ONE OF THE MOST IMPORTANT FIGURES in the New York ballet world has been Lincoln Kirstein, a man who, like Diaghilev, could call himself neither a dancer nor a choreographer. Although he became a novelist, a poet, and a critic, he was always haunted by ballet. One of the saddest occasions of his childhood was the day when his parents decided that, since he was only nine, he was too young to see Diaghilev's Ballets Russes. At last, in 1924 when he was seventeen, he did see that company and he felt as if he had reached the promised land.

Then, in 1929, he had an experience so strange that he could only interpret it as an omen. While sightseeing in Venice during a European visit, his wanderings brought him to a church, in front of which was moored a black gondola. Inside, Kirstein saw a crowd of mourners and, though he knew no one there, they looked curiously familiar. They had come to attend a funeral, which Kirstein discovered was being conducted according to the Eastern Orthodox liturgy. Only later did he learn that he had unwittingly attended the funeral of Diaghilev and that the mourners were Diaghilev's dancers.

There are those who would say that Kirstein eventually became an American Diaghilev. Yet, for all his respect for Diaghilev and his company, Kirstein was not content to be a fan of foreign dancers. He envisioned an American ballet company with a school attached to it that could train dancers in a distinctively American style. In 1933 he and a friend, Edward M. M. Warburg, decided to make that dream a reality. They persuaded George Balanchine, the choreographer Kirstein most admired, to come to America to direct a new school and company. It was a risky prospect, but Balanchine was out of work and jobs were scarce during those Depression years. Balanchine accepted the offer, telling Kirstein that he would love to visit a country that had produced women as lovely as Ginger Rogers. On New Year's Day, 1934, the School of American Ballet opened in a Manhattan studio that had once belonged to Isadora Duncan. The students who enrolled ranged from experienced dancers who desired to appear with a serious ballet company to awkward beginners. Whatever the level of their training, all were enthusiastic and Balanchine soon started choreographing for them.

At first, his choreographic work-in-progress seemed to grow according to happenstance. Once, when he was rehearsing a passage in which the ensemble ran offstage, a dancer fell down. Balanchine kept the incident in his ballet. At another rehearsal, a dancer entered late. That too was incorporated into the choreography. The ballet that resulted from all this was *Serenade,* a tenderly lyrical abstract piece that many companies still perform.

When Balanchine had completed several works, the dancers offered a New York season in 1935, calling themselves the American Ballet. The repertoire, though small, contained several Balanchine creations that would be recognized as important—*Serenade, Errante,* and *Mozartiana.* Nevertheless, it failed to please John Martin, dance critic of *The New York Times,* who chided the company for what he called its decadent "Riviera

The Bolshoi Ballet in *Serenade*, choreographed by Balanchine in 1934 for American Ballet, forerunner of New York City Ballet. *Alamy Stock Photo.*

esthetics." He even suggested that Balanchine should be dismissed. Martin, who reviewed dance for the *Times* from 1927 to 1962, was one of America's first major dance critics. Since he was intelligent, well informed, and totally devoted to dance, a denunciation from him was not to be taken lightly. In time, he came to support Balanchine. But for Martin in 1935, the American Ballet seemed insufficiently American. A review of some history may suggest why this was so.

The 1930s—from the Great Depression to the outbreak of World War II—were years of social upheaval and intense nationalism. Political and economic troubles focused attention on working-class struggles, the plight of farmers, and the growth of labor unions, and Americans were urged to join together to achieve national unity. Because ballet was born in the courts of Europe, many people considered it an art for an oppressive aristocracy that had no place in democratic America. Instead of adopting ballet, these theorists argued, America should create a totally new dance.

The dance form they advocated was modern dance; and modern dance certainly deserved support. Yet if its partisans were right to claim its validity, they were wrong about ballet. Despite its origin in European courts and its emphasis on dignity of carriage (a virtue that need not be restricted to aristocrats), ballet does not inherently reflect any specific social system. Instead, it could be compared with a language. Just as English, German, and Spanish are, in themselves, neither moral nor immoral, they can be put to moral or immoral uses by the speakers and writers who employ them. Ballet is similarly flexible. In the seventeenth century it may have glorified monarchy; in our own century it has been used to praise communism. In its early days, ballet borrowed elements from elegant court ceremonies as well as from robust commedia dell' arte farces. Later, folk forms were translated into balletic character dances. Throughout history, imaginative choreographers have devised new balletic steps and have found fresh uses for old ones. Surviving both autocracies and proletarian revolutions, ballet has been able to depict princes and peasants, kings, commoners, and cowboys.

BALANCHINE AND KIRSTEIN PERSEVERED in the face of criticism, as did the pioneers in Philadelphia, Chicago, and San Francisco. However, in the mid-1930s, all American ballet troupes found themselves confronted by a formidable rival: a company that prided itself on its glamour and Russianness. Wishing to perpetuate the Diaghilev tradition, René Blum and Col. Wassili de Basil formed the Ballets Russes de Monte Carlo in 1932, which was a sensation when it made its first American tour the following year. Ballet goers had legitimate reasons for rejoicing. The company's repertoire included old favorites from the Diaghilev era and important new works by Léonide Massine. Some of Diaghilev's dancers, including the scintillating Alexandra Danilova, headed the roster. And there were three well-publicized teen-aged prodigies, the so-called "baby ballerinas": Tamara Toumanova, Irina Baronova, and Tatiana Riabouchinska. American ballet-lovers took them to their hearts, just as moviegoers adored child stars like Shirley Temple.

Blum and de Basil may have wished to be second Diaghilevs, but it soon became apparent that neither possessed Diaghilev's authority or his organizational skill. Factions arose and split off from the company, including one headed by Blum himself, and questions of legal rights to ballets became increasingly complex. In eight years, de Basil changed his company's name six times, at last settling on Original Ballet Russe. After 1938 his Ballet Russe was in direct competition with another Ballet Russe, the Ballet Russe de Monte Carlo, which had been founded when Massine and a group of dancers became dissatisfied with de Basil. World War II separated both Ballets Russes from Europe. The Original Ballet Russe spent much of the war in Latin America, then returned to Europe and finally disbanded. The Ballet Russe de Monte Carlo, under the direction of Sergei Denham, a Russian-born banker, toured the United States regularly until 1962, becoming in effect (if not in name) an American institution—and in many cities a beloved one. The managerial intrigues of both companies could serve as material for farce, if it were not for one tragic footnote: René Blum, a cultivated, much respected patron of the arts and the brother of French Socialist leader Léon Blum, died in a Nazi concentration camp.

Neither Ballet Russe attained the stature of the Diaghilev Ballet, and de Basil, Blum, and Denham may have learned through experience that Diaghilev was inimitable. Yet the two companies accomplished a great deal. By touring incessantly and emphasizing a sparkling dancing style, they introduced ballet to many people throughout North and South America. They helped Americans acquire the habit of ballet going. And they also presented important ballets, particularly by Massine. The most durable have been *Le Beau Danube* and *Gaîté Parisienne,* two frothy comedies. But Massine was also acclaimed for *St. Francis,* a retelling of legends about the medieval saint; and his most controversial productions of the 1930s were his "symphonic ballets," choreographic interpretations of famous symphonies. *Choreartium* was a massive abstraction to Brahms's Fourth Symphony. *Symphonie Fantastique,* to Berlioz's work of the same name, followed the composer's own scenario about a young artist's opium dreams. *Les Présages* (Tchaikovsky's Fifth Symphony) and *Rouge et Noir* (Shostakovitch's First Symphony) allegorically depicted the conflicting forces that can shape man's destiny, and *Seventh Symphony* (to Beethoven) was based on myths of the Creation.

Both de Basil and Denham increasingly employed American dancers, and Denham's Ballet Russe de Monte Carlo eventually consisted almost entirely of Americans. But because these directors' companies contained such words as "Russe" and "Monte Carlo" in their names, they may—especially in their earlier days—have reinforced the notion that ballet was a foreign art.

It is not surprising that in the 1930s Kirstein's American Ballet was in trouble: for lovers of modern dance it was not American enough; for some fans of the Ballet Russe it was too American. Nevertheless, it struggled along for several seasons as the resident ballet company of the Metropolitan Opera until Balanchine's unconventional choreography shocked conservative operagoers. Yet, if outraged socialites found Balanchine controversial, he managed to wow Broadway and Hollywood by producing dance sequences for musical comedies, such as *On Your Toes* (with its "Slaughter on Tenth Avenue" gangster ballet) and *Babes in Arms*, and for films, such as *The Goldwyn Follies* and *I Was an Adventuress*. At a time when the choreographer of a Broadway show was usually referred to as a "dance director," Balanchine insisted on the now-familiar credit line of "choreography by . . ." in Broadway playbills.

To give his dancers additional employment and to encourage young American choreographers, Kirstein organized a second company, a touring group called Ballet Caravan, in 1936. As titles such as *Pocahontas* and *Yankee Clipper* suggest, the repertoire featured American themes and the company's choreographers sought to demonstrate that ballet was capable of treating American subject matter. Two works created by Ballet Caravan are still danced today. Lew Christensen's *Filling Station,* to a score by Virgil Thomson, is a ballet in the style of a comic strip; its hero is a filling-station attendant and other characters include truck drivers, passing motorists, and a gangster pursued by state troopers. Eugene Loring's *Billy the Kid,* to music by Aaron Copland, juxtaposes scenes from the life of the notorious outlaw with panoramic depictions of the settling of the West to imply that, despite their superficial glamour, lawless characters like Billy cannot be tolerated if civil order is to prevail.

World War II forced both the American Ballet and Ballet Caravan to disband. Balanchine served briefly as a resident choreographer for the Ballet Russe de Monte Carlo during the war. With the coming of peace, he and Kirstein embarked in 1946 on a new project. They formed Ballet

Society, a noncommercial organization designed to offer experimental works for a limited subscription audience. Two years later, Ballet Society presented some performances at the New York City Center of Music and Drama, an auditorium the city acquired in 1943 to be a performing arts center with its own resident opera and theatre companies. The company so impressed Morton Baum, chairman of the City Center finance committee, that he offered to make Ballet Society an official part of City Center, even though a friend who remembered the financially beleaguered American Ballet warned him, "You play around with Balanchine and Kirstein and you'll lose your shirt." Kirstein in turn was struck speechless by Baum's offer. Then he replied, "If you do that for us, I will give you in three years the finest ballet company in America."

Many dance writers would say he kept his promise. The New York City Ballet, as Ballet Society was renamed, is now considered one of the world's great dance companies and since 1964 has had handsome quarters at Lincoln Center. Although many choreographers have produced works for the company, the repertoire was dominated by Balanchine during his lifetime and it was Balanchine who was responsible for the company's distinctive style. A prolific, even-tempered, and imperturbable worker, Balanchine created ballets in a steady flow of inspiration, saying that his muse came to him "on union time." Even if critics used flowery language to describe his ballets, he eschewed rhetoric when he talked about choreography, preferring to liken his craft to skills such as carpentry and cooking.

Balanchine's ballets range from a serene *Orpheus* to a sprightly adaptation of *A Midsummer Night's Dream.* Yet Balanchine was best known for his plotless, or abstract, ballets. He did not invent the abstract ballet—Fokine probably did that with *Les Sylphides*— but no other choreographer explored this genre more thoroughly. Despite his ability to tell effective balletic stories when he chose to do so, he was essentially an antiliterary choreographer. "Why should we do Shakespeare?" he once remarked. "Shakespeare's already done Shakespeare." Balanchine often removed elaborate settings and costumes as well as complicated plots from his ballets. Instead, he put his faith in the power and beauty of movement, and his faith was deep.

The steps in Balanchine's abstractions were always closely interwoven with the music, yet these ballets were more than animated music appreciation lessons. Each of his abstractions reflected Balanchine's personal response to a score. Balanchine once termed music a "floor for dancing," and using music as a solid base he was capable of building remarkable choreographic structures. The rigor of Bach's Concerto for Two Violins is reflected in the crisp, bracing *Concerto Baracco*. The choreography for *Divertimento No. 15* is as gracious as its Mozart score. *Kammermusik No. 2,* to Hindemith, has the power and energy of some complex machine.

Newcomers to Balanchine need not feel intimidated by the word "abstract." One does not have to master erudite theories to appreciate his choreography; one need only watch closely as the choreography proceeds. Through changes of movement quality, it often evokes moods or personal relationships. The movement may be tense or relaxed, abrupt or flowing, carefree or somber; and the ways the dancers move in space may suggest love or hate, attraction or repulsion. Patterns form and dissolve and the sum of these patterns gives each ballet its particular emotional character. For example, the steps in *The Four Temperaments* (Hindemith) look as enigmatic as the symbols of a medieval alchemist. One episode of *Scotch Symphony* (Mendelssohn) introduces a woman who seems as ethereal as any sylphide of the Romantic era; the ballet can therefore be interpreted as a tribute to Romanticism. *Liebeslieder Walzer* (Brahms) simply shows young people waltzing in a ballroom. Yet the shifting patterns of their waltzes hint at flirtations, infatuations, and lovers' pangs.

Balanchine's movement vocabulary is that of classical ballet inherited from Petipa, and in homage to his Mariinsky training Balanchine produced his own versions of scenes from *Raymonda* and *Swan Lake.* But when he used contemporary music he often distorted academic technique with unexpected shifts of weight or energy—not merely to shock, but to revitalize tradition, just as a poet may revitalize language by putting familiar words or verse forms to new and unexpected uses. Among modern composers, Balanchine particularly admired Stravinsky and set ballets both to concert works by Stravinsky and to scores especially written for the dance. The most famous Balanchine-Stravinsky collaboration is probably *Agon* (1957). Its title is the Greek word for "contest," and it could be regarded as a set of games or athletic events—Olympian games for young gods—because the ballet's atmosphere is so electric and the dancers triumph without ever losing their elegance. *Agon* is sometimes regarded as one work in a trilogy of Balanchine-Stravinsky ballets deriving from Greek sources, the others being *Apollo* (1928) and *Orpheus* (1948). Each celebrates the civilizing powers of art, *Apollo* and *Orpheus* expressing this idea through stories drawn from mythology, *Agon* doing so abstractly.

Although Russian-born, Balanchine admired America's vigor and physicality and the freshness of the American people at their best. Occasionally, he made use of specific American themes in his works. He created ballets to Sousa marches (*Stars and Stripes*) and Gershwin songs (*Who Cares?*), and his *Square Dance* ingeniously combines classical steps, square dance patterns, and Baroque music. Even at their most nonrepresentational, Balanchine's works could still be considered American in spirit because of their energy and athleticism. Their language may be classical, but Balanchine choreographed classical ballets with an American accent.

After Balanchine's death in 1983, Lincoln Kirstein continued as general director of the New York City Ballet and Peter Martins and Jerome Robbins were named ballet-masters-in-chief (1983–1989). Both Martins, who later became sole ballet master (1990–2018), and Robbins contributed new works to the repertoire, and the company has preserved its legacy of Balanchine ballets.

AMERICA'S OTHER LARGE-SCALE BALLET COMPANY is American Ballet Theatre, founded in 1939 as Ballet Theatre. The company was an outgrowth of the Mordkin Ballet, a group directed by Mikhail Mordkin that offered familiar classics and new works choreographed by Mordkin in a traditional Russian style. But Richard Pleasant, Ballet Theatre's first director, had bolder ambitions. He dreamed of a company that, like a great art museum, could offer significant examples of many styles and historical periods. Therefore, for Ballet Theatre's first season in 1940, Pleasant assembled works by eleven choreographers, ranging from masters such as Fokine and Nijinska to comparative unknowns. After Pleasant entered military service in World War II, the company was run by several directors and managers until Lucia Chase and the scene designer Oliver Smith became codirectors in 1945. As a wealthy young widow, Chase had become seriously interested in dance and had appeared with the Mordkin Ballet. She helped finance Ballet Theatre's first season and continued to contribute to the company in the seasons that followed. Entering the dance field as a rich amateur, she became a thorough professional, single-minded in her devotion to ballet. When Chase and Smith retired as directors in 1980, they were succeeded by the Russian-born, Kirov-trained Mikhail Baryshnikov, one of the great male dancers of our century. Baryshnikov left American Ballet Theatre in 1989 and was replaced by a new team of codirectors: Jane Hermann and, in a return to the company, Oliver Smith. In late 1992, Kevin McKenzie became director.

Over the years, American Ballet Theatre has tried to remain true to the spirit of Pleasant's original concept, and its directors have often characterized it as a museum of the dance. It has produced classics, such as *Swan Lake, The Sleeping Beauty, Giselle, La Sylphide, Les Sylphides, Petrouchka,* and *La Bayadère;* it has commissioned new ballets, and has revived contemporary works first staged by other organizations—among them Eugene Loring's *Billy the Kid,* created for Ballet Caravan in 1938, and Agnes de Mille's *Rodeo,* which received its world premiere by the Ballet Russe de Monte Carlo in 1942.

The year 1942 was a significant one for American ballet, for *Rodeo's* production by the Ballet Russe was a sign that the company, separated by war from Europe, was willing to Americanize itself. *Rodeo,* to a score by Aaron Copland, tells of a tomboyish cowgirl who realizes that, to compete with frilly young ladies for the attention of the ranch hands, she too has to dress in a ladylike fashion. An ingenious device employed in both *Billy the Kid* and *Rodeo* is the use of a bowlegged, bent-kneed stance to make the dancers resemble cowboys riding horses.

GRANDDAUGHTER OF ECONOMIST HENRY GEORGE, daughter of writer-director William C. de Mille, and niece of movie director Cecil B. DeMille, Agnes de Mille was particularly interested in the introduction of American subject matter into ballet. One of her best-known pieces for American Ballet Theatre is *Fall River Legend,* based on the story of Lizzie Borden, the shy New England woman who, in a sensational murder trial, was accused of killing her father and stepmother. De Mille also choreographed many successful musical comedies, including *Oklahoma!, Bloomer Girl,* and *Carousel.*

The most influential of these shows was *Oklahoma!* (1943), the Western musical by Richard Rodgers and Oscar Hammerstein II, de Mille was invited to choreograph because of the success of her cowboy ballet, *Rodeo,* the previous year. All of de Mille's dances for the show possessed gusto. But the one that prompted the most comment was "Laurie Makes Up Her Mind," a miniature ballet in which, during a dream, the heroine (represented here by a dancing alter ego) comes to terms with her feelings about two young men.

The creators of the best musical comedies of the past had always tried to establish believable pretexts for dance numbers. But admirers of "Laurie" claimed that it significantly advanced the show's plot, and de Mille was lauded for having integrated dance with the production's dramatic values. As a result, some critics declared that *Oklahoma!* revealed the growing sophistication of the American musical. Yet it could also be argued that the older musicals possessed a sophistication of their own because of the way plot, songs, dances, and comedy routines were skillfully treated in them as separate but equal components of a total theatrical entity, just as mime and dance existed as separate parts of a Petipa ballet. Given the vigor of *Oklahoma!,* such arguments would have sounded merely theoretical to audiences of 1943; *Oklahoma!* established a trend, and for a decade or more miniature ballets were important parts of many Broadway musicals.

OF ALL FOREIGN CHOREOGRAPHERS INTRODUCED to American audiences by Ballet Theatre, the most important has been British-born Antony Tudor, who was a clerk in London's Smithfield Market until performances by Pavlova and the Diaghilev Ballet made him decide to study dance. He soon attempted choreography, creating works such as *The Planets, The Descent of Hebe,* and his first masterpieces, *Jardin aux Lilas* and *Dark Elegies,* in England before leaving for New York to participate in Ballet Theatre's debut season.

Like Balanchine, Tudor extended the range of ballet—but in a totally different direction. Whereas Balanchine often gloried in movement for its own beauty, Tudor used movement to explore psychological states. Through movement, he made thoughts and feelings visible, thereby enriching the possibilities of narrative ballet. Tudor's ballets—there are not many, for he was a painstaking craftsman—always employ the classical vocabulary, yet he could modify traditional steps to suggest the changes of a character's

American Ballet Theatre principal dancers Diane Richards and Royes Fernandez in Tudor's *Jardin aux Lilas (Lilac Garden). Photograph by Jack Mitchell/Getty Images.*

mind or the way that character may be pulled by conflicting desires. For Tudor, small gestures could be as significant as big leaps and he made the wave of a hand or the flick of a wrist reveal much about a person.

Tudor's ballets often combine psychological insight with social comment. *Jardin aux Lilas* (*Lilac Garden*) concerns a woman about to be wed in a marriage of convenience to a man she does not love. Among the guests at a party in her honor are both the man she loves and her husband's former mistress. The ballet becomes a series of furtive meetings and hasty partings, the characters always taking care to conceal their true feelings behind a mask of polite manners. The final irony of the situation is that, although these people are well-to-do, their concern for social position hinders them in their search for personal happiness. *Pillar of Fire* depicts the anguish of a shy woman who fears spinsterhood; because she wrongly suspects that the man she loves does not love her, she commits what her prim neighbors would call a moral indiscretion with another man. Other major works by Tudor include *Undertow,* an examination of the social and psychological forces that cause a young man from the slums to commit a sex crime; *Dark Elegies,* a ritual of mourning; and *Romeo and Juliet,* a choreographic adaptation of Shakespeare's play that often resembles a set of Renaissance paintings in motion. Whereas Balanchine emphasized the extroversion of American dancers, Tudor concerned himself with the direct expression of personal feelings. Together, they have profoundly influenced American ballet style.

So HAS NEW YORK–BORN JEROME ROBBINS, whose first work, *Fancy Free* (to music by Leonard Bernstein), was an immediate hit at its premiere by Ballet Theatre in 1944. Its plot was as simple as it was genial—three sailors on shore leave during World War II try to pick up some girls—but it was tightly constructed and demonstrated Robbins's ability to fuse ballet with Broadway, jazz, Harlem, and Hollywood dance styles. If its World War II setting now makes *Fancy Free* seem a "period piece," its sense of fun has not dimmed.

In Jerome Robbins's World War II ballet, *Fancy Free* (1944), three sailors (Robbins, John Kriza and Harold Lang) try to attract the attention of Muriel Bentley and Janet Reed. *Photograph by George Hurrell. Courtesy of the Dance Collection, The New York Public Library.*

Fancy Free's mixture of classical and popular dance idioms is typical of Robbins's approach to choreography. Working for both American Ballet Theatre and New York City Ballet, he proved thematically and stylistically eclectic. His *Interplay* is a perky jazz suite. *Afternoon of a Faun,* his meditation on themes from Nijinsky's ballet, transforms the faun into a young dancer rehearsing in a studio. *Moves* is a ballet in silence that appears to be abstract, but proves rich in emotional implications. *Dances at a Gathering,* to Chopin piano music, is also plotless. Nevertheless, its witty and tender episodes suggest much about human relationships. *The Cage* created a scandal at its premiere in 1951 because it implied that the way female insects such as the mantis devour their male partners after mating may have parallels in human behavior. In contrast, *Ma Mère l'Oye* (*Mother Goose*) is a sweetly whimsical and deliberately childlike retelling of old French fairy tales; and in *Glass Pieces* Robbins made a balletic commentary on the experimental "minimalist" music of Philip Glass. Robbins's theatricality also helped him become an important choreographer and stage director on Broadway, where his successes have included *West Side Story, Gypsy,* and *Fiddler on the Roof.* Thanks to the influence of Robbins—and of de Mille, who also both stage-directed and choreographed Broadway productions—choreographers are now often asked to direct musicals as well as to create dances for them.

CONCEIVABLY, THE FASCINATION WITH DIVERGENT DANCE styles that Robbins displayed could only have developed in a nation like America that was settled by people of many cultural and social backgrounds. Equally eclectic in his approach to dance is Eliot Feld, who once danced the Little Prince in Balanchine's *Nutcracker,* appeared in both the stage and movie versions of Robbins's *West Side Story,* and whose choreographic debut, *Harbinger,* was presented by American Ballet Theatre in 1967. He has headed several companies of his own. Believing that all children should have access to dance training, he and the dancer Cora Cahan founded the tuition-free Ballet Tech School in 1978, and in 1982 they supervised the renovation of an old movie house which, now named the Joyce Theater, has become one of New York City's leading centers for dance performances.

A comparable eclecticism has been displayed by the Joffrey Ballet, which Robert Joffrey and Gerald Arpino founded in 1956 when they and a few other dancers rented a station wagon and went off on a tour of one-night stands. Despite adversity, the company persisted, then prospered. In its choice of repertoire, the company exhibits an intriguing split personality. Some of its ballets have been deliberately trendy and topical: for instance, Joffrey's *Astarte* was a mixed-media spectacular that combined live dancers with films and psychedelic lighting effects. But the company has also offered a representative sampling of time-tested works by Bournonville, Fokine, Massine, Balanchine, and Robbins, as well as *The Green Table,* an antiwar ballet by the German Expressionist choreographer Kurt Jooss. Contrasting satirical scenes of bombastic diplomats gathered around a conference table with grim vignettes showing the devastation of war, *The Green Table,* choreographed in 1932, was obviously inspired by World War I. Unfortunately, given the political state of the world, it continues to seem all too timely. After Joffrey died in 1988, the company under Arpino moved from New York to Chicago in 1995, and appointed Ashley C. Wheater, a former company dancer, as director in 2007.

AT THE TURN OF THE CENTURY, American ballet was insignificant. Just over 100 years later, America has now become, along with England and Russia, one of the "big three" nations of the ballet world and the one in which ballet is most diversified in its manifestations. Like American culture as a whole, American ballet has absorbed many influences.

Professional companies have developed in many cities. Among them are the Boston Ballet, the Pennsylvania Ballet of Philadelphia, the Washington Ballet, the Cincinnati Ballet, the Atlanta Ballet, Miami City Ballet, Ballet West of Salt Lake City, the Tulsa Ballet, the Houston Ballet, the San Francisco Ballet, and Pacific Northwest Ballet of Seattle. Many introduce standard repertoire to their audiences, others feature their own choreographers, and several have special emphases, among them the Sarasota Ballet in Florida which, under the direction of Iain Webb and Margaret Barbieri, has become a repository for ballets by Frederick Ashton.

In 1968, Arthur Mitchell, a leading dancer of the New York City Ballet, founded Dance Theatre of Harlem to demonstrate that, contrary to the claims of the bigoted or the misinformed, blacks were capable of excelling in classical ballet. Despite periods of financial adversity, the company has persisted, offering both classical and contemporary works.

An enormously important, if unexpected, influence on American ballet has been modern dance. Some of the modern dance pioneers may have scorned ballet and some of their balletic contemporaries may initially have been mystified by modern dance. Yet modern dance choreographers have done much to enliven the ballet repertoire. As far back as 1947, Valerie Bettis choreographed for Ballet Russe de Monte Carlo and Merce Cunningham choreographed for Ballet Society. Since then, works by Cunningham, Paul Taylor, Martha Graham, José Limón, Twyla Tharp, and other modern dance choreographers have been staged by many ballet companies.

In the twentieth century, America developed two principal forms of theatrical dancing: ballet and modern dance. From antagonistic beginnings, they have come to be on friendly terms.

As THE LAST CENTURY DREW TO A CLOSE, ballet appeared to be flourishing throughout North America. Cities large and small had ballet companies of their own. There were many good schools and an abundance of fine dancers.

Yet some observers began to feel that a creative spark was vanishing from ballet. One of the most plaintive laments came from the dance writer Jennifer Homans who, in her 2010 history of ballet, *Apollo's Angels,* titled her final chapter "The Masters Are Dead and Gone," concluding that after a lifetime of balletgoing, "I now feel sure ballet is dying." She voiced a number of complaints about the dance scene in general, including the charge that ballet was becoming an art for the wealthy—a view which audiences of divergent artistic and political temperaments might share. But her main cause for dismay was her belief that after the death of Balanchine and other balletic leaders there were no great new talents to take their place.

Homans's book prompted many outcries, including one by the critic Roslyn Sulcas that appeared in *The New York Times* on April 23, 2017, with the headline "Three Kings of Ballet Choreography," in which she singled out three choreographers, all associated at one time or another with the New York City Ballet, who in her opinion have infused ballet with fresh excitement: Alexei Ratmansky, Christopher Wheeldon, and Justin Peck.

Alexei Ratmansky, artistic director of the Bolshoi Ballet from 2004 to 2008, is shown here at a rehearsal of a new staging of *Leah*. He continues to be artist in residence at American Ballet Theatre. *Alamy Stock Photo.*

Ratmansky, born in 1968, is the oldest of the three. Although a native of St. Petersburg, he studied ballet at the Bolshoi School in Moscow and danced with several international companies including the Ukrainian Ballet, the Royal Winnipeg Ballet, and the Royal Danish Ballet; he directed the Bolshoi Ballet from 2004 until 2008. New York-based since then, he has choreographed for both American Ballet Theatre and New York City Ballet and was appointed ABT's choreographer in residence in 2009; he has also worked with a host of other troupes.

Unusually prolific, Ratmansky is something of a choreographic sponge, soaking up artistic influences everywhere. Seriously interested in dance history, he has supervised carefully researched and reconstructed stagings of 19th-century ballets, including *Sleeping Beauty, Swan Lake,* and *Paquita,* learning the old Stepanov system of notation in order to do so. He has created new versions of his own of other ballets, including *Firebird* and *Whipped Cream* (his English title for *Schlagobers,* a pastry-shop fantasy with music by Richard Strauss produced in Vienna in 1924). Ratmansky has also remade such once-famous ballets of the Soviet era as *Bright Stream* and *The Bolt,* revising them so that their political content is minimized while their lively plots are preserved.

Like many contemporary choreographers, Ratmansky can devise works which, though plotless, seem rich in thematic implications. Several ballets to scores by Shostakovich are of this sort. Thus his *Symphony #9* (produced by American Ballet Theatre in 2012) appears festive, yet its frolics sometimes seem compulsive, as if an invisible taskmaster were ordering, "Rejoice! You must rejoice—or else!" Audiences were free to ponder the history of twentieth-century authoritarian regimes and interpret this as they wished.

Interpretative ambiguities caused trouble in 2017 when Ratmansky created *Odessa* for New York City Ballet. It contained a tumultuous scene in which a woman was tossed about by five men; some viewers took this as an image of gang rape. But no context was provided for it. Because *Odessa* was set to music that Leonid Desyatnikov had composed for a Russian film about gangsters, there was speculation that the troublesome sequence was a passing reference to that movie. But the movie is not widely known in America and many American audiences were left mystified.

Fortunately, American Ballet Theatre audiences in 2016 found no troubling images in Ratmansky's *Serenade after Plato's Symposium,* to music by Leonard Bernstein inspired by a great Platonic dialogue about the nature of love. For much of its duration it is an all-male ballet; the ways its men interact make it clear that they are discussing serious matters, and when the cast's one woman eventually enters, she seems Plato's wise seer Diotima.

LIKE RATMANSKY, CHRISTOPHER WHEELDON shuttles back and forth from company to company in country after country. Born in England in 1973, he studied at the Royal Ballet School, danced with the Royal Ballet, then joined the New York City Ballet in 1993, and began choreographing for it and, later, other companies in 1997.

Wheeldon is remarkably versatile, capable of producing the rigorously abstract *Polyphonia* (to Ligeti) and the ingenious *Scènes de Ballet,* in which two lines of dancers facing each other appear to be performing before an invisible mirror. One of his most frequently danced compositions is the *pas de deux*

Ballet comes to Broadway: director and choreographer Christopher Wheeldon and leading man Robert Fairchild on a triumphant opening night of *An American in Paris* (2015). Fairchild, a principal with the New York City Ballet, left in 2017 to focus on an independent career. *Photograph by Jemal Countess/ Getty Images.*

from *After the Rain,* originally a section from a longer work to ethereal music by Arvo Pärt. The slowly unwinding duet requires intricate partnering, but its progression must seem utterly effortless so that its two bodies seem to involve what the Australian dancer Amber Scott has called "an entwining of souls."

Wheeldon formed his own troupe, Morphoses/The Wheeldon Company, in 2006. But he found his schedule so crowded with projects that he could not devote sufficient attention to it and relinquished its direction in 2010, which should serve as a cautionary reminder that busy choreographers should not become too busy. Since then, Wheeldon has remained choreographically ever-active, for the Royal Ballet and American troupes, and he directed and choreographed the musical success *An American in Paris.*

Justin Peck, born in 1987 and the youngest of the three choreographers Sulcas singled out for attention is, like Ratmansky and Wheeldon, esthetically inquisitive, open to many influences. He was inspired to dance after seeing tap dancing and became addicted to ballet by a performance of

Justin Peck in 2014, the year he was appointed Resident Choreographer for the New York City Ballet. He had become soloist at the NYCB in 2013. *Photograph by Yana Paskova for The Washington Post via Getty Images.*

Giselle by American Ballet Theatre. He studied at the School of American Ballet, joined the New York City Ballet in 2006, began choreographing in 2009, and in 2014 was named the company's resident choreographer, succeeding Christopher Wheeldon.

One never knows what to expect of him. In *Rodeo: Four Dance Episodes* he took some of the music Aaron Copland composed for Agnes de Mille's Western ballet *Rodeo* and, discarding its specifically cowboy references, made it the basis for a lusty work for fifteen men and only one woman during which the men partner one another in both lyrical and energetic passages. Although born in Washington, D.C., Peck grew up in San Diego. A sense of beach life and perpetual sunshine can be detected in both *Heatscape,* for the Miami City Ballet and *Paz de La Jolla,* in which the corps de ballet sometimes seems to resemble ocean waves. Fascinated by compositional strategies, he made *New Blood* a series of interlocking duets: at the end of each, a dancer exits, to be replaced by a newcomer, and so the ballet proceeds.

It is no surprise that Peck titled one of his ballets *Everywhere We Go*, for he can go everywhere in search of steps and ideas. He is attuned to today's social and political climate as well as to the possibilities of technique. Genres and styles are thoroughly mixed in *The Times Are Racing*, which includes sequences for dancers in sneakers, a softshoe duet which, depending upon the casting, can be performed either by two men or a man and a woman, and fast-paced ensembles suggesting companionship, danger, and rescue, all of which race by in what may seem an evocation of the tumultuous pace of our times.

The emergence of new choreographers suggests that ballet remains very much alive.

Related Readings

Balanchine on Abstract Ballet

I am so often told that my choreographic creations are "abstract." Does abstract mean that there is no story, no literary image, at best a general idea which remains untranslated in terms of reality? Does it mean the presentation of sound and movement, of unrelated conceptions and symbols in a disembodied state?

I said on another occasion that no piece of music, no dance can in itself be abstract. You hear a physical sound, humanly organized, performed by people, or you see moving before you dancers of flesh and blood in a living relation to each other. What you hear and see is completely real. But the afterimage that remains with the observer may have for him the quality of an abstraction. Music, through the force of its invention, leaves strong after-images. I myself think of Stravinsky's *Apollon,* for instance, as white music, in places as white-on-white. . . .

For me whiteness is something positive (it has in itself an essence) and is, at the same time, abstract. Such a quality exerts great power over me when I am creating a dance; it is the music's final communication and fixes the pitch that determines my own invention.

George Balanchine's deeply serious *Don Quixote,* which he created for the New York City Ballet in 1965, is very different in mood from Marius Petipa's light-hearted 19th century adaptation of Cervante's classic novel that Balanchine knew in St. Petersburg. Like many Balanchine works, dramatic and abstract alike, its cast includes a questing male figure searching for a woman (originally Suzanne Farrell) who appears to symbolize the ideal. Balanchine, who occasionally danced Quixote, is shown rehearsing the ballet with Kay Mazzo, watched by Carol Sumner and Frank Ohman. *Photograph by Gjon Mili/The LIFE Picture Collection/Getty Images.*

Some choreographers seem to be so uncertain of their own medium that not only do they seek the ballet that "has a story" but they also have the story told in words. To me these are no longer ballets, they are choreographic plays. Any amplification necessary must come from the music which may, at times, make use of a chorus. Much can be said in movement that cannot be expressed by words. Movement must be self-explanatory. If it isn't, it has failed.

The dance has its own means of telling a story and need not invade the field of the drama or the cinema. The quality of the movement and the choreographic idea decide whether the story is understandable. In most cases, the criterion of success or failure lies in the choice of the subject matter.

Music is often adjectived as being too abstract. This is a vague and dangerous use of words and as unclear to me as when my ballets are described that way. Neither a symphony nor a fugue nor a sonata ever strikes me as being abstract. It is very real to me, very concrete, though "storyless." But storyless is not abstract. Two dancers on the stage are enough material for a story; for me, they are already a story in themselves.

(George Balanchine, "Marginal Notes on the Dance," in Walter Sorell, ed., *The Dance Has Many Faces*. 3rd ed. Pennington, N.J.: a cappella books, 1992, pp. 98–99)

The Ideals of Ballet Theatre

1. There already exist opera theatres, symphony theatres, sports, moving-picture, painting and dramatic theatres. In each of these cases the term, "theatre," is inclusive. . . . All the dramas, all the comedies, all the burlesques, all the revues during a certain period make up what we call that season's Theatre.

2. Ballet Theatre, accordingly, is incomplete if director or audience, because of personal preference or prejudice, narrows the concept of theatrical dance as a whole. From the whole being greater than any of its parts, comes the Ballet Theatre conviction that the whole must never be ruled by any of its parts, no matter how great. This applies not only to individuals but also to types and styles of dancing.

3. The Gallery Idea is a translation from museum to dance terms of a system which can comprehend the collection and display of masterpieces of all times, places and creators with the provision that they attain a certain standard of excellence. The Ballet Theatre's first repertory was not a random collection, but an attempt to show at least one masterpiece from each of the greater periods. . . .

4. . . . Ballets are the most ephemeral of art works because they can always disappear when the mind that remembers them dies. Ballet Theatre has assumed the duty of keeping for this time and this place the most authentic copies of the best of the past. Not only have they intrinsic interest but they are a constant admonitory standard to the young dancer and choreographer of today.

5. A true ballet theatre cannot stop with being a collector. Its duty to the present is to be a contemporary Lorenzo di Medici to choreographers, designers, composers who require as material a company for creating the classics of tomorrow. The past must not be let to die; neither should the present.

6. Ballet is a community art. . . . A ballet director does well to consider himself the mayor of a small community and in recognition of this Ballet Theatre dancers are chosen for citizenship as well as for dancing ability.

7. Citizenship is fostered by Fair Play, sometimes called Democracy. It means in general the right in every individual to advance as far as his native abilities, enhanced by uniform educational opportunities, will allow. To Ballet Theatre it means alternation of roles, suppression of favoritism, etc.

8. No artistic dictatorship is a Ballet Theatre policy. No one choreographer has artistic, financial or political control over the work of another choreographer. . . .

9. A financial freedom as well as moral freedom. At the outset Ballet Theatre unionized its own dancers. . . . dancers (contrary to a romantic fallacy Ballet Theatre tries hard to kill) prefer to be freestanding individuals, earning salaries rather than favors and, by this self-respect, they expand as artists.

(Unsigned statement in Ballet Theatre souvenir program, 1941)

Working with Tudor

You can't be a dancer in Tudor ballets. Everything is based on classical technique, but it must look non-existent. The structure is emotional; the technique is twisted, disguised. The flow of the movement phrase must never be broken, and this is what makes his choreography so difficult technically. He may want—and expect you to be able to do—four pirouettes, but you can't let the preparation for the pirouettes show. The turns are part of a phrase that may be saying "I love you, Juliet," and you must not interrupt that phrase to take a fourth position preparation, because then you are paying attention to yourself as a dancer and not to Juliet.

Antony Tudor rehearsing his ballet *Pillar of Fire* with the American Ballet Theatre at Lincoln Center in July 1975. Considered one of Tudor's greatest ballets, it was the first he created in the United States after coming to America from London in 1942. The cast of the first performance included Tudor, Nora Kaye and Jerome Robbins. *Photograph by Jack Mitchell/Getty Images.*

Tudor sometimes seems hard and vicious, but he has respect for his performers. You are not his tool; his string pulling lets you be alive on the stage. You must be serious and dedicated, because he demands that you enter completely into a role. Once he knows you understand the character, he will trust you creatively. He never set my final walk off—now a quite famous one—in "Pillar of Fire." I knew there had to be something vulgar and nasty in it, and something of the arrogance of a strutting sailor. So I just walked, with hips tight and shoulders up, and Tudor said that was just right.

(Hugh Laing, Interview by Selma Jeanne Cohen. *Dance Perspectives 18,* 1963, 79)

British dancer *Hugh Laing* (1911–1988) worked with Tudor in both London and New York. He portrayed major roles in the premieres of many important Tudor ballets, including *Jardin aux Lilas* and *Pillar of Fire.*

9

The Phoenix of Modern Dance

N O ONE HAS EVER REALLY LIKED THE TERM "modern dance." Dancers, choreographers, and critics have found it awkward, or confusing. At times, some of modern dance's most passionate devotees themselves have had difficulty defining just what modern dance is. Nevertheless, the term has stuck and the art has flourished.

One reason modern dance is hard to define is that it is not so much a system or technique as an attitude toward dance, a point of view that encourages artistic individualism and the development of personal choreographic styles. According to this philosophy, there are as many valid ways of dancing as there are talented choreographers; as Helen Tamiris wrote in a program note for a concert she gave in 1927, "There are no general rules. Each work of art creates its own code." Modern dance can be likened to the phoenix, the magical bird of Arabian mythology that, after living out a cycle of years, regularly burned itself upon a funeral pyre, only to arise renewed from its ashes. The phoenix of the arts, modern dance has had its own cycles of creation, and it remains in a perpetual state of metamorphosis.

MANY OF THE FOUNDERS OF MODERN DANCE were Americans, and the art developed in response to varied cultural influences. Toward the end of the nineteenth century educators began to praise dancing as a healthful form of exercise, and dance—or at least choric movement—began to be incorporated into civic pageants on inspirational or patriotic themes. It was in such an artistic climate that visionary dancers attempted to discover their own artistically valid approaches to movement. One of these iconoclasts was Maud Allan, known both for lyrical solos to classical music and for an emotionally intense dance inspired by the story of Salome. Loïe Fuller, another innovator, was a pioneer in what today would be termed mixed media. A trouper all her life, Fuller had been a child temperance lecturer and a singer before she decided to devote herself to dance. She became celebrated for works exploiting the effects caused by colored light falling upon scarfs or veils. In her *Serpentine Dance* of 1892 she wore a costume made of hundreds of yards of China silk, and as she manipulated the fabric and let it billow about her, the lighting made it seem to catch fire and take shapes reminiscent of flowers, butterflies, birds, and clouds. Standing on a piece of glass that was lighted from below, she appeared to be gradually consumed by flames in *Fire Dance,* another of her solos. Fuller created theatrical magic, and an admiring William Butler Yeats wrote a poem in her honor.

DANCERS SUCH AS FULLER AND ALLAN seem of secondary importance in comparison with Isadora Duncan. Fond of saying that she first danced in her mother's womb, Duncan danced as if by instinct from early childhood on. She picked up a smattering of training in various dance styles, and by the time she was in her teens she felt confident enough to march into the office of theatrical manager Augustin Daly, where she pronounced herself to be the spiritual daughter of Walt Whitman and declared, "I have discovered the dance, I have discovered the art which has been lost for two thousand years."

If no one knows what Daly thought of her rhetoric, he must have considered Duncan talented, for he gave her jobs in shows. Yet Duncan desired more than to appear in a famous manager's productions: she wished to present dance concerts of her own. To raise money, she endured the humiliation of entertaining millionaires' wives by dancing in their drawing rooms, after which she would beg them for financial assistance to further her projects. Thinking that her ideas might be better appreciated abroad, she and her family sailed to Europe on a cattle boat. In time, she acquired the reputation of being eccentric—as did her mother, her sister, and her brother. Only an idealistic but impractical family like the Duncans would try to build a palatial residence and art center in their beloved Greece without realizing that their property was totally devoid of drinking water. And only someone as contradictory as Isadora—she was known everywhere by her first name—would both preach the cause of socialism and commend British servants for their obedience.

But Isadora was more than eccentric. Her life and thought were shaped by some of the major social and ideological forces of the twentieth century. Feeling herself torn between liberalism and repression, she called herself "a Pagan Puritan, or a Puritanical Pagan." She espoused the cause of feminism and proclaimed the right of women to marry and bear children as they pleased. She herself had a much-publicized affair with the English actor and stage director Edward Gordon Craig, after which she lived for a time with Paris Singer, whose father had founded the Singer sewing-machine company. Still later, she married Sergei Essenin, a gifted but temperamentally unstable Russian poet. Her love life may have provided items for gossip columnists, but she always remained a serious artist who, wishing to free America from Puritanism, dared to dance and to dream of all America dancing along with her.

There were times when she seemed to live a charmed life. All these idylls were interrupted by some monstrous trick of fate. One of the most macabre of them was the freak accident in Paris that claimed the lives of her children. During a drive with their nurse, the car stalled. When the chauffeur stepped outside to crank up the engine, he accidentally put the car into reverse and it rolled over an embankment into the Seine. Isadora herself died in an equally bizarre auto accident. On September 14, 1927, she decided to go for a ride in an open car. But the fringe of the long shawl she was wearing caught in the spokes of a wheel and the very first turn of the wheels broke her neck. Those present remember that when she stepped into the car Isadora exclaimed, *"Adieu, mes amis. Je vais à la gloire."*

"I go to glory." Isadora Duncan attained glory as a prophet of what is now called modern dance. Although she did try to train children who occasionally appeared with her in concerts, the typical Duncan program consisted of solos to composers such as Gluck, Beethoven, Wagner, Chopin, and Scriabin. Wearing simple tunics or robes, she danced barefoot (which some audiences found as startling as nudity) on a bare stage hung with blue curtains. Because she could be overwhelming in her stage presence and because she sometimes burst into impromptu speeches in which she let her audience know her thoughts on the issues of the day, some people assumed that her dances were essentially improvisatory. Certainly, Duncan could be unpredictable. Nevertheless, those works that her disciples preserved and taught to other dancers all prove to be carefully shaped.

Their movement vocabulary is limited to variations on basic actions—walks, skips, jumps, runs. Yet they are neither easy to perform nor dull to watch. Among the things that make them eloquent are their dynamic shadings, their rhythmic variety, their artful contrast between moments of stillness and activity, and their ebb and flow of movement. Because for every action in them there is a counteraction, they may bring to mind phenomena such as the ocean tides, the movement of grass in the wind, and the inhalations and exhalations of the breath itself. Always, Duncan made her search for choreographic truth a kind of religious quest.

So DID ANOTHER MODERN DANCE PIONEER, Ruth St. Denis. She too was an artist of contradictions, simultaneously attracted to metaphysics and sentimental romances, to mysticism and showbiz glamour. She also resembled Duncan in the thoroughly miscellaneous dance training she received. She studied a bit of ballet and ballroom dancing, could do some Broadway high kicks, and knew something about a form called "Delsarte." Let an old song help explain just what Delsarte was:

Every little movement has a meaning all its own.
Every thought and feeling by some posture may be shown.

This was one of the hit tunes from *Madame Sherry,* a musical comedy of 1910, and it pokes fun at a system of movement study devised by François Delsarte, who died in 1871. Believing that movement is the outward manifestation of inner feelings, Delsarte tried to make a scientific examination of the ways in which emotions are reflected in posture and gesture. However, some of his well-meaning, but foolish, disciples reduced his findings to a collection of decorative and graceful poses. High-minded suburban clubwomen were particularly taken by this version of Delsarte and would sometimes do Delsartian exercises on their lawns in springtime.

Wishing a career in the theatre, the adolescent Ruth Dennis (which was Ruth St. Denis's real name) decided to storm Broadway. Knowing nothing about managers or impresarios, she started dancing for the first theatrical employee she encountered: a ticket seller. Fortunately, the man was kind enough to help arrange a proper audition for her. She toured in shows, including several productions by the great stage director David Belasco, who, as she used to say, "canonized" her by changing her surname from Dennis to St. Denis. One day, while on tour with a show in Buffalo, she was idly sipping an ice cream soda in a drugstore when her eye fell on a poster on the wall—and her life was forever changed. An advertisement for a brand of cigarettes called Egyptian Deities, the poster showed the goddess Isis enthroned in a temple. The design was in no way archaeologically accurate, yet it obsessed St. Denis and made her long to create a dance inspired by the figure in the poster.

The dance programs she eventually developed emphasized works in an Oriental style. If the steps were not always authentic, the dances were lush and lovely and managed to combine mystical messages with appeals to the senses in such a way that, like Bakst's Oriental designs for Diaghilev, they constituted an assault on turn-of-the-century propriety. Several of St. Denis's solos made artful use of only a few gestures. For example, in her *Incense* she rippled her body as she contemplated the smoke of burning incense ascending toward the gods in heaven; and in *The Cobras* she transformed her arms into two coiling snakes. As a dancer, St. Denis was beautifully proportioned, and although her hair started to turn white before she was thirty, that somehow made her all the more entrancing. She also knew how to manipulate veils and scarfs to maximum effect, so that the moving fabrics, far from being merely decorative, seemed magical extensions of her own dancing body.

In 1914 a young man named Ted Shawn came to St. Denis as a pupil. Before long, he was her partner, and then her husband. Shawn had been studying for the ministry when he contracted diphtheria. The serum that saved his life temporarily paralyzed him and he took up dancing as a physical therapy. The more he learned about dance, the more he wished to devote his life to the art, even though his startled friends kept warning him, "But, Ted, men don't dance." Together, St. Denis and Shawn organized a school and a company in Los Angeles called Denishawn. Thoroughly eclectic, Denishawn's curriculum included Oriental dance, Spanish dance, Native

Ruth St. Denis in her Oriental solo, *The Peacock,* and Ted Shawn as the Aztec emperor in *Xochitl* influenced generations of modern dancers. *Ruth St. Denis photograph by Arnold Genthe. Ted Shawn photograph by Nicholas Muray.*

American dance, basic ballet, and just about any other dance form that struck the fancy of its directors. The touring Denishawn companies were equally eclectic, and Denishawn programs might contain Hindu dances, hulas, dances based on myths or ancient history, rhythmic interpretations of concert music, and demonstrations of the latest ballroom dance crazes.

Denishawn concerts were well paced and had something for everybody. No wonder, then, that troupes of Denishawn dancers would serve both as serious cultural attractions and as units in such spectacular revues as the *Ziegfeld Follies*. Branch schools of Denishawn opened around the country and Denishawn survived as an institution until 1931, when its founders separated (although they were never divorced). St. Denis came to specialize in religious dances and Shawn started to devote himself to the cause of male dancing, organizing an all-male company that toured successfully in the 1930s. He also founded the Jacob's Pillow Dance Festival on some property he owned in Massachusetts; the festival is still flourishing.

At its height, Denishawn attracted such talented students as Martha Graham, Doris Humphrey, and Charles Weidman. They knew Denishawn would provide them with sound training and valuable theatrical experience. Nevertheless, they gradually became discontented. They feared that Denishawn's eclecticism allowed them to learn a little about many dance forms without becoming masters of any single one of them. They charged that a cult of personality had developed around Shawn and Miss Ruth (as students called her). And they complained that Denishawn too easily compromised its ideals in pursuit of commercial success. Therefore rebellious students started walking out on Denishawn. Graham was among the first.

Other defections occurred after a Denishawn staff meeting in 1928, at which Doris Humphrey accused Miss Ruth and Shawn of cheapening their presentations when they danced in the *Ziegfeld Follies*. Shawn snapped back at her, "Do you mean to say that Jesus Christ was the less great because he addressed the common people?"

"No," said Humphrey, "but you're not Jesus Christ."

Shawn retorted, "But I am. I am the Jesus Christ of the dance."

After that, Humphrey felt she could no longer remain with Denishawn, and she and her partner Charles Weidman left to form a company of their own.

All across America, there would soon be rebellious young dancers questioning the values and standards of the dance world in which they found themselves. Modern dance has continued to develop as a result of young dancers learning from and then going beyond—or even actively rebelling against their elders. It is surely significant that the two nations in which early modern dance prospered, America and Germany, had no creatively significant ballet companies at the time. Therefore, idealistic dancers felt obliged to reinvent dance as they went along. Since America has often liked to call itself a nation "on the move," it could be argued that modern dance represents one way of channeling the energy for which Americans are famous. Modern dance can also be said to exemplify both American self-reliance and, in its creatively permissive spirit, American ideals of democracy and nonconformity.

The early days of modern dance—the 1920s and 1930s—were, as the critic John Martin once described them, "days of divine indiscipline." Despite the consternation of audiences unaccustomed to choreographic experimentation, there was a sense of adventure in the air. Modern dancers occasionally took their iconoclasm to extremes. Because ballet was suspect to them and ballet movements were often curved and symmetrical, modern dancers reveled in angular asymmetries. Early modern dance tended to be fierce; it emphasized the ground rather than the air and disdained frills and glamour.

Except for Germany's Harald Kreutzberg, Ted Shawn, Charles

Léon Bakst sketched Isadora Duncan in her heroic solo to the *Marseillaise*, the French national anthem. From Ilya Schneider, *Isadora Duncan: The Russian Years.*

Weidman, and Lester Horton in America, and some few others, most of the important early modern dancers were women. Men were discouraged from studying dance by a prejudice against male dancers, but women were tolerated as dancers, even though—especially in ballet—their virtue was suspect. Modern dance allowed women to proclaim their independence from both artistic and social stereotypes.

For the most part, the moderns were concerned with the expressive power of movement. So, of course, were Isadora Duncan and Diaghilev's choreographers, but Duncan and Diaghilev sought to combine movement with fine music—and in Diaghilev's case with fine art as well—to demonstrate

Mary Wigman's solo, *Song of Fate*, showed a masked figure struggling against destiny. *Courtesy of the Dance Collection, The New York Public Library.*

that movement could hold its own as an ally of the other arts. Many of the early moderns, in contrast, minimized the other arts. Music for a dance was sometimes composed after that dance had been choreographed and it occasionally consisted only of percussion rhythms. Costumes were spartan—so much so that some wits dubbed this the "long woolens" period of modern dance.

MODERN DANCE DEVELOPED INDEPENDENTLY in America and Germany, where the art was known as *Ausdruckstanz* (expressive dance). However, German modern dance was blighted by Nazi oppression, and by the end of World War II it had been left artistically weakened. Before the war, however, the most important of Germany's modern dance choreographers was Mary Wigman. She was the pupil of both Émile Jaques-Dalcroze, founder of a system of movement exercises designed to develop rhythmic awareness, and Rudolf von Laban, a theorist who tried to analyze movement in terms of scientific principles. By balletic standards, Wigman was a somewhat stocky, muscular dancer, and although many people found her eloquent, few considered her conventionally pretty. Her choreography was noted for its intensity, even the lyrical dances. Many of her most famous dances were somber works that called attention to primitive drives that still existed in supposedly "civilized" people. Because Wigman felt her dancing made contact with primordial forces that could take possession of her as she moved, she often wore masks in her dances in order to escape from or transcend her ordinary personality and let those forces take command.

Although Wigman was the most famous of the German modern dancers, she was not the only significant German choreographer; nor did all German choreographers create works in her style. Between World War I and World War II, modern dance in Germany—as well as in other Central European nations—was remarkable for its variety and quality.

Less internationally celebrated than Wigman because she did not tour as extensively, Gret Palucca was considered by some German critics to be Wigman's choreographic equal. Unlike Wigman, who was her teacher, Palucca specialized in dances of dynamism and elan, and the structural logic of her compositions caused her to be admired by German abstract painters. Oskar Schlemmer, who was a painter as well as a choreographer, experimented with theatrical abstractions, attaching sticks and hoops to dancers' bodies to affect the way they looked as they moved through space.

Rosalia Chladek, a Czech-born Austrian dancer, was trained in the Dalcroze system. Like many other choreographers at the time, she created suites or cycles of dances consisting of episodes that were simultaneously self-contained and thematically related to one another. Some of these cycles depicted scenes from the lives of historical or religious figures such as Joan of Arc and the Virgin Mary. Others were studies in dynamics or movement qualities, for instance, a suite of marches that offered examples of festive, sad, heroic, and barbaric ways of marching.

Still other dancers were known for character sketches. As a portrayer of jesters, aristocrats, biblical angels, and people from the Middle Ages, Harald Kreutzberg was praised for the deftness and elegance of his gestures. In contrast, Valeska Gert's solos were rowdy and often bitterly satirical. She was fond of playing unruly figures such as boxers, strippers, prostitutes, and squalling babies. She developed what she called *tontänze* (sound dances) in which bodily movements were combined with vocal sounds ranging from spoken words to grunts, screeches, and squeals. These raucous compositions prefigured some of the experiments in mixed-media and dance-theatre made from the 1960s through the 1980s.

After touring America in the early 1930s, Wigman sent one of her assistants, Hanya Holm, to New York to open a branch of the Wigman school. Holm soon realized that American bodies and temperaments were so different from those of German students that she asked, and received, permission to change the name of the school to the Hanya Holm Studio and to run it as an independent institution. Holm formed her own company and choreographed for it her most important work, *Trend* (1937), which concerned the survival of society in a time of chaos. She also created the dances for a number of Broadway musicals, including *My Fair Lady* and *Kiss Me, Kate*.

AMONG AMERICAN MODERN DANCERS, the most influential were Doris Humphrey and Martha Graham. Doris Humphrey grew up in the Chicago area, where her parents managed a hotel that catered to a theatrical clientele. As a girl, she took ballet lessons, and her teachers exemplify the uneven standards of American dance training in the early twentieth century. For example, one teacher was a Viennese woman who claimed that a diet of gooseberries would develop physical agility. Another teacher was a gentleman who delighted in pinching little Doris as she went through her exercises. Fortunately, in addition to such eccentrics, she managed to study with real masters. Humphrey joined Denishawn in 1917, then rebelled against it eleven years later and started a group of her own in collaboration with Charles Weidman, her partner.

Weidman was particularly known for his deft and witty mimetic pieces. *Flickers* (1941) was a spoof of silent films. *And Daddy Was a Fireman* (1943) contained affectionate portraits of members of Weidman's family. Weidman created several dances inspired by the comic drawings and stories of James Thurber: *Fables for Our Time* (1947), *The War Between Men and Women* (1954), and *Is Sex Necessary?* (1960). However, his compassion and concern for social justice occasionally led him to choreograph serious, even somber, works, among them *Lynchtown* (1936), a depiction of mob violence during a lynching, and *A House Divided* (1945), a tribute to Abraham Lincoln.

Humphrey almost invariably chose serious themes. Like Graham, she developed a technique from a study of elementary principles of movement. But whereas Graham emphasized the breath, Humphrey stressed balance. Her key words were "fall" and "recovery" and her choreography made much of the contrasts between yielding to gravity and resisting gravity to restore equilibrium. In *Water Study* (1928) Humphrey made use of fall

In *Duodrama* Doris Humphrey and Charles Weidman examined male-female relationships over the centuries. *Photograph by Edward Moeller.*

and recovery to suggest the movements of waves. However, since conflict is inherent in the muscular drama of balance and imbalance, it is not surprising that many of Humphrey's works were studies of human conflict. *The Shakers* (1931) was based on the ceremonies of a nineteenth-century celibate sect that believed one could free oneself of sin by literally shaking it out of the body. *Inquest* (1944) concerned nineteenth-century slum life. *Day on Earth* (1947) was a symbolic study of young love, maturation, marriage, and family responsibilities. *Ruins and Visions* (1953) depicted the folly of trying to isolate oneself from reality.

Humphrey choreographed her most ambitious study of conflict, the *New Dance* trilogy, during 1935 and 1936. Although each work in this sequence was a self-sufficient creation, all three were related thematically. *Theatre Piece* satirized the rat race of competitive society. *With My Red Fires* was an attack on possessive love personified by a mother who attempts to thwart her daughter's romantic yearnings. But Humphrey's idealism always prevented her from falling into pessimism. Therefore, after deploring both communal and personal failings, Humphrey visualized an ideal social order in which the individual and the group could exist in accord. This finale, called simply *New Dance*, was plotless, but its choreographic patterns could be said to symbolize individuals simultaneously independent from and in harmony with their fellow beings.

MARTHA GRAHAM ONCE SUMMED UP HER APPROACH to choreography by saying that she considered each of her works to be "a graph of the heart." An incident from her childhood that she never forgot was when her father, a physician specializing in nervous disorders, told her never to lie to him because he would be able to tell when she was lying by her bodily tensions. She always tried to tell the truth in her dances, however unpalatable the truth may be.

Like that other artistic innovator, Gertrude Stein, Graham was born in Allegheny, Pennsylvania. Capable of tracing her ancestry back to Miles Standish, Graham was raised in an atmosphere of middle-class rectitude. But when her family moved to Santa Barbara, California, because of her sister's asthma, Graham found herself in an environment that was less stern in both its climate and its concern for propriety; she thrived there.

Attending a performance by Ruth St. Denis made her realize that she wanted to dance. Fearing parental disapproval, she did not dare attend the Denishawn school until after her father's death. The conflict she felt then between personal desires and traditional canons of respectability eventually became one of her choreographic themes.

Graham was urged to leave Denishawn and follow an independent career by Louis Horst, at that time Denishawn's musical director. Later, he served as accompanist, composer, and father confessor to the entire early generation of American modem dancers, and he taught hundreds of young dancers elementary principles of dance composition until his death in 1964. An opinionated, irascible man, Horst enjoyed giving the impression of being an ogre. But it was with his encouragement that Graham started offering programs in which Denishawn's softly curving and exotic movements gave way to an insistent angularity.

Her debut concert in 1926 so bewildered some people that one of her acquaintances felt obliged to exclaim, "It's dreadful! Martha, how long do you expect to keep this up?"

"As long as I have an audience," Graham answered.

In addition to performing, she began teaching, and her reputation for dramatic power attracted acting students as well as dancers to her classes. She taught one young actress, Bette Davis, to fall down a flight of stairs in such a spectacular fashion that Davis got a job on the basis of that stunt alone.

As modern dancers often do, Graham developed her technique according to her expressional needs, the kinds of movements she emphasized in her classes reflecting the creative problems with which she was preoccupied. Early Graham technique was notable for its nervous energy. Yet it was in no way arbitrary, for Graham based it on a study of one of the fundamental facts of life: breathing. From examining the bodily changes that occur during inhalation and exhalation, Graham developed the principles of "contraction" and "release," built a whole vocabulary of movements upon them, and experimented with dynamics. Whereas classical ballet often sought to conceal effort, Graham revealed it, allowing contractions to attain whiplash intensity in the belief that life itself is effort. In time, her technique became more lyrical, but her dances never ceased to be passionate. The austerity of

Martha Graham's *Primitive Mysteries* reflects religious rituals of the American Southwest. *Photograph by Barbara Morgan; Courtesy of Barbara Morgan.*

some of her early productions also gave way to a greater richness of stage design and she often collaborated with the sculptor Isamu Noguchi.

Graham's percussive style made it a vehicle for the expression of heightened emotions and some of her dances could combine agony with rapturous exaltation. Graham's most acclaimed early work in this vein is *Primitive Mysteries* (1931), a study of the rites of Christianized Indians in the American Southwest that shows a cult of women adoring the Virgin Mary, sinking into grief at the Crucifixion, and rejoicing at the Resurrection.

During the Great Depression, many choreographers created dances of social protest. Graham was seldom overtly political, but during the 1930s and 1940s she did choreograph works concerning some of the forces that helped to shape American culture. *American Provincials* (1934) was a bitter attack on Puritanism. The solo *Frontier* (1935) offered a portrait of a pioneer woman coming to terms with the vastness of the American continent. Graham again examined Puritanical repression in *Letter to the World* (1940), which contrasted the New England poet Emily Dickinson with the figure of a domineering ancestress, who symbolized the repressive power of tradition. However, in *Appalachian Spring* (1944), though an evangelist gesturally preaches a hellfire-and-damnation sermon to a young couple at a housewarming, the newlyweds' love for each other and the calm wisdom of an older pioneer woman prevail. Graham often commissioned new music for her dances; for *Appalachian Spring,* in which she made a kind of peace with her American heritage, Aaron Copland composed a particularly notable score.

From the 1940s onward, Graham created dance-dramas inspired by history, mythology, and literature, and the characters in them often served as symbols of psychological traits. Thus, although *Errand Into the Maze* derives from the Greek myth of Theseus and the Minotaur, it does not literally retell that story; rather, it depicts a woman shuddering through a labyrinth in which lurks a creature—part man, part monster—who personifies her deepest fears. The conquering of that monster represents the overcoming of terror. At one point in *Cave of the Heart,* which is based on the myth of Medea, the protagonist shuts herself inside an awesome, spiny construction designed by Noguchi. This sequence is a reminder that Medea—who so loathes her faithless husband that she is willing to kill his new bride and her own children—is a sorceress wielding terrible power, and it is also a visual image of the way that an all-consuming hatred can set a person totally apart from the rest of the world.

Many of Graham's dramatic dances are about women. Because they frequently begin at a climactic moment in the heroine's life and then move through past events toward her destiny, past, present, and future may be choreographically blended. A particularly complex example of this fluid dramatic structure was the evening-length *Clytemnestra,* in which the ancient-Greek queen, condemned to Hades after her death, looks back on her violent past and gradually comes to understand herself and her motives. Another of Graham's favorite structural devices is the splitting up of a character into several parts, each personified by a different dancer: in *Seraphic Dialogue,* the spirit of Joan of Arc contemplates images of herself as village maiden, warrior, and martyr.

Until her death in 1991, Graham never stopped prompting admiration and controversy. Some dancegoers were puzzled by her occasional obscurity;

others found her almost shockingly frank. But no one ever could question her sincerity, integrity, or genius.

HUMPHREY AND GRAHAM WERE BY NO MEANS the only influential American modern dancers of their time. There was Helen Tamiris, who was born Helen Becker, but whose change of name was inspired by a poem about a Persian queen, which contained the line, "Thou art Tamiris, the ruthless queen who banishes all obstacles." At a time when many dancers sought to demonstrate their seriousness by adopting a severe or spartan manner, Tamiris was flamboyant and what a Hollywood agent might have termed a "glamour girL" Fascinated by American history, she choreographed dances to Walt Whitman poems, Revolutionary War songs, and bayou ballads. By dancing solos to two spirituals at a program in 1928, she became one of the first white choreographers to take black culture seriously. She continued to dance to spirituals throughout her career, eventually assembling a whole suite of such solos. As vigorous a choreographer on Broadway as she was for the concert stage, Tamiris created the dances for several musicals, including *Annie Get Your Gun* and *Up in Central Park.*

ANOTHER VIVIDLY THEATRICAL CHOREOGRAPHER was Lester Horton. Between 1928 and his death in 1953, he directed dance groups in Los Angeles, which demonstrated that modern dance could flourish outside New York. Like Tamiris, Horton had a social conscience. He was deeply interested in Mexican and Native American culture, and his company is believed to be the first modern dance troupe in America to be racially integrated. His most famous single work is *Salome,* a highly dramatic study of the biblical temptress.

BECAUSE MODERN DANCE STRESSED individual creativity, choreographers often worked in isolation. However, several important attempts were made to bring them together. The best known of these projects were the Bennington Festivals, held in summer during the 1930s on the campus of Bennington College in Vermont. After a hiatus during World War II, the American Dance Festival was established in 1948 at Connecticut College and is now located in Durham, North Carolina.

José Limón's *The Moor's Pavane* (1949, with Limón, Lucas Hoving, Pauline Koner, and Betty Jones) recreated Shakespeare's *Othello* in courtly dance terms, and has been danced by both modern and ballet companies. *Photograph by Walter Strate. Courtesy of the Dance Collection, The New York Public Library.*

THE STRESS ON INDIVIDUAL CREATIVITY also led dancers to study with established figures, then to break away and found their own companies. Just as Graham and Humphrey left Denishawn in order to choreograph, so did some of their own students. Anna Sokolow left Graham in 1939; she later became known for works, often to jazz scores, about the loneliness and frustration of people in big cities. A Humphrey-Weidman dancer who headed an important company of his own was José Limón. Humphrey served as a choreographer and artistic adviser for his company until her death in 1958. Limón's choreography tended to be dramatically turbulent and, with his combination of tragic dignity and proud defiance, the Mexican-born dancer was a striking figure on stage. His best-known work is *The Moor's Pavane*

(1949), a retelling of Shakespeare's *Othello* that derives its power from the way the jealousy of Othello and the evil machinations of Iago are placed within the formal confines of Renaissance court dances. Limón's company attracted many fine dancers, among them Pauline Koner, who also had an independent career as a choreographer of both lyrical and dramatic works.

ANOTHER MAJOR AMERICAN CONTRIBUTION to world choreography has been made by black dancers. Contemporary black dance is an amalgam of elements derived from jazz, modern dance, and the history and folklore of Africa, the Caribbean, the American South, and the metropolitan ghetto. The result is a dance form of great energy that can both rage at oppression and comfort the afflicted.

Black dancers constantly struggled against prejudice. Bigots scorned all manifestations of black culture. There also were certain white dancegoers who, though they professed to admire blacks for their theatrical vitality, warned them not to attempt forms such as ballet and modern dance; paradoxically, as they were trying to set limitations upon black dance, some of these same observers were praising white modern dancers for their total freedom of expression.

Yet black dancers persisted and choreographically explored both specifically African-American themes and ideas drawn from many world cultures. In 1931, Edna Guy and Hemsley Winfield organized the New Negro Art Theatre Dance Group in New York, which featured works by Winfield—an actor turned dancer—in an eclectic style that blended African-American and German Expressionist influences. Unfortunately, Winfield died suddenly of pneumonia in 1934, when he was only twenty-seven.

A MAJOR PIONEER OF BLACK DANCING during the 1930s was Asadata Dafora, who staged dance-dramas concerning African tribal life. Among the black dancers who gained prominence during the 1940s are Katherine Dunham and Pearl Primus, both of whom were university-trained anthropologists as well as choreographers. Dunham made use of Caribbean and American black themes in a series of revues that successfully combined anthropological research with Broadway flair. Primus's repertoire extended from restagings of African rituals to *Strange Fruit,* a study of lynching in the South.

Alvin Ailey based his fervent *Revelations* (1960) on spirituals. *Photograph by Bill Hilton.*

Among the acclaimed dances on black themes that have been staged since the 1950s are Talley Beatty's *The Road of the Phoebe Snow,* based on childhood memories of growing up beside the railroad tracks; Donald McKayle's *Rainbow 'Round My Shoulder,* a portrait of convicts on the chain gang, and his *District Storyville,* a look at New Orleans during the early days of jazz when musicians entertained in brothels in order to earn a living. One of the most popular of all American dance companies is the predominantly black Alvin Ailey American Dance Theatre. Ailey's own choreographic works include *Revelations,* a rousing and eloquent tribute to black religious music, and several dances to works by the jazz composer Duke Ellington. As a director, Ailey commissioned new works from established choreographers, such as Beatty and McKayle, and from new choreographers who have emerged since the 1960s, including Eleo Pomare, Dianne McIntyre, Billy Wilson, and Bill T. Jones. After Ailey's death in 1989, his company continued to thrive under the direction of, first, Judith Jamison and, later, Robert Battle.

BY THE 1950S, MODERN DANCE HAD BECOME RECOGNIZED as one of the great American arts. At the same time, there were observers who charged that some of its original fervor had dissipated. Rebellious young choreographers even claimed that modern dance had become so preoccupied with dramatic narrative that it had declined into a ponderous form of pantomime.

Some rebellious choreographers created deliberately severe, blunt plotless pieces. Simone Forti (who also danced under the names of Simone Morris and Simone Whitman) emphasized simple, repetitive actions. Fascinated by the sheer physicality of bodies and objects, she had people clamber up an inclined plane in one work and form football huddles in another. In yet another composition, two people did nothing more than shut themselves up inside boxes, from which whistling noises emerged; when the noises stopped, the two people came out of the boxes and the dance was over.

Forti was one of many iconoclastic dancers who studied with Anna (also known as Ann) Halprin, a San Francisco choreographer who often based her experiments on task activities. Some conservative theatergoers refused to regard such productions as dance. But audiences, tired of choreographic fussiness and bombast, found their very plainness refreshing.

Believing that movement could be beautiful and enjoyable for its own sake, other, newer choreographers advocated a dance that was abstract, evocative, and nonliteral. Erick Hawkins, a dancer for Graham and her former husband, came to emphasize movement qualities rather than explicit themes in his choreography, the qualities he particularly favored being softness, gentleness, and ceremoniousness.

Paul Taylor proved to be a choreographic chameleon capable of working in several disparate styles. Certain of his dances of the 1950s were studies in everyday, ordinary movement that contrasted spurts of activity with long periods of stillness. Then in 1962 he choreographed *Aureole,* a lyrical work that has often been termed classical in spirit because of its grace, harmony, and lucidity. It has even been compared with classical ballet, although its

A versatile choreographer, Paul Taylor borrows from many styles. Although abstract, his *Images*, to Debussy, evokes through movement and costumes an archaic culture like that of Minoan Crete. *Photograph by Costas. Courtesy of the Paul Taylor Dance Company.*

actual steps would amaze Petipa. Whereas ballet may disguise bodily weight and effort, Taylor makes clearly weighted bodies seem ultimately graceful. Several later works by Taylor, including *Airs* and *Arden Court,* are also in this vein, and in addition to being performed by his own company, they have entered the repertoires of ballet companies. Classically trained dancers adapt easily to Taylor's lyricism, but find themselves challenged by his concept of weighted movement.

As soon as one comes to expect one sort of dance from Taylor, he may suddenly choreograph something completely different. Just as in some of his early pieces, Taylor used nothing but ordinary movements in *Esplanade.* But these familiar steps—running, skipping, jumping—are taken to such virtuosic extremes that they seem extraordinary. *American Genesis* gave American settings to well-known Bible stories—Noah's ark becomes a Mississippi riverboat—and Taylor's version of Stravinsky's *Le Sacre du Printemps,* which he calls *Le Sacre du Printemps (The Rehearsal),* is simultaneously a detective-story ballet, a dance about a dance company rehearsing a detective-story ballet, and a commentary on Nijinsky's original theme of sacrifice. A choreographic wit, Taylor is also something of a moralist—but never doctrinaire in either his optimism or his pessimism. *Company B,* to songs that became popular during World War II, sung in recordings by the Andrews Sisters, at first seems a romp for dancers cavorting downstage. But in the shadows upstage dancers appear to be soldiers in battle, their grim reality intruding upon the frivolity. Few contemporary choreographers are as versatile as Taylor.

ALWIN NIKOLAIS ONCE PROCLAIMED HIMSELF an artistic polygamist. By this he meant that in his productions he sought "a polygamy of motion, shape, color, and sound." For his abstract multimedia works, Nikolais, in addition to choreographing their dances, usually composed their electronic scores and designed their scenery, costumes, and lighting. He became a complete man of the theatre—and with his love of technological wizardry, a most up-to-date one. Yet his productions also recall the past: Viganò is his precursor as a choreographer-composer, and courtly masques and spectacles prefigure the

Alwin Nikolais altered the natural lines of the body with props and costumes not only to create unusual spatial patterns but also to comment on human behavior patterns, as he did in the Boulevard episode in *Imago* (subtitled *The City Curious)* in 1963. *Alamy Stock Photo.*

splendor of his mixed-media pieces, which pay tribute to the electronic age rather than to monarchy. Nikolais often transforms dancers by encasing them in fantastic costumes or by attaching sculptural constructions to them that change the appearance of the body's natural shape. And he floods dancers with patterns of light in such a way that reality and illusion are confused, so that audiences may not be able to tell which moving figures before them are real dancers and which are merely shadows or projections. Although he likes to play theatrical conjuring tricks, Nikolais had also hoped to make spectators think seriously about their relation to their environment.

MERCE CUNNINGHAM PROVED TO BE an unusually influential experimentalist. His company's performance style was often almost balletically lucid, even though his dancers seldom tried to look ethereal. Despite this latent classicism, Cunningham's productions—many of them collaborations with composer John Cage—aroused much controversy. Three aspects of Cunningham's choreographic theories have been especially provocative: his use of chance and indeterminacy; his treatment of stage space as an open field; and his tendency to regard the components of a dance production as independent entities.

Wishing his dances to possess some of the unpredictability of life itself, Cunningham began to make choreographic use of chance. But for Cunningham chance did not mean chaos and his dances are not improvisations or free-for-alls. Typically, Cunningham will prepare in advance a multitude of movement possibilities—more than he may actually need in a work— and then decide on the sequences he would use by some simple device such as flipping a coin. Sometimes a work would have episodes that could have been performed in any order. Since Cunningham prepares so much, it may be asked why he bothers with chance at all. He would reply that chance can reveal to a choreographer ways of combining movements that the rational, conscious mind might not otherwise have thought of on its own. All people are, to some extent, prisoners of their mental habits. But Cunningham believed that through chance, choreographers may free themselves from habit and discover attractive new movement sequences.

A theatrical preoccupation with indeterminacy is perhaps to be expected in this age of mechanical forms, such as films, recordings, and television.

The great 20th century artist Robert Rauschenberg designed the set for Merce Cunningham's witty, colorful and elegant *Travelogue* (1977). *Photograph by Jack Vartoogian.*

One characteristic of the mechanical is its fixity: once something is on film, it will stay that way forever—or at least until the film decays. But even when performers are trying to speak the same words, sing the same music, or dance the same steps, every live performance differs, if only slightly, from every other live performance. Therefore, it can be argued that, in his concern for choreographic indeterminacy, Cunningham was calling attention to the indeterminacy inherent in all live theatre.

A second characteristic of Cunningham's choreographic approach was his treatment of stage space. Whereas many dances are often structured around a central focus—a ballerina or *danseur,* or a hero or heroine, who may be framed by an ensemble—Cunningham gives equal importance to all parts of the stage. Corners and sides can be as important as stage-center, and many things can happen simultaneously in different stage areas. Instead of being choreographically guided toward a single point, the spectator's eye is left free to roam as it pleases across a field of activity. This need not create any perceptual difficulties, for our eyes regularly adjust to everyday situations of far greater visual complexity that can be found in most dances.

Finally, Cunningham regarded the components of a production—movement, music, decor—as coexisting independent entities. The dancers' steps are not phrased to coincide with the musical phrases; the scenery does not illustrate the choreography. Dance, music, and scenery simply occupy the same space and time. The most radical manifestations of Cunningham's belief in the independence of theatrical elements occured in his "Events." These ninety-minute productions, performed without intermission, consist of choreographic sequences from dances already in the Cunningham company's repertoire. Yet the sequences are not presented as detached excerpts; instead, they are woven together and performed to scores other than those for the works from which they derive. Thus Events presented old movements in a new context, and the change of context often drastically altered the effect of the movements. Through his Events, Cunningham emphasized that everything is subject to change.

For all his concern for change, each of Cunningham's dances manages to have its own special climate. Although there is nothing literally tropical about *Rainforest,* the choreography is sensuous and Andy Warhol's decor of floating silver pillows somehow seems appropriate to such a lush creation. *Summerspace* shimmers like a hot August afternoon. *Winterbranch* contains so many images of struggle and oppression that it has reminded audiences of the horrors of war. *Sounddance,* with its blasts of movement to blasts of sound, could be called a choreographic holler or shout. And because in *Quartet*—which, despite its title, is a dance for five—one outsider keeps trying in vain to join a group of four people, the dance can be interpreted as an image of social ostracism or of the gulf between generations. Cunningham's dances may consist of many different things but, like objects in a landscape, they may cohere to produce an unmistakable atmosphere.

THE EARLY 1960s SAW A REMARKABLE UPSURGE of dance experimentation in New York City. Perhaps the most significant of all the experimental concerts of the 1960s occurred on July 6, 1962, when some young choreographers—including Yvonne Rainer, Steve Paxton, David Gordon, and Deborah Hay—gave a concert of works at the Judson Memorial Church, a Baptist church in Greenwich Village that had long supported liberal social action and artistic endeavors, even though the grandmother of one of its ministers once warned him, "A praying knee and a dancing foot never grew on the same leg." For many years thereafter, the Judson Church served as a center for innovative dance. The choreographers who prepared the first program there had been members of an experimental dance composition workshop led by Robert Dunn and, objecting to what they regarded as a rigid codification of both ballet and modern dance techniques, they asked questions about the nature of performance. Similar questions continue to be asked, both by choreographers associated with Judson and by choreographers who have experimented totally apart from the Judson milieu. The answers to those questions have often been stimulating and provocative.

Experimentation focused on several issues—for example, the kinds of movements that may be used in a dance. It now appears that almost any movement from the simplest to the most complex may legitimately function as a dance movement. As an example of complexity, one may point to the works of Twyla Tharp, who has developed a rhythmically supple way of moving in which sharply thrusting steps may suddenly give way to seemingly offhand shrugs and, with equal unexpectedness, shrugs may explode into lunges and leaps. Murray Louis has favored a dry, witty style that draws on the ability of well-trained dancers to isolate parts of their bodies and to move them in seeming independence of the rest of their bodies. Rudy Perez has devised movement that is rich in emotional implications, yet he has measured it out on stage with tight, stoic control. Moving from New York City and establishing himself in Los Angeles which, since the time of Lester Horton, had become a lively modern dance center (Bella Lewitzky was a major choreographer and teacher), Perez, always fascinated by the rhythms of everyday life, continued to choreograph into his eighties, even though legally blind.

Believing that too much of contemporary dance—modern dance as well as ballet—has adopted a balletic lightness, Senta Driver deliberately introduced weightedness into her choreography. She has also exploded many theatrical stereotypes and conventions. In her dances it is not surprising to see women partner men and lift them into the air.

Many of the Judson choreographers and the choreographers influenced by them used ordinary, even totally mundane, movements, or borrowed movements from games and work activities. Choreographers have even utilized nondancers in order to give their works an unadorned appearance, just as in certain sculptures the wood or stone is left deliberately unpolished. Thus Yvonne Rainer, one of the leading Judson choreographers, was noted for dances that had a rough-and-tumble look. The emphasis on ordinary movement can also have social implications.

The rise of the Judson choreographers coincided with the rise of the civil rights and peace movements, and these political concerns as well as issues such as feminism, gay liberation, and ecology have engaged many choreographers. Steve Paxton, for instance, developed a form he called contact improvisation, which emphasizes people moving cooperatively together and which can serve as a testament to human dignity.

Yet it appears that, for all their affirmations of the ordinary, choreographers and audiences alike also love display and virtuosity. Because they wish to avoid the clichés of both classical ballet and the standard modern dance techniques, choreographers have developed new forms of virtuosity. Sports and acrobatics have been particularly influential. One of the most spectacular examples of this influence is Pilobolus, a collectively run dance group founded by some former Dartmouth College students. In the creations of Pilobolus, bodies entwine, cling together, and break apart in ways that can be grotesque, surprising, and breathtakingly virtuosic in their defiance of gravity. Equally virtuosic in their own way are some of the dances of Molissa Fenley, whose choreography stresses endurance and requires seemingly unlimited reserves of stamina. One of her most unusual pieces is *State of Darkness,* a solo version of Stravinsky's *Le Sacre du Printemps*—a

In *The Floor Dance (Requiem for the Living),* choreographed in 1989 in response to the devastation of an oil slick, Molissa Fenley never rose to her feet, but spent the entire solo twisting and turning on the ground. *Photograph by Jack Mitchell Getty Images.*

Trisha Brown Dance Company in her *Glacial Decoy* (1979), with costumes and visual design by Robert Rauschenberg and danced in silence. Photogaph by *Jacques Demarthon / Getty Images.*

composition lasting more than half an hour—in which Fenley appears to be not a sacrificial victim, but a female warrior.

Stephen Petronio's dances often proceed with great bursts of energy. But because every effect is carefully controlled, Petronio's tumultuousness can be exhilarating rather than intimidating. Garth Fagan, director of Garth Fagan Dance (a company from Rochester, New York, that was formerly known as the Bucket Dance Theatre), favors deliberately roughhewn movement notable for its sharp changes in dynamics.

Some choreographers blend modem dance with other dance forms—most frequently, with ballet. Lar Lubovitch has created intricate works for ballet and modem dance groups. The hard-edged choreography of Karole Armitage reflects her background as a former member of both Merce Cunningham's company and the Geneva Ballet. Her productions also attest to her interest in pop musical styles and the latest, and often most outrageous, fashion trends.

In addition to exploring different kinds of movement, choreographers have experimented with dance structure. Trisha Brown, for example, choreographed several dances that have an accumulative structure: a step or gesture is introduced, followed by another step or gesture; both are repeated and a third introduced; then the three are repeated and a fourth added. Such dances are like choreographic equivalents of the song "The Twelve Days of Christmas." Other dances by Brown challenge a viewer's capacity to see and assimilate movement. Complex phrases occur with such rapidity in them, each new phrase virtually erasing the last, that the spectator's mind is forced to dance along with the performers on stage.

Some choreographers have been influenced by the so-called "minimalist" or "pattern" music associated with composers such as Steve Reich and Philip Glass. In this sort of music, patterns are established and developed in a complex manner, but with few changes of tempo or dynamics. Lucinda Childs has become known for dances in which a limited number of steps are varied and developed in so many ways that, far from looking plain or spare, the resultant choreography may seem as intricate as the designs on an Oriental rug. Comparable intricacies can be found in the choreography of Laura Dean, who has favored geometric patterns and repeated passages of spinning movements.

Many of the early productions at the Judson Church were deliberately plotless as choreographers reacted against the dramatic, allegorical, or literary dances that were prevalent at the time. As James Waring, one of the Judson choreographers, put it in an essay, "Dance itself is not a symbol of anything." But implicit or explicit dramatic content seeped back into much contemporary choreography, although it is expressed far differently from how it probably would be in a work by a choreographer like Martha Graham. James Waring choreographed a dance version of *Phantom of the Opera,* and loving tributes to great dance figures of the past, as in his *Mazurkas for Pavlova*. Ralph Lemon has created dances about varied matters such as the fading of the romance of the Old West, the emotional auras and energies of fairy tales, and the inevitability of death. Ann Carlson has concerned herself with American patriotism, people's work patterns, and the similarities and differences between human beings and animals.

Meredith Monk usually both choreographs the movement and composes the music for her multimedia spectacles. Monk is particularly adept at creating fantastic, emotionally evocative images, and she has staged works both in proscenium theatres and in nonproscenium spaces. *Juice* took place inside New York's Solomon R. Guggenheim Museum, Monk's dancers moving along the great spiral ramp designed by Frank Lloyd Wright; and in *Needle Brain Lloyd and the Systems Kid* she filled the Connecticut College lawn with a motley array of characters, including croquet players, gangsters, pioneers, and motorcycle riders. Among her other imagistic works are *Quarry,* which presented the rise of a dictatorship as seen through the eyes of a sick child, and *Education of the Girlchild,* which showed the course of life from birth to old age, then reversed the process to make time run backward to birth. Kei Takei, a Japanese-born dancer, devoted herself to a seemingly endless cycle of dances called *Light,* concerning the bearing of burdens and the stoic facing of adversity. Eiko and Koma, two other Japanese-born, New York-based dancers, are known for their collaboratively choreographed evocations of the forces of nature. Their pieces seldom last long in actual time; yet, to suggest the passage of centuries or even eons, they are performed in slow motion. Mesmeric slow motion is also associated with Robert Wilson, who became famous for vast theatrical epics about historical figures such as Albert Einstein, Joseph Stalin, and Sigmund Freud and went on to direct plays and operas.

ONE AMERICAN CHOREOGRAPHER whose career seems to embody many divergent trends of modern dance is Mark Morris. Born in Seattle in 1956, he was inspired to study dance at the age of eight after seeing a performance by José Greco's flamenco troupe. He studied ballet and modern locally, began dancing with a Balkan folk dance ensemble, and moved to New York where he performed with several companies, including those of Lar Lubovitch, Laura Dean, and Eliot Feld. He formed his own Mark Morris Dance Group in 1980, attracting almost immediate attention for his versatility.

His productions have ranged from a choreographic setting of Vivaldi's exultant *Gloria,* to *Championship Wrestling,* based upon an essay on that sport by the French philosopher Roland Barthes. The tone of his pieces is often unpredictable. Whereas the boisterous *Grand Duo,* to Lou Harrison, seems to resemble a polka for belligerent gnomes, *Spring, Spring, Spring,* his treatment of *Le Sacre du Printemps,* looks carefully controlled, with few hints of primordial wildness, even though it is set to a jazz-based version of Stravinsky's tumultuous score.

The Mark Morris Dance Group in his masterpiece *l'Allegro, il penseroso ed il moderato*. The evening length dance is based on poems by John Milton with music by Handel. *Alamy Stock Photo.*

Morris has especially liked creating dances to great choral music and operas, and his successful productions of this kind have included *L'allegro, il penseroso ed il moderato,* to Handel's fanciful evocations of character types, and Purcell's opera *Dido and Aeneas*, in which Morris himself originally danced the leading female roles of both the tragic heroine Dido and the malevolent Sorceress. A passionate advocate of live music for dance programs, Morris formed the Mark Morris Dance Group Music Ensemble in 1996 and, on occasion, has conducted vocal and instrumental performances. In 2001 he opened the Mark Morris Dance Center in Brooklyn, which serves as his group's headquarters, a school, and a community center.

OBSERVING THE DANCE SCENE IN THE EARLY twenty-first century, some commentators might have declared that the influence of the post-modernists was waning. Several died, among them Robert Ellis Dunn in 1996 and Trisha Brown in 2017. Laura Dean had apparently lost interest in choreography; Meredith Monk was devoting herself to music, rather than dance, and Robert Wilson had become associated with operatic and theatrical stage direction. But this may have been a misleading view of the situation.

So-called post-modernism was still in evidence. Thus Monk's musical compositions often include rhythmic motions for their performers. After a period in which she devoted herself to film-making, Yvonne Rainer returned to choreography. Trisha Brown's works continued to be staged by her former dancers and were in demand by other companies. Lucinda Childs has been extremely influential in France and has brought her company to New York. If post-modernism no longer inspires artistic uproars, that may be because it has been integrated into the fabric of dance as a whole.

At the same time, the established modern dance choreographers continue to be honored. Employing both his own dancers and guest companies, Paul Taylor has produced revivals by such choreographers as Graham, Humphrey, and Cunningham. So, too, Stephen Petronio has honored his heritage with productions by Cunningham, Rainer, Paxton, and Anna Halprin, among others. The Graham and Limón companies continue, both offering new works by many choreographers and preserving dances of the past. Although some of their commissions have met with mixed success, their revivals can come as revelations. Thus, today, the patterns of social unrest in Graham's *Chronicle* (1936) can seem eerily timely, while Humphrey's *Passacaglia* (1938) can still be said to offer an inspiring vision of social harmony.

Modern dance, in all its forms, remains capable of remarkable self-renewal. Like the mythical phoenix, it is forever rising from its own ashes, transforming itself and making itself creatively new.

Related Readings

Duncan Dancing

Isadora's pantomimic interpretation of the *Marseillaise,* given in New York before the United States had entered the World War, aroused as vehement and excited an expression of enthusiasm as it would be possible for an artist to awaken in our theater today. . . . In a robe the color of blood she stands enfolded; she sees the enemy advance; she feels the enemy as it grasps her by the throat; she kisses her flag; she tastes blood; she is all but crushed under the weight of the attack; and then she rises, triumphant, with the terrible cry, *Aux armes, citoyens!* Part of her effect is gained by gesture, part by the massing of her body, but the greater part by facial expression. In the anguished appeal she does not make a sound, beyond that made by the orchestra, but the hideous din of a hundred raucous voices seems to ring in our ears . . . and finally we see the superb calm, the majestic flowing strength of the Victory of Samothrace. . . .

In the *Marche Slav* of Tchaikovsky Isadora symbolizes her conception of the Russian moujik rising from slavery to freedom. With her hands bound behind her back, groping, stumbling, head bowed, knees bent, she struggles forward, clad only in a short red garment that barely covers her thighs. With furtive glances of extreme despair, she peers above and ahead. When the strains of *God Save the Czar* are first heard in the orchestra she falls to her knees and you see the peasant shuddering under the blows of the knout. The picture is a tragic one, cumulative in its horrific details. Finally comes the moment of release and here Isadora makes one of her great effects. She does not spread her arms apart with a wide gesture. She brings them forward slowly and we observe with horror that they have practically forgotten how to move at all. They are crushed, these hands, crushed and bleeding after their long serfdom; they are not hands at all but claws, broken, twisted piteous claws! The expression of frightened, almost uncomprehending, joy with which Isadora concludes the march is another stroke of her vivid imaginative genius. . . .

Those who like to see pretty dancing, pretty girls, pretty things in general will not find much pleasure in contemplating the art of Isadora. She is not pretty; her dancing is not pretty. She has been cast in nobler mold and it is her pleasure to climb higher mountains. Her gesture is titanic; her mood generally one of imperious grandeur. She has grown larger with the years— and by this I mean something more than the physical interpretation of the word, for she is indeed heroic in build. But this is the secret of her power and force. There is no suggestion of flabbiness about her and so she can impart to us the soul of the struggling moujik, the spirit of a nation, the figure on the prow of a Greek bark. . . . And when she interprets the *Marseillaise* she seems indeed to feel the mighty moment.

(Carl Van Vechten, "The New Isadora," in Paul Magriel, ed., *Nijinsky, Pavlova, Duncan* [Part three; Duncan]. New York: Da Capo, 1977, pp. 30–33)

Ruth St. Denis on Body and Soul

As I see it, the deepest lack of Western cultures is any true workable system for teaching a process of integration between soul and body. Obviously, no effort has been made by the church as a whole, probably because of its long fostered conflict between the Goodness of the Soul and the supposed Badness of the Body. I yield to no one in my admiration for the character of St. Paul, but I have ever profoundly disagreed with his attitude of spirit versus the life of the senses. His doctrines, spread over the Western world, have led to such a contempt for the body and its functions that we have a divided and disintegrating consciousness regarding our total personalities.

The great mission of the dancer is to contribute to the betterment of mankind. I have written elsewhere, "the highest function of the dance is to ennoble man's concept of himself." This cannot be accomplished until the creative artist, whatever his field, becomes aware of himself as a citizen of the world and of his responsibility to lead instead of follow, to unfold instead of repeat and to bring self-realization to its highest point of expression. Some illumined seer has proclaimed that the artist of today is the prophet of tomorrow. But in order to attain the fullest self-realization through the dance we must understand that the arts—not just dancing but all of them—are never a religion in themselves, never objects of worship, but are the symbol and language for communicating spiritual truths.

(Ruth St. Denis, "Religious Manifestations in the Dance," in Walter Sorell, ed., *The Dance Has Many Faces.* 3rd ed. Pennington, N.J.: a cappella books, 1992, pp. 13–14)

The Perils of One-Night Stands

It was in a little town in Tennessee that I found my prize example of a stage door. After going around the whole block containing the theatre three times, I went to the box-office and inquired of the ticket seller, "Is there a stage door, and if so, where?" Following his directions, I found an opening which I passed up three times as being impossible to consider as a place of entrance or exit for human beings. This opening was only four feet high and had a hinged lid which swung upward and was tied in place by a frayed rope. It was surrounded by many evidences of its manifold uses, for unquestionably ashes and garbage and trash-barrels had been brought out of this hole for many years, paying toll as they passed through. Coal and wood had gone in this way, also leaving souvenirs of their passing. Looking in, I was unable to penetrate the utter darkness of the interior. But taking nose in hand, I doubled over and gave myself up to the adventure. After sliding down an incline of several feet, I found myself in a furnace room, and as my eyes gradually accustomed themselves to the dim light, I saw a decrepit furnace man who assured me that this was indeed the stage door, and the only stage door. He pointed into the deep recesses of the cellar to a stairway, toward which I began to pick my way. But before I reached the stairway, a smell reached me, a smell with real authority. . . . Tracked to its lair, I found that the source of the smell was in buckets of bill-posting paste which had soured to the point of being a possible ingredient for bootleg. Not pausing over this rich find, I climbed the stairs, testing each as I went, and only resting my weight on such as did not break under my experiments, and eventually emerged onto the stage where we were to play that night. But what a stage!

Evidently the house had been used for small time vaudeville at some time during its past, and the remarks of these now dead-and-gone vaude-villians had been responsible for a large sign which greeted me—"We know the stage is rotten—how's your act?" At least no one, management included, had any illusions on the subject of the stage.

Then I visited my dressing room! Here words fail me! I have dressed in many strange places—in an empty swimming pool, in a billiard room where for "skin" changes I squatted behind one pool table and the girls behind another, in the tax collector's office of a City Hall, in classrooms of high schools. . . . But for sheer, putrid perfection, this Tennessee dressing room was unrivalled. This would all have less point except for the fact that the lobby and auditorium of this theatre were newly decorated and kept moderately clean. There is a strange kink in the psychology of the theatre that this could be possible.

(Ted Shawn, "One Night Stands in Darkest America" [August 1927], in Doris Hering, ed., *Twenty-Five Years of American Dance*. Rev. and enl. ed. New York: Dance Magazine, 1954, pp. 132–133)

The Making of Wigman's Witch Dance

Sometimes at night I slipped into the studio and worked myself up into a rhythmic intoxication in order to come closer to the slowly stirring character. I could feel how everything pointed toward a clearly defined dance figure. The richness of rhythmic ideas was overwhelming. But something was opposed to their becoming lucid and orderly, something that forced the body time and again into a sitting or squatting position in which the greedy hands could take possession of the ground.

When, one night, I returned to my room utterly agitated, I looked into the mirror by chance. What it reflected was the image of one possessed, wild and dissolute, repelling and fascinating. The hair unkempt, the eyes deep in their sockets, the nightgown shifted about, which made the body appear almost shapeless: there she was—the witch—the earthbound creature with her unrestrained, naked instincts, with her insatiable lust for life, beast and woman at one and the same time.

I shuddered at my own image, at the exposure of this facet of my ego which I had never allowed to emerge in such unashamed nakedness. But, after all, isn't a bit of a witch hidden in every hundred-per-cent female, no matter which form its origin may have?

All that had to be done was to tame this elemental creature, to mold her and to work on one's own body as on a sculpture. It was wonderful to abandon oneself to the craving for evil, to imbibe the powers which usually dared to stir only weakly beneath one's civilized surface. But all this had to be surrendered to the rules of creation, the rules which had to be based on the essence and character of the dance-shape itself to define and reflect it truly once and for all. I had to take this into consideration and to be extremely careful so that the original creative urge was neither weakened nor blocked in the process of molding and shaping.

Does not the power, the magnificence of all creative art lie in knowing how to force chaos into form? . . .

. . . the *Witch Dance* mask possessed its own personal life. Every movement of the body evoked a changed expression of the face; depending on the position of the head, the eyes seemed to close or open. As a matter of fact, even around the mouth—intimated with a few strokes of the brush—there seemed to play a smile which, in its unfathomableness, was reminiscent of the Sphinx. The body, too, burdened with heaviness, possessed something of the lurking animal-like quality in the image of the enigmatic Sphinx, even though only by way of intimation.

(Mary Wigman, *The Language of Dance* [1963], trans. by Walter Sorell. Middletown, Conn.: Wesleyan University Press, 1966, pp. 40–42)

Doris Humphrey on Basic Principles

In the human animal, the walk is the key pattern of fall and recovery, my theory of motion—that is, the giving in to and rebound from gravity. This is the very core of all movement, in my opinion. All life fluctuates between the resistance to and the yielding to gravity. Youth is "down" as little as possible; gravity holds him lightly to earth. Old age gradually takes over and the spring vanishes from the step until the final yielding, death. There are two still points in the physical life: the motionless body, in which the thousand adjustments for keeping it erect are invisible, and the horizontal, the last stillness. Life and dance exist between these two points and therefore form the arc between two deaths. This lifetime span is filled with thousands of falls and recoveries—all highly specialized and exaggerated in the dance—which result in accents of all qualities and timings. If these movements, especially of the feet, augmented by other parts of the body, are organized into rhythmic patterns, they are connected as by an umbilical cord to everybody's life. . . .

A movement without a motivation is unthinkable. Some force is the cause for change of position, whether it is understandable or not. This applies not just to dancing, but to the physical world in general. Choreographers can and do ignore motivation, making no explanation to themselves or others, but try as they may to be abstract, they cannot avoid saying, "I live, therefore I move!" The cessation of movement is death, but before that the dancer at least makes the minimal statement, "I am a live human being." The only way I can think of to avoid this is to encase the body in a sort of box costume in which no part of the anatomy shows, and nothing reveals a living muscle underneath. Anybody want to try this? It might really be an abstraction, as it would be cause for conjecture whether a human being inhabited the outfit, or a mechanism. Even here motivation is at work; someone must have been inspired to invent the mechanism.

Obviously I am for conscious motivation, and therefore in favor of communication about people to people. I insist from the beginning of class work, and with professional dancers, too, that movement should be supported by a purpose, even that no move be made until a reason, simple as it may be, demands it.

(Doris Humphrey, *The Art of Making Dances.* New York: Rinehart, 1959; repro. Princeton, N.J.: A Dance Horizons/Princeton Book Company, Publishers, 1990, pp. 106, 110)

Martha Graham on Dancing

I am a dancer. I believe that we learn by practice. Whether it means to learn to dance by practicing dancing or to learn to live by practicing living, the principles are the same. In each it is the performance of a dedicated precise set of acts, physical or intellectual, from which comes shape of achievement, a sense of one's being, a satisfaction of spirit. One becomes in some area an athlete of God.

Practice means to perform, over and over again in the face of all obstacles, some act of vision, of faith, of desire. Practice is a means of inviting the perfection desired.

I think the reason dance has held such an ageless magic for the world is that it has been the symbol of the performance of living. Many times I hear the phrase . . . the dance of life. It is close to me for a very simple and understandable reason. The instrument through which the dance speaks is also the instrument through which life is lived . . . the human body. It is the instrument by which all the primaries of experience are made manifest. It holds in its memory all matters of life and death and love. Dancing appears glamorous, easy and delightful. But the path to the paradise of that achievement is not easier than any other: There is fatigue so great that the body cries, even in its sleep. There are times of complete frustration, there are daily small deaths. Then I need all the comfort that practice has stored in my memory, and a tenacity of faith that Abraham had wherein he "Staggered not at the promise of God through unbelief."

It takes about ten years to make a mature dancer. . . . The body is shaped, disciplined, honored and, in time, trusted. Movement never lies. It is the barometer telling the state of the soul's weather to all who can read it. . . .

And there is grace. I mean the grace resulting from faith . . . faith in life, in love, in people, in the act of dancing. All this is necessary to any performance in life which is magnetic, powerful, rich in meaning.

In a dancer there is a reverence for such forgotten things as the miracle of the small beautiful bones and their delicate strength. In a thinker there is a reverence for the beauty of the alert and directed and lucid mind. In all of us who perform there is an awareness of the smile which is part of the equipment or gift of the acrobat. We have all walked the high wire of circumstance at times. We recognize the gravity pull of the earth as he does. The smile is there because he is practicing living at the instant of danger. He does not choose to fall.

(Martha Graham, statement in Martha Graham Dance Company souvenir program, 1985)

Limón's Choreographic Credo

I view myself as a disciple and follower of Isadora Duncan and of the American impetus as exemplified by Doris Humphrey and Martha Graham, and by their vision of the dance as an art capable of the sublimity of tragedy and the Dionysian ecstasies. I try to compose works that are involved with man's basic tragedy and the grandeur of his spirit. I want to dig beneath empty formalisms, displays of technical virtuosity, and the slick surface; to probe the human entity for the powerful, often crude beauty of the gesture that speaks of man's humanity. I reach for demons, saints, martyrs, apostates, fools, and other impassioned visions. I go for inspiration and instruction to the artists who reveal the passion of man to me, who exemplify supreme artistic discipline and impeccable form: to Bach, Michelangelo, Shakespeare, Goya, Schönberg, Picasso, Orozco.

With the years, I have become blind to the blandishments and seductions of the romantics. I am impatient with the sounds of the Schumanns, the Mendelssohns, the Gounods, and the Massenets. The literature of the romantics, their architecture, and their fashions arouse in me a feeling of aversion. The undisciplined and sometimes fatuous exhibition of the romantic soul in exquisite torment—whether in music, painting, or dance—leaves me cold. This saccharine and maudlin view of the human condition is to me specious and decayed. I am happy that the Cézannes, the Debussys, the Duncans, the Ibsens, the Dreisers, and the O'Neills have given us back a more adult view of our humanity.

I deplore the artist who makes of his art a withdrawal from the travail of his time; who sterilizes and dehumanizes it into empty formalism; who renounces the vision of man as perfectable, a "golden impossibility," and makes him into the shabby scarecrow of the beatniks; who forgets that the artist's function is perpetually to be the voice and conscience of his time. It was Doris Humphrey who first taught me that man is the fittest subject for choreography. And Martha Graham continues triumphantly to prove that his passions, grandeurs, and vices are the ingredients of great dance, great theatre, and great art.

(José Limón, "An American Accent," in Selma Jeanne Cohen, ed., *The Modern Dance: Seven Statements of Belief.* Middletown, Conn.: Wesleyan University Press, 1966, pp. 23–24)

Cunningham on Dance and Chance

If a dancer dances—which is not the same as having theories about dancing or wishing to dance or trying to dance or remembering in his body someone else's dance—but if the dancer *dances,* everything is there. The meaning is there, if that's what you want. It's like this apartment where I live—I look around in the morning and ask myself, what does it all mean? It means: this is where I live. When I dance, it means: this is what I am doing. A thing is just that thing. In painting, now, we are beginning to see the painting, and not the painter or the painted. We are beginning to see how a painted space is. In music, we are beginning to hear free of our well-tempered ears.

In dance, it is the simple fact of a jump being a jump, and the further fact of what shape the jump takes. This attention given the jump eliminates the necessity to feel that the meaning of dancing lies in everything but the dancing, and further eliminates cause-and-effect worry as to what movement should follow what movement, frees one's feelings about continuity, and makes it clear that each act of life can be its own history: past, present and future, and can be so regarded, which helps to break the chains that too often follow dancers' feet around.

There doesn't seem to me the need to expound any longer on the idea that dance is as much a part of life as anything else. Since it takes place in one form or another almost constantly, that is evidence enough. The play of bodies in space—and time. When I choreograph a piece by tossing pennies—by chance, that is—I am finding my resources in that play, which is not the product of *my* will, but which is an energy and a law which I too obey. Some people seem to think that it is inhuman and mechanistic to toss pennies in creating a dance instead of chewing the nails or beating the head against a wall or thumbing through old notebooks for ideas. But the feeling I have when I compose in this way is that I am in touch with a natural resource far greater than my own personal inventiveness could ever be, much more universally human than the particular habits of my own practice, and organically rising out of common pools of motor impulses.

(Merce Cunningham, "The Impermanent Art," in Fernando Puma, ed., *Seven Arts No.3*. Indian Hills, Colo.: The Falcon's Wing Press, 1955, pp. 70–71)

Rainer's Unenhanced Physicality

The choices in my work are predicated on my own peculiar resources—obsessions of imagination, you might say—and also on an ongoing argument with, love of, and contempt for dancing. If my rage at the impoverishment of ideas, narcissism, and disguised sexual exhibitionism of most dancing can be considered puritan moralizing, it is also true that I love the body—its actual weight, mass, and unenhanced physicality. It is my overall concern to reveal people as they are engaged in various kinds of activities—alone, with each other, with objects—and to weight the quality of the human body toward that of objects and away from the super-stylization of the dancer. Interaction and cooperation on the one hand; substantiality and inertia on the other. Movement invention, i.e., "dancing" in a strict sense, is but one of the several factors in the work.

(Yvonne Rainer, program note for the dance work *The Mind Is a Muscle, 1968*)

10

Ballet Around the World

THE TWENTIETH CENTURY MAY HAVE USHERED in a golden age of dance. Today, most major cities possess dance companies, and wherever dance prospers it soon acquires its own stylistic accent. This is true even of ballet, an art based upon a specific technical vocabulary that is taught in ballet classrooms everywhere.

Great Britain has several companies, of which the foremost is the Royal Ballet. Despite its imposing name, the Royal Ballet was not born in the lap of luxury; its origins were quite humble. In certain ways, the conditions of British dance in the early years of the twentieth century were akin to those that prevailed in America at that time. Both countries welcomed dancers from abroad, yet few attempts were made to establish native companies. Dancing, many people seemed to feel, was best left to the Russians or the French. Fortunately, some determined women thought otherwise.

ONE WAS AN IRISH-BORN WOMAN whose real name was Edris Stannus, but who is far better known under her stage name, Ninette de Valois. After dancing with Diaghilev's Ballets Russes for several years, de Valois left the company in 1925 and started teaching and choreographing in England. She soon became involved with several important repertory theatres— the Festival Theatre in Cambridge, the Abbey Theatre in Dublin, and London's Old Vic—staging dances often of a considerably experimental nature for them. These theatres were usually richer in idealism than in hard cash, and because they were situated in unfashionable, out-of-the-way neighborhoods, de Valois's mother once asked her despairingly why she always had to work on "the wrong side of the river."

London's Old Vic Theatre was definitely on the shabby side of the Thames. Nevertheless, it was a remarkable institution; under the guidance of Lilian Baylis, it offered drama and opera at the lowest possible prices. De Valois managed to persuade Baylis to present ballet as well. When Baylis opened a second theatre, the long-derelict Sadler's Wells, in 1931, de Valois became director of the Vic-Wells Ballet which, as its name suggests, performed alternately at the two theatres. Later, when the Old Vic was used exclusively for drama and opera and dance moved to Sadler's Wells, the ballet company became known as the Sadler's Wells Ballet It retained that name when in 1946 it moved again—this time to the Royal Opera House. By the 1950s, the Sadler's Wells Ballet was regarded as one of the world's great companies and in 1956 it received a Royal Charter and a new name, the Royal Ballet. Unlike Europe's other royal companies, Britain's Royal Ballet was not founded to provide entertainment for aristocrats; rather, it is the outgrowth of a real community theatre movement. The company has not forgotten its origins: at various times it has organized what are referred to as "second companies" in residence at Sadler's Wells. The first of them was called Sadler's Wells Theatre Ballet. A newer Royal company toured extensively and in 1990 moved its home to the city of Birmingham, England, where it is now known as the Birmingham Royal Ballet, is independent of the Royal Ballet in London, and can no longer be considered "second" to any other group.

In the early years of the Vic Wells, there were ballet goers who scoffed at the idea of British ballet. Yet the company had its partisans and it kept winning friends. In 1933, the Camargo Society, an organization dedicated to the sponsorship of new British ballet productions, turned over all its funds to the Vic-Wells. What made the young company worth encouraging were the dedication of its dancers and the fortitude and vision of its director. Although de Valois choreographed less often as her administrative duties increased, she was an effective choreographer in a strongly dramatic style and three of her ballets have survived. *Checkmate* depicts an allegorical chess game between love and death. Her other two surviving works were inspired by British art: *Job* is based on William Blake's illustrations for the Old Testament story, and *The Rake's Progress* derives from a set of engravings by Hogarth showing a fashionable young man's descent into debauchery.

Erina Takahashi, senior principal dancer with the English National Ballet, as The Chosen One in Kenneth MacMillan's *Rite of Spring. Photograph by Robbie Jack/ Corbis via Getty Images.*

When de Valois retired as director in 1963, she was followed by a succession of directors, including Frederick Ashton, Kenneth MacMillan. Norman Morrice, Anthony Dowell, Monica Mason, and, Kevin O'Hare.

MACMILLAN BECAME ASSOCIATED WITH turbulently dramatic ballets about the frustrations, dark passions, and unfulfilled desires that may lurk within the human psyche, and though his choreographic vocabulary is essentially classical, he could treat classical steps in an almost violently Expressionist manner in order to reveal the fears and longings of his characters. Among his most intense works are *The Invitation,* a ballet about seduction and the loss of innocence; *Mayerling,* a choreographic account of the moral decline of Crown Prince Rudolph of Austria-Hungary, and *Song of the Earth,* a meditation on the inevitability of death.

AS THE ROYAL BALLET'S FIRST DIRECTOR, Ninette de Valois was neither glamorous in appearance nor extravagant in manner. Instead, she impressed her associates as being well organized, firm, and even slightly prim; some of her colleagues have suggested that if she had not gone into ballet direction, she might have been a schoolmistress or, possibly, a member of Parliament. Altogether different in temperament was another great lady of British ballet, Marie Rambert, whose real name was Cyvia Rambam (although she also called herself Myriam Ramberg). Born in Warsaw of cultivated parents in 1888, she inherited the family blessing of literacy and the family curse of insomnia. Her parents read *War and Peace* aloud to each other when they could not sleep and Rambert whiled away her own sleepless nights by reciting poetry to herself in several languages. A fidgety child, she received bad marks for conduct in school and, as she grew up, her intellectual restlessness led her to participate in radical politics. Fearing that she might get herself into trouble with the authorities in Warsaw, her parents sent her off to Paris to study medicine.

There, however, she discovered, and idolized, Isadora Duncan—an important influence, for Rambert was always interested in choreographic experimentation. However, her initial training was in eurhythmics, the method of rhythmic analysis developed by Émile Jaques-Dalcroze. Because of her knowledge of eurhythmics, she came to the attention of Diaghilev, who hired her to help Nijinsky analyze Stravinsky's complex score for *Le Sacre du Printemps.* (Later in her life, she confessed that she fell in love with Nijinsky, although she dared not admit it publicly at the time.) Her association with Diaghilev led her to respect the art of ballet as she never had before and when she eventually settled in London, she opened a ballet school there.

A tempestuous and unpredictable woman, Rambert astonished people. Sedate Londoners were surprised by her love of turning cartwheels in public. Until her seventieth birthday, she turned cartwheels everywhere, including around the Mozart monument in Salzburg and in London's Trafalgar Square. As an elderly woman, she regretted the loss of this ability and assured young skeptics that turning cartwheels had done wonders to clear her brain. Since she lived to be ninety-four, she may have been right. However, even more astonishing was Rambert's ability to discover young choreographers. An extraordinary number of Britain's most talented choreographers worked with Rambert at one time or another early in their careers.

In 1931—the same year in which the Vic-Wells Ballet made its debut—Rambert's husband, the playwright Ashley Dukes, converted an old parish hall into a theatre, which he named the Mercury. There, Rambert founded her own dance group, the Ballet Club. But the Ballet Club was no Vic-Wells. The Mercury stage was tiny—scarcely larger, it seemed, than a postage stamp. Moreover, Rambert lacked de Valois's cool head and organizational firmness. Indeed, her fits of temper were legendary. Yet she could work wonders. She was forever encouraging young choreographers and, although these discoveries eventually left the Mercury for companies that danced on larger stages, talented newcomers were somehow always to be found.

Renamed Ballet Rambert, the company outgrew the Mercury, becoming in time one of the institutions of British ballet. But, like its founder, it remained surprising. Thus in 1965 Rambert and Norman Morrice, her newest choreographic discovery at the time, completely reorganized the company to stress modern dance. After that year, Rambert, though no longer actively in charge of the company, followed its transition with interest right up to her death in 1982.

THE GREATEST TALENTS NURTURED BY RAMBERT were Antony Tudor and Frederick Ashton. Tudor choreographed for the Ballet Club before moving to America in 1939 to participate in the first season of Ballet Theatre. Ashton, who spent his childhood in South America, has nevertheless been termed a quintessentially English choreographer whose tender and gracious works reveal much about the English temperament. Rambert produced Ashton's earliest works.

In 1935 he joined the Vic-Wells Ballet and his choreography developed along with the company. A versatile choreographer, Ashton created serene abstractions (*Symphonic Variations*) and scintillating ones (*Scènes de Ballet*), bittersweet romantic dance-dramas (*A Month in the Country*) and fantasies (*Cinderella, Ondine*, and *The Dream,* based on Shakespeare's *A Midsummer Night's Dream*). One of Ashton's most unusual works is *Enigma Variations,* a portrait of the composer Edward Elgar and his friends that lovingly evokes the Edwardian era with a wealth of realistic detail. Ashton was also one of our century's leading comic choreographers. Two of his

Margot Fonteyn (at left) in *Symphonic Variations*, a lyrical abstract ballet by Frederick Ashton. *Photograph by Baron.*

finest comic works are *A Wedding Bouquet*, accompanied by the recitation of a nonsensical text by Gertrude Stein depicting absurd misadventures at a provincial wedding, and a sunny new version of *La Fille Mal Gardée*.

A master of lyrical choreography, Ashton developed the lyricism of his dancers. One of the greatest exponents of the style was Margot Fonteyn, who joined the Vic-Wells during the 1934–1935 season. A musical dancer blessed with exquisite line, Fonteyn was England's leading ballerina from the 1930s to the 1970s, and her notable partners included Robert Helpmann, Michael Somes, David Blair, and the fiery Russian-born Rudolf Nureyev.

SEVERAL BRITISH COMPANIES EXIST in addition to the Royal Ballet and the Rambert. English National Ballet (the former London Festival Ballet), founded in 1950 by Alicia Markova and Anton Dolin, tours extensively, in addition to performing in London. Although it has had several directors since its inception, it has always stressed a repertoire of familiar classics and modern works of general appeal. Two companies—Scottish Ballet in Glasgow and Northern Ballet in Manchester—represent attempts to develop ballet in cities outside London.

LIKE THE UNITED STATES, GREAT BRITAIN is a nation in which two ways of dancing—ballet and modern dance—have taken root and have developed in new ways. Nevertheless, serious British dance of any kind, like serious American dance, is a relatively recent phenomenon. Other nations can look back on centuries-old traditions. One such nation is Russia, where ballet has survived both changes of taste and changes of government. The Russian Revolution of 1917 inspired wild experimentation, and some zealots arose who claimed that, because it had been fostered by the tsars, ballet was a decadent art that deserved to perish along with the old regime. Other theorists, whose views ultimately prevailed, claimed that ballet could be shaped to meet the demands of the new Soviet society. The development of ballet in the early years of the Soviet government was supervised by Anatoly Lunacharsky, the first Soviet Commissar of Education, who managed to encourage experimentation without letting ballet fall into the hands of those who demanded its total abolition.

Among the most innovative of the Soviet choreographers of the 1920s were Fyodor Lopukhov and Kasian Goleizovsky. Lopukhov combined ballet with acrobatics and in his *Dance Symphony* (1923), to Beethoven's Fourth Symphony, he created an essentially abstract work that attempted to express the wonders of the universe. The cast included the young George Balanchine, whose own choreographic development may have been influenced by Lopukhov. Balanchine also admired Goleizovsky who, like Lopukhov, utilized acrobatics and whose choreography, in its time, was considered erotic.

Neither Lopukhov nor Goleizovsky came to dominate the scene. Instead, Soviet ballet, especially since the early 1930s, emphasized full-evening narrative works, often derived from history or literature, featuring vigorous stage action and heroic or optimistic themes. Precursors of this trend include *the Red Poppy,* choreographed by Vassily Tikhomirov and Lev Laschilin in 1927, and Vassily Vainonen's *The Flames of Paris* of 1932. The latter concerned the French Revolution. The former, a story about striking coolies who are aided by Russian sailors, is known for its rousing score by Reinhold Gliere. Important later examples of Soviet narrative ballet include Rostislav Zakharov's *The Fountain of Bakhchisarai* (1934), adapted from Pushkin, and Leonid Lavrovsky's *Romeo and Juliet* (1940), with a score by Prokofiev that ranks among the great ballet scores of the century. More recently, Yuri Grigorovich won praise for choreographing ballets such as *The Stone Flower, Spartacus,* and a new version of *Nutcracker.*

At its best, Soviet choreography has an epic sweep; at its worst, it can be bombastic. Yet, in mediocre works as well as fine ones, Russian dancing can be exciting. The style stresses high elevation, a fluidity of the arms and upper body, and amplitude of movement. Two great ballerinas who came to exemplify various aspects of this style were Galina Ulanova and Maya Plisetskaya. Ulanova's body could register the slightest nuances of characterization. Plisetskaya danced with enormous passion in serious ballets and with zest and sparkle in lighter roles.

Mikhail Lavrovsky leads a slaves' revolt in Yuri Grigorovich's *Spartacus* for the Bolshoi Ballet. From Alexander Demidov, *The Russian Ballet: Past and Present.*

A standard training method came to dominate Russian schools, based on the theories of Agrippina Vaganova, one of the twentieth century's most important teachers. Nevertheless, although all ballet students are trained according to the same principles, local differences still exist. Just as Moscow and St. Petersburg were balletic rivals during the last century, so they remain today. Moscow's Bolshoi Ballet prides itself on its flair, whereas St. Petersburg's Mariinsky Ballet considers itself unequaled for purity of style.

The Soviet era also saw the establishment of what might be termed folkloric ballet companies, which adapt the folk dances of a region so that they will be theatrically effective on stage. While such editing may cause the dances to lose a measure of strict authenticity, it is hoped that they will thereby have gained in entertainment value. One of the leading folkloric companies in the Soviet Union was the State Folk Dance Ensemble, founded in 1937 by Igor Moiseyev, which devoted itself to dances from all parts of the U.S.S.R. as well as from some of the countries it visited on its many tours. The Soviet bloc is not the only group of countries to send folkloric ballets on tour. Other nations have their own such troupes—for example, Mexico's Ballet Folklórico and the Bayanihan Dance Company of the Philippines. Many groups of this kind can be called travel brochures in motion because they invariably give a rosy view of the countries from which they hail. If they are propagandistic in a sense, their choreographic propaganda is far more entertaining than political speeches.

WHEN THE SOVIET UNION WISHED to impress other countries, it often sent dancers and dance teachers there. After the Chinese Revolution in 1949, Russian ballet teachers traveled to China to stage Western classics, such as *Swan Lake* and *Giselle*. The Sino-Soviet rift a decade later caused these productions to fall out of favor. For a time, Chinese officials allowed only a limited repertoire of ballets on Chinese historic and patriotic themes. But in more recent years China has welcomed both ballet and modern dance groups from abroad and there appears to be a genuine curiosity about the dance styles of other countries.

Cultural exchanges between East and West have often included visits by dance companies. For the most part, the world's dancers live in a peaceful coexistence that politicians might envy. Yet the dance world has known its own political tensions. Several noted Soviet dancers, among them Rudolf Nureyev, Natalia Makarova, Mikhail Baryshnikov, and Valery and Galina Panov, have gone to Western companies because of dissatisfaction with conditions in Russia. And international problems can threaten dance companies everywhere. Nevertheless, dance companies continue to be among the world's true internationalists and their world of art often recognizes no boundaries.

WHEREVER ONE TRAVELS, ONE IS APT to find dance. Italy continues to produce fine individual dancers, but it has declined in importance as a choreographic center. The Royal Danish Ballet preserves its Bournonville repertoire. At the same time, it seeks to develop new choreographers. Although Denmark has never found another choreographer to equal Bournonville, Harald Lander choreographed important works for the Danes during the 1930s and 1940s, among them *Études*. This tribute to a dancer's daily training, which begins with elementary exercises and becomes both more technically demanding to perform and more exhilarating to watch as it proceeds, has been produced by companies around the world since its premiere in Copenhagen in 1948.

FRENCH BALLET HAS WITNESSED PERIODS OF TRIUMPH and travail. At the end of the nineteenth century, the Paris Opéra Ballet began to decline as a center of important new choreography. In comparison with the excitement of the Paris seasons by Diaghilev's Ballets Russes, the Opéra Ballet even seemed stodgy, although the company's school trained fine dancers and the classical tradition was preserved by Léo Staats, a choreographer known for his stylistic refinement. A fresh burst of excitement came in 1929 with the arrival of Serge Lifar as choreographer for the Opéra. Lifar, a former star of Diaghilev's company, dominated the Opéra for more than three decades. On stage as a dancer he had a charismatic presence; offstage he was a *bon vivant,* fond of mingling with the smart set. As a choreographer, Lifar could show off both himself and his dancers and, early in his career, he developed some controversial theories.

Like many of the early modern dancers, Lifar felt that in dance productions, the choreographer could easily become subordinate to the composer or designer. He therefore proclaimed the autonomy of dance and, occasionally, as with his *Icare* of 1935, created his entire ballet in silence, then noted down its choreographic rhythms and sent them off to be orchestrated by an obliging composer. However, just as certain French wines do not travel well, so Lifar's Parisian choreography has not always pleased ballet lovers from other countries, who may find his works mannered, rather than stylish. Nevertheless, Lifar did revitalize the Opéra. Since the 1960s, the Opéra Ballet has had several directors, all of whom have complained about the bureaucratic red tape in which such a venerable institution can be entangled. Despite such problems, the Paris Opéra Ballet remains a major company and its school is one of the finest in the world.

Several attempts have been made to develop French ballet outside the Opéra. Boris Kochno, Diaghilev's former secretary, founded Les Ballets des Champs-Elysées in 1945, with the encouragement of Jean Cocteau and the designer Christian Bérard. Until it was disbanded in 1951, the company possessed a freshness and chic that delighted audiences weary of the austerities that had been imposed upon them by World War II.

Kochno encouraged two young choreographers, Janine Charrat and Roland Petit. Petit's *Le Jeune Homme et la Mort,* choreographed under Cocteau's supervision, became simultaneously a scandal and a triumph. The ballet's story is about a young man who commits suicide after being scorned by his beloved. Then the personification of Death comes to claim him. But when she removes her mask, Death proves to be the young woman of the preceding scene. Together, they walk across the rooftops of Paris into eternity. Two things made the ballet remarkable. First, its choreography combined classical steps with realistic everyday movement; second, Petit's use of music was unconventional. He rehearsed the ballet to jazz and it was not until the ballet was completed that the dancers learned that, at Cocteau's suggestion, the actual score was to be a Bach passacaglia—the grandeur of Bach's music serving as an ironic counterpoint to the sordid action.

Petit founded his own Ballets de Paris in 1948, for which he created several works, of which the most talked-about was an adaptation of *Carmen* starring his wife, Renée ("Zizi") Jeanmaire. After that, Petit divided his time between creating works for ballet companies and staging musical numbers for films and revues.

One of the most lavish of French ballet companies was Le Grand Ballet du Marquis de Cuevas. In the age of the welfare state, this large troupe was something of an anachronism, for it was run at the whim of a Chilean-born nobleman of Spanish descent whose wife was John D. Rockefeller's granddaughter. Almost as if he were trying to emulate Louis XIV, the marquis lived in grand style, was impeccably well mannered, and dispensed kisses so lavishly that he was nicknamed the "kissing marquis." Should someone offend him, he would challenge the miscreant to a duel. But fortunately all the duels of this theatrical marquis turned out to be harmless if well-publicized affairs. To no one's surprise, Le Grand Ballet did not long survive its founder's death in 1961.

More recently, the French government has decentralized the arts so that Paris does not have a total cultural monopoly. Arts centers have been established in many cities and regional ballet companies have their headquarters in places such as Marseille, Nancy, the area near the Rhine, and the industrial north of France.

Maurice Béjart, one of the most controversial of French choreographers, directed ballet companies of his own in Brussels, Belgium, and Lausanne, Switzerland, and these groups have attracted both cheers and boos wherever they have appeared. Béjart's choreography is high in energy and often, as in his versions of *Le Sacre du Printemps* and Ravel's *Bolero,* high in erotic content as well. But Béjart also tackled social and political issues. In his adaptation of *Firebird,* the title character is not a ballerina, but the male leader of a guerrilla band, and his *Romeo and Juliet* uses Shakespeare's story to preach "make love, not war." Béjart's company danced both on proscenium stages and in vast arenas, for which he created works such as a ballet to Beethoven's Ninth Symphony that is a choreographic ode to world brotherhood. Béjart's detractors may charge that his works lack subtlety, but no one can say that they lack impact.

ALTHOUGH IN NO WAY SIMILAR TO THOSE OF BÉJART, John Cranko's ballets also prompted critical debates. The South African choreographer first attracted attention in the late 1940s and early 1950s for his ballets for the Sadler's Wells Theatre Ballet. But he achieved international fame when he became director of the Stuttgart Ballet in 1960. Stuttgart had a long tradition of ballet—Noverre had been ballet master there in the eighteenth

John Cranko's *Onegin*, for the Stuttgart Ballet, with Marcia Haydée. *Photograph by Hannes Kiliån. Courtesy of the Dance Collection, The New York Public Library.*

century—and, when he arrived, Cranko found a competent and successful (although to some tastes slightly provincial) troupe. Within a few years, it became a company of international importance. Cranko's best-known productions for it were evening-long ballets based on literary sources: *Romeo and Juliet, Onegin* (after Pushkin's *Eugene Onegin*), *Carmen, The Taming of the Shrew.* Admired for their clear characterizations and swiftly paced, easily comprehensible action, they have also been accused of being obvious and superficial. Yet everyone agreed that Cranko was a fine company director, and his sudden death in 1973 on his way home from an American tour came as a shock. Nevertheless, the Stuttgart Ballet has successfully carried on, building a mixed repertoire of both classical and contemporary pieces. And the spirit of creativity that Cranko encouraged continues in Stuttgart.

The Stuttgart Ballet is only one of many notable German ballet companies. All the leading German cities have ballet troupes attached to their opera houses or municipal theatres, and although artistic standards may vary from city to city, several have maintained a consistently high standard. Because there are so many companies, all in need of new productions, Germany offers employment opportunities for foreign as well as native-born choreographers: for instance, Milwaukee-born John Neumeier, a former dancer with the Stuttgart Ballet who in 1973 became director of the Hamburg Ballet. Under his guidance, the company has achieved an eminence rivaled only by that of the Stuttgart Ballet, with which Neumeier once danced. Neumeier's ballets are often passionate and brooding, and many are filled with a complex literary symbolism that makes them intellectually fascinating to some dancegoers and unduly ponderous to others. Neumeier feels a special temperamental affinity with the spiritually exalted works of Bach—he has choreographed both Bach's St. Matthew Passion and his Christmas Oratorio—and with the introspective compositions of Gustav Mahler. He has set ballets to several Mahler symphonies, one of his finest achievements being *Mahler's Third Symphony,* a study of a lonely outsider who rejects power in favor of love.

In contrast to the neo-Romanticism of Neumeier, the choreography of William Forsythe, another American expatriate, and Stuttgart Ballet

Members of the Frankfurt Ballet perform *Skinny,* choreographed by William Forsythe. Forsythe's steps derive from the classical vocabulary yet his themes and the turbulence of his productions seem aesthetically akin to recent modern dance. *Photograph by Linda Vartoogian.*

alumnus, is sharp-edged and abrasive. Based in Frankfurt, he has created works which, though plotless, appear to be commentaries on power struggles between people and the difficulties of bringing order to a disorderly world. Forsythe's steps derive from the classical vocabulary; nevertheless, the turbulence of his productions often makes them seem aesthetically akin to many recent developments in modern dance.

One of Cranko's last protégés was Uwe Scholz, a classicist by temperament who was nevertheless willing to incorporate several styles of contemporary dancing into his choreography and who, before his untimely death in 2004, was associated with companies in Zurich and Leipzig.

BALLET AND MODERN DANCE HAVE TAKEN ROOT in nations as culturally and geographically disparate as the Netherlands, Israel, and Japan, both forms of dance developing side by side in these countries. The Netherlands,

Sinfonietta is an example of Jiri Kyliǎn's inventive and lyrical choreography. *Photograph by Jack Vartoogian.*

for instance, has two important ballet companies: the National Ballet, in Amsterdam, and Netherlands Dance Theatre, in The Hague. These two groups have commissioned works from both modern dance and ballet choreographers. Various modern dance influences can be discerned in the tightly controlled choreography of Hans van Manen, who has been associated with both companies, and in the rhapsodically surging creations of Czech-born Jiri Kylian, who became director of Netherlands Dance Theatre.

Glancing at the dance map of the world, one finds ballet companies everywhere. Oslo, Stockholm, Prague, and Budapest have ballet companies. So do communities such as Zagreb, Zurich, Geneva, Basel, Tokyo, and the major cities of South Africa. A large ballet company with a large repertoire is attached to the Teatro Colón in Buenos Aires. Other Latin American cities have their own dance companies. The National Ballet of Cuba was founded by the great ballerina Alicia Alonso. There are several ballet and modern dance companies in Australia and New Zealand. And Canada supports both estimable modern dance and ballet companies. Ballet is a dance language virtually the whole world has learned. And wherever it has developed, it has acquired its own local accent.

Related Readings

Ashton and the Purity of Dancing

With every new ballet that I produce I seek to empty myself of some plastic obsession and every ballet I do is, for me, the solving of a balletic problem. . . .

I personally am not fond of the literary ballet, because it seems to me that there comes a hiatus always in which one longs for the spoken word to clarify the subject. And these ballets seem to lead always more to miming than to dancing, thereby invading the functions of the drama or the cinema. In my balletic ideology it is the dancing which must be the foremost factor, for ballet is an expression of emotions and ideas through dancing, and not through words or too much gesture, though naturally these can play their part. But I am against the overlapping of one into the other, except in the case of intentional music drama, when all the arts are welded into a whole.

This brings me to . . . taking one's lead directly from the music, and this is the method which I now prefer. Through it one gets the purity of the dance expressing nothing but itself, and thereby expressing a thousand degrees and facets of emotion, and the mystery of poetry of movement; leaving the audience to respond at will and to bring their own poetic reactions to the work before them. Just as the greatest music has no program, so I really believe the greatest ballets are the same, or at any rate have the merest thread of an idea which can be ignored, and on which the choreographer may weave his imagination for the combination of steps and patterns. . . .

Please don't misunderstand me and think that, by saying this, I mean there are not great ballets which are literary and pictorial. What I do mean to say is that they are isolated examples, and that if this line is pursued too strongly it will bring about the decadence of the dance. If the ballet is to survive, it must survive through its dancing qualities, just as drama must survive through the richness of the spoken word. In a Shakespearean play it is the richness of the language and the poetry that are paramount; the story is unimportant. And it is the same with all the greatest music, and dancing and ballets. In a ballet it is the dance that *must* be paramount.

(Frederick Ashton, "Notes on Choreography" [1951], in Walter Sorell, ed., *The Dance Has Many Faces*. 2nd ed. New York: Columbia University Press, 1966, pp. 89, 91–92)

Remembering the Mercury Theatre

Even I am staggered at the amount and quality of theatrical art born on that stage, and with infinitesimal finance. I consider this the greatest tribute to Ashley's vision.

The theatre had only a hundred and fifty seats, plus standing room for about twenty-five. The stage was only eighteen feet deep, including the apron, and the proscenium also measured only eighteen feet.

Looking back, one can hardly believe that such miracles were performed in that tiny space and that Fred Ashton, Antony Tudor, Andrée Howard, Walter Gore and so many others created ballets for it. The proximity of the audience made it very difficult to create any illusion, one had to make a strenuous effort of imagination to produce works that would transport the audience away from reality into a world of fantasy. Absolute sincerity was required from the artist and complete identification with the part, as the smallest pretence would be felt by the audience immediately. It was a hard school for the choreographers, but it taught them to use every gesture imaginatively, every step, and of course every dancer. Later when Ashton began to create for larger stages it was much easier for him to obtain new effects with that experience behind him.

As for the dancers themselves, it required special virtuosity to make no noise whatever, and do in height what they could not do in width. After that, when they came on to a bigger stage, it gave them tremendous élan. People often think it is difficult to dance on a big stage after a small one, but it is not so. In fact the reverse is true. When the Bolshoi company came to Covent Garden, they found it very difficult to dance there. In three jumps they had crossed the stage and had to fill up the musical phrase with a pose instead of the fourth jump. Their stage in Moscow is much bigger.

(Marie Rambert, *Quicksilver: An Autobiography.* London & New York: St. Martin's Press, 1972, pp. 137–140)

11

International Contemporary Dance

EVER SINCE THE BEGINNING OF THE TWENTIETH CENTURY, skeptics have snorted that modern dance is only a passing fad that cannot possibly last. But the art certainly has survived. It has prospered as well—and in countries throughout the world.

GREAT BRITAIN HAS ALWAYS CONSIDERED ITSELF a nation of balletomanes. Nevertheless, modern dance tried to take root there on several occasions, and it is now very much part of the British cultural scene.

Early in the twentieth century, Ruby Ginner, a former ballet student who had become appalled by what she considered a lack of soul in most dancing, turned to the arts of ancient Greece for inspiration and developed a technique, which she called the Revived Greek Dance, that emphasized natural movements such as walking, running, leaping, and skipping. This dance form was one of many choreographic responses to the Hellenism of Isadora Duncan that occurred throughout the world. Margaret Morris, who had studied with Isadora Duncan's brother, Raymond Duncan, also developed her own system of freestyle dancing and opened a London school in 1910.

In the flurry of British dance activity during the early 1930s, there was modern dance as well as ballet. Margaret Barr, who had studied with Martha Graham in America in 1928, founded the Dance Drama Group at Dartington Hall, a progressive British school with a strong emphasis on the arts. Her group's first productions—many of them dealing with contemporary social problems—were given in 1931, and in 1934 her company moved to London. That same year, the Ballets Jooss, fleeing the Nazi regime in Germany, was offered a residency at Dartington Hall. Other modern dance troubles also attempted to establish themselves, most of them on a shoestring budget. But the austerities and restrictions of World War II brought an end to these ventures and, with the coming of peace, ballet was left as England's dominant dance form for almost two decades.

However, Marie Rambert, the Duncan admirer and eurhythmics student who founded one of England's most important ballet companies, always remained interested in new ways of dancing. Her fascination with modern dance increased during the 1960s and she eventually turned her own company into a modern dance group. Martha Graham, an indirect inspiration to some of the British modern dance of the 1930s, significantly assisted the British modern dance that developed in the 1960s.

Both Rambert and Graham supported the efforts of Robin Howard, a London restaurateur and patron of the arts who lost both of his legs during military service in World War II. As he once put it, he found himself increasingly drawn to dance "partly because it was a total contrast to warfare." He was so impressed by performances of the Graham company on tour that he became determined to bring modern dance to Britain. He established the London School of Contemporary Dance in 1966, out of which emerged a company, the London Contemporary Dance Theatre, which flourished from 1967 until it was disbanded in 1994. Under the direction of Robert Cohan, a former member of the Graham company, the London group was heavily influenced by Graham. Yet, in the true spirit of modern dance, it developed its own new choreographers, including Richard Alston, Robert North, and Siobhan Davies. Since the 1960s, smaller modern dance groups have also been formed, many of them directed by former students of the London School of Contemporary Dance.

Alston, possibly the most important of the British modern dance choreographers, developed a style that emphasizes speed, lightness, and clarity. Although trained at the Graham-oriented London School of Contemporary Dance, he rejected Graham's turbulence, allowing himself to be influenced instead by Cunningham's abstractions and by the lyricism and musicality of England's great ballet choreographer, Sir Frederick Ashton. Far from feeling that Alston had betrayed his teachers, Robin Howard encouraged the young choreographer, saying that only when Alston emerged did he feel that London Contemporary was a real artistic success. Alston's choreography demonstrated that Howard's organization was capable of producing independent thinkers and not merely imitators of its faculty.

The range of British modem dance has steadily widened. Davies is known for her lucid, understated choreography. Christopher Bruce, a dancer with Ballet Rambert who stayed with it when it became a modem dance group, blends classical and contemporary influences in his works, many of which, though plotless, are strongly dramatic in quality and show a concern for the oppressed that makes them implicitly political.

Lloyd Newson's choreography for his DV8 Physical Theatre can be extremely taxing in its demands. Newson uses strong, at times almost reckless, movements to comment on loneliness, sexual stereotyping, and the struggles of people to assert themselves and to relate to one another.

Several British choreographers have been influenced by popular culture. Michael Clark, a highly disciplined choreographer fond of anarchic-looking productions, scorns artistic, social, and sexual conventions in dances that may involve cross-dressing, nudity, and thunderous rock music. Lea Anderson directed an all-female group called the Cholmondeleys, which took its name from an old English surname pronounced "Chumley." Anderson devises sharp, succinct, often comic dances that she hopes will have the impact of pop songs. She also organized a comparable all-male group called the Featherstonehaughs (from another improbable surname, pronounced "Fanshaw").

LIKE GREAT BRITAIN, FRANCE HAS HAD a long love affair with ballet. Yet modem dance has never been totally excluded from its culture. Loïe Fuller spent much of the last part of her life in Paris, where audiences adored her. During the early 1920s, eurhythmics classes were introduced into the curriculum of the Paris Opéra Ballet School, and the eurhythmics teachers occasionally staged productions of their own at the Opéra.

The 1920s were not the only time when modem dance established a special enclave within the precincts of the venerable Opéra. In 1974, the American dancer Carolyn Carlson organized a special modem dance ensemble at the Opéra. She eventually pursued her career elsewhere. But, in 1980, Jacques Garnier founded another modern dance group at the Opéra: G.R.C.O.P. (Groupe de Recherche Chorégraphique de l'Opéra de Paris), a repertory

Karole Armitage's *Living Toys* with the Rambert Dance Company at Sadler's Wells, London. Armitage has studied with such diverse masters as George Balanchine, Léonide Massine, and Merce Cunningham, and was called the "punk ballerina." *Photograph by Johnny Green; Alamy Stock Photo.*

company that performed creations by both European choreographers and Americans such as Karole Armitage, Lucinda Childs, Paul Taylor, and David Gordon. The Paris Opéra Ballet itself has danced works by Merce Cunningham, Alwin Nikolais, and Mark Morris.

Maguy Marin is among the most prominent of the French choreographers who have emerged since the 1970s. Like many of the newer European choreographers, she can be intensely emotional. In addition, she possesses a satirical gift. Produced in 1989, the bicentennial of the French Revolution, *Hey, What's All This to Me?!* was a deflation of political rhetoric and posturing in which authority figures sent people off to war and the heroes of the Revolution were nothing but doddering fogies in a nursing home. Marin's

Two masked dancers of the Lyons Opera Ballet embrace in Maguy Marin's *Cinderella*. *Photograph by Jack Vartoogian.*

ballet *Cinderella,* for the Lyons Opéra Ballet, a troupe hospitable to contemporary styles, retold the familiar fairy tale. But all the characters were masked and costumed to resemble dolls and the action took place in a giant dollhouse. The production therefore seemed to concern the way children often express their own hopes and fears through the stories they tell and the games they play with their dolls.

BEFORE WORLD WAR II, GERMANY WAS a major center of modern dance. But the art withered under Nazi rule and ballet quickly supplanted it in popularity with the coming of peace. Dore Hoyer, one of the few German choreographers to be recognized as important immediately after the war, worked with both Gret Palucca and Mary Wigman. In her own choreography, she combined the latter's sense of drama with the former's concern for structure. She was especially famous for choreographic sketches that sought to express the essence of states of mind and feeling. As the years passed, Hoyer felt herself increasingly exiled from the ballet-oriented German dance scene, and she committed suicide in 1967.

Ironically, only a few years after her death there occurred an unusual resurgence of German modern dance. Much of it is highly emotional and stylistically Expressionistic, and because its choreographers are fond of devising dramatic situations in which dance may be combined with dialogue, this new German modem dance is occasionally referred to as *Tanztheater* (dance-theatre). Its best-known exponent was Pina Bausch, who directed a company in the small industrial city of Wuppertal and whose productions are known for their dreamlike imagery, their dramatic intensity, and their preoccupation with human frailties and cruelties. Bausch was particularly concerned with the emotional wars that may be fought between men and women.

Her *Bluebeard,* for instance, shows a man and a woman constantly tormenting each other, and its setting—a crumbling house with a floor strewn with dead leaves—becomes a visual symbol of their decaying

Human relationships are regarded despairingly by a hippopotamus in Pina Bausch's *Arien*, for her Wuppertaler Tanztheater. *Photograph by Ulli Weiss.*

romantic relationship. To emphasize the solidity, and the messiness, of the material world, Bausch frequently covered the stage with earth, plants, or water. In *Arien,* dancers wade through a pool of water until their costumes are bedraggled. The stage in *Carnations* is transformed into a field of thousands of flowers. But before the piece is over, the lovely blossoms are trampled underfoot, with Bausch thereby implying that, all too often, people emotionally trample one another.

Other major practitioners of *Tanz-theater* include Reinhild Hoffmann, who has depicted the perils of being an international celebrity in *Callas* and the violent motifs in fairy tales in *Machandel,* and Johann (also known as Hans) Kresnik, who combines psychological and political themes and is particularly fascinated by the way societal conditioning may affect an individual's behavior. Susanne Linke, a compelling performer, has tried to show the relationship between the new German dance and *Ausdruckstanz* by choreographing dramatic sketches as a tribute to Dore Hoyer.

THE JAPANESE DEVELOPED THEIR OWN neo-Expressionist modern dance form known as *Butoh* (or dark soul dance). The choreographic imagery in *Butoh* productions by such choreographers as Kazuo Ohno, Tatsumi Hijikata, and Min Tanaka can be startling indeed. As performed by a company called Sankai Juku, Ushio Amagatsu's *Jomon Sho,* an evocation of prehistory, begins with dancers being lowered head downward toward the stage with ropes attached to their ankles. The troupe has occasionally performed this sequence outdoors, with the dancers being lowered from the tops of buildings—on one occasion in 1985 with tragic consequences. In Hijikata's *Forbidden Colors,* a dancer has sex with a chicken squeezed between his thighs, and in *Rose Dance* Hijikata painted his body to look as if his skin had been peeled away.

Such theatrical effects may strike some observers as extremist. But many *Butoh* performers vividly recall relatives and family friends describing the horrors of the 1945 atomic bomb attacks on Hiroshima and Nagasaki. *Butoh* represents a post-Hiroshima generation's response to world tensions. *Butoh* may be grotesque. But so is the world we have created for ourselves. *Butoh's* grotesquerie can also be viewed as a sign of artistic rebellion against conventionality for, traditionally, Japan has been a nation preoccupied with etiquette and refined concepts of beauty.

MODERN DANCE IS OFTEN SAID TO BE not so much a specific technique as a point of view or state of mind. It is no wonder, then, that some companies, like the National Ballet and the Netherlands Dance Theatre of The Netherlands, though trained according to the pedagogical methods of classical ballet, reveal close affinity to modern dance in their choreographic choices. The members of Australia's Sydney Dance Company are also balletically trained. But the productions of its founding director, Graeme Murphy, were often unconventional. Thus, in his version of Ravel's *Daphnis and Chlöe,* Cupid rides a skateboard, nymphs sweep on stage in roller skates, and villainous pirates prove to be members of a motorcycle gang.

The growth of Australian modern dance was aided by several pioneering teachers and choreographers. Margaret Barr went from London to Australia in the late 1930s and opened a studio in Sydney. An even more influential figure was Gertrud Bodenwieser, a Viennese choreographer who also made Sydney her home after she fled the Nazis in 1939. The energetic Bodenwieser trained several generations of Australian dancers and teachers.

WITH THE RISE IN POPULARITY OF DANCE around the world has come a renewed interest in the problems of recording and preserving choreography. Since the time of Beauchamps and Feuillet there have been sporadic attempts to devise systems of dance notation. Arthur Saint-Léon, Friedrich Albert Zorn, and Vladimir Ivanovich Stepanov invented their own notation systems in the nineteenth century. Early in our century, choreographers such as Vaslav Nijinsky and Léonide Massine developed idiosyncratic variants of Stepanov's system.

However, one of the most important—and certainly one of the most successful—twentieth-century notation systems was that invented by Rudolf von Laban in 1926. Although he called his system Kinetographie, it is usually known as Labanotation, and it is considered notable for its comprehensiveness and accuracy. Another influential system is Choreology (or Benesh notation, after the names of Rudolf and Joan Benesh, who invented it in 1955). Still other systems exist and, recently, attempts have been made to record dances with the aid of film, video, and computers. The Dance Notation Bureau, founded in New York in 1940, is an organization dedicated to the study of all forms of notation, with a special emphasis on Labanotation.

Dancers increasingly realize that theirs is an art of preservation as well as invention.

Related Readings

Pina Bausch Interviewed

Is this always how you begin work now, by asking questions?

Well, of course, I have asked hundreds of questions. The dancers have answered them, tried something out. . . . Everyone has a think about it and gives an answer. Sometimes we'll be trying to put things into words. Various things. And then we all take a look at them. . . .

So the piece doesn't begin with a movement then, but with a level of conscious-ness—in the head, rather than in the legs?

The steps have always come from somewhere else—never from the legs. The movements are always worked out in between times. And gradu-ally we build up short dance sequences which we memorize. I used to get scared and panic and so I would start off with a movement and avoid the questions. Nowadays I start off with the questions. . . .

What particular questions did you ask this time?

That's difficult to summarize; recently somebody said, "That was the one hundred and twenty-first question."

Do you remember what the first one was?

I might have asked them about Christmas. I always ask about Christ-mas—well, not always, but fairly often. Each time it's a different ques-tion. This time everybody in the company described Christmas dinner, the things they normally eat. Yesterday I asked if anyone had ever been so frightened they'd messed their pants and when was the first time they'd felt they were a man or a woman. Good questions but they didn't lead us anywhere. Sometimes I think I've got some really good questions, but they lead nowhere. And then sometimes I ask a similar kind of question in a totally different way, until in the end I've changed it completely—and then sometimes I get there in a roundabout way.

That really no longer sounds as if it has anything to do with dance. How is it that you still end up with something which is in fact a dance piece? How do these questions become dance?

In the end, it's composition. What you do with things. There's nothing there to start with. There are only answers: sentences, little scenes someone's shown you. It's all separate to start with. Then at a certain point I'll take something which I think is right and join it to something else. This with that, that with something else. One thing with various other things. And by the time I've found the next thing I think is right, then the little thing I had is already a lot bigger. And then I go off in a completely different direction. It starts really small and gets gradually bigger.

(Interviewed by Jochen Schmidt, November 29, 1982; in Norbert Servos, *Pina Bausch-Wuppertal Dance Theater, or the Art of Training a Goldfish: Excursions into Dance,* trans. by Patricia Stadie. Cologne: Ballett-Bühnen-Verlag, 1984, pp. 235–236)

Meditations of a Butoh Choreographer

When I was in the mountains which surround the Dead Sea, I turned toward the sun and I felt that the movement of the continental shelves, which has been going on since the world was created, was reflected in the depths of my heart. In this Butoh space, which the Dead Sea represents, I heard, out of nowhere, a requiem which engulfed me. Facing the sun I allowed everything I possessed to slip away. . . . It was an infinite movement. I heard great things, comparable to the Sermon on the Mount, but I did not realize it.

I thought that no beast could live in such a place, so I was surprised when I saw innumerable animals running over the mountains. They looked like weasels and they jumped around the sun-charred slopes making a lot of noise. Their cries resounded across the universe like an immense choir. Death, birth, life, all of this is the same.

Mankind has a story as does the cosmos. Superimposed on the story of the cosmos, man's story unfolds. Within this cosmological superimposition emerges the path that leads from birth through maturity to death. The Butoh costume is like throwing the cosmos onto one's shoulders. And for Butoh, while the costume covers the body, it is the body that is the costume of the soul. . . .

In life there is, without a doubt, something beyond the brashness of youth which bursts like summer light. There is something between life and death. This part of ourselves is like the wreck of an abandoned car; if we fix it, it could start up again.

Simply thinking about it sets my heart beating. Butoh's best moment is the moment of extreme weariness when we make a supreme effort to overcome exhaustion. That reminds me of my show in Caracas. I was covered in sweat. My body had grown old and I was working like a rickety old car, but I was happy. Is that what we call wearing oneself out for glory?

The dead begin to run.

(Kazuo Ohno, in Ethan Hoffmann and Mark Holborn, *Butoh: Dance of the Dark Soul*. New York: Sadev / Aperture, 1987, p. 36)

12

Ballet Modern

Ongoing Exploration

THE DAWNING OF THE TWENTY-FIRST CENTURY brought ballet and modern dance both triumphs and fresh challenges. Cities throughout North and South America and across Europe have their own dance companies, sometimes, as in Europe, attached to opera houses or municipal theatres. Standards of dance training have risen, and some old aesthetic conflicts have been more or less peacefully resolved: for instance, the battles between ballet and modern dance fought—often fiercely—for part of the twentieth century. Many schools teach both forms, many companies expect their dancers to be proficient in both, and some choreographers are comfortably eclectic in their choice of movements.

Articulating an increasingly prevalent pedagogical philosophy, Caroline Wright, principal of Centre Point, a dance school in Manchester, England, declared in 2017 that "Our students are up one minute for a ballet pirouette and then rolling on the floor the next. We're being creative and really trying to break boundaries." Commenting on the scene as whole, she noted, "Every classical company now has a strong modern basis."

There are those who might consider her views overly optimistic, dancers and teachers who fear that a mixture of techniques may dilute the special character of the forms being mixed, distorting classical ballet's purity of line or taming the vigor of modern dance. Yet it could be argued that this need not occur, given intelligent teaching, coaching, and choreography.

Britain's Royal Ballet, occasionally accused of being overly conservative in outlook, took a bold step in 2006 when it appointed Wayne McGregor resident choreographer, for McGregor is a modern dancer associated with a sharp and often angular style. While in residence with the Royal Ballet, McGregor also choreographs for his own modern dance troupe.

Some institutions, for various reasons, are not so welcoming. When the Théâtre de la Monnaie, the Brussels opera house, changed its overall direction in 1988, Maurice Béjart's Ballet of the Twentieth Century, the theatre's resident dance company, moved to Lausanne, Switzerland, and was replaced by the Mark Morris Dance Group. Whereas Béjart was celebrated throughout Europe as an important choreographer, Morris, at least to Europeans, was then little-known; he was also brash and outspoken, and his Brussels tenure lasted only until 1991, when he returned to America. His successor at the Monnaie was the Belgian-born Anne Teresa de Keersmaeker, who had once studied at the Béjart school.

The venerable Paris Opéra and its Paris Opéra Ballet have long been centers of controversy, its artistic and administrative affairs constantly ensnarled in bureaucratic red tape—as its ballet directors have repeatedly discovered. Among them was Benjamin Millepied, appointed director in 2013. Although French-born—his mother was a modern dancer, his father an athlete—he was trained entirely outside the Opéra; he came to New York in 1992 to attend the School of American Ballet, joined the New York City Ballet, where he was mentored by Jerome Robbins. He began both to choreograph and to show an interest in company direction.

Heading the Paris Opéra Ballet and faced with the problem of preserving its great traditions while at the same time encouraging innovation, he staged works by Balanchine, Robbins, and Cunningham and commissioned pieces by Justin Peck, William Forsythe, and Wayne McGregor, among others, yet found it difficult to work with the institution's authorities. Married to the actress Natalie Portman, he moved to Los Angeles in 2016 where he founded and directs the L.A. Dance Project, a company seeking to promote collaborations between dancers and artists.

Dance can face many sorts of problems. In 2016, for instance, the Cape Town City Ballet, founded in 1934 by Dulcie Howes, a pioneer of dance education in South Africa, was evicted from its home, the University of Cape Town School of Dance. Although the university continued to offer contemporary and African dance, ballet was deemed too "Eurocentric and colonial"—an attitude that may reflect revulsion against South Africa's apartheid past.

Nevertheless, throughout much of the world, dance has adapted itself to changing cultural and political conditions. Change can be slow, however. Black dancers still struggle to be accepted, yet some companies and dancers have achieved renown, the internationally acclaimed Alvin Ailey American Dance Theatre being prominent among them. Also enterprising is Philadanco, which Joan Myers Brown established in Philadelphia when she found that black dancers were often denied entrance into local dance organizations.

Some black companies have special emphases. Evidence, Ronald K. Brown's troupe, blends traditional African dance, especially that of Senegal, with contemporary idioms, often investing productions with spiritual significance. Urban Bush Women, founded by Jawole Willa Jo Zollar offers works by her and other choreographers focused on social justice issues viewed from a feminist perspective, as well as the history, culture, and spiritual problems of the African Diaspora. Bill T. Jones has created vehement dances on political themes, American history, and the AIDS crisis.

Lester Horton and Martha Graham were among the earliest white modern dance directors to welcome performers of all races, and many troupes, but by no means all, are now equally hospitable. But black ballet dancers still have a difficult time, even some of the most talented finding classical companies closed to them. Janet Collins, a gifted ballet dancer, found no company willing to accept her until she became ballerina of the Metropolitan Opera Ballet in 1951 at the age of 34. When the Ballet Russe de Monte Carlo hired Raven Wilkinson in 1956, it became the first touring American ballet company to employ a black dancer. But because it regularly toured the segregated South, Wilkinson found herself under attack by bigots; she eventually left the troupe and joined the Dutch National Ballet which, like several other European companies, welcomed diversity. Among other African-Americans in that troupe were Sylvester Campbell, a dancer known for his classical style, and Billy Wilson, who gravitated between ballet and musical theatre.

Misty Copeland, principal dancer of the American Ballet Theatre, performs a new work at the Marian Anderson Award gala 2015, held at the Kimmel Center in Philadelphia. *Alamy Stock Photo.*

In 2015, Misty Copeland became the first African-American woman to be appointed a principal dancer with American Ballet Theatre, although in previous years Anne Benna Sims and Nora Kimball had been soloists with that company. Nevertheless, there still have been few black dancers with ballet troupes. In response to this situation, several directors and choreographers have established ballet companies explicitly for dancers of color. Despite occasional financial setbacks, Dance Theatre of Harlem survives and artistically prospers. Ballet Black was founded in England in 2001 by Cassa Pancho in what she declared in a policy statement was a visionary attempt "to see a fundamental change in the number of black and Asian dancers in mainstream companies, making that vision wonderfully unnecessary."

Feminist dancers began to wonder why there were so few women ballet choreographers and directors, although earlier in the twentieth century there had been such important choreographers as Bronislava Nijinska, Ninette de Valois, and Agnes de Mille. And among the founders of ballet companies were de Valois (Royal Ballet), Marie Rambert (Ballet Rambert), Lucia Chase (American Ballet Theatre), Gweneth Lloyd (Royal Winnipeg Ballet), Ludmilla Chiriaeff (Les Grands Ballets Canadiens), Celia Franca (National Ballet of Canada), Peggy van Praagh (Australian Ballet), and the pioneering leaders of companies associated with the American regional ballet movement, including Dorothy Alexander (Atlanta Ballet), E. Virginia Williams (Boston Ballet), Josephine and Hermene Schwarz (Dayton Ballet), and Barbara Weisberger (Pennsylvania Ballet).

As a result of directorial soul-searching some companies resolved to pay greater attention to staging ballets by women. The Royal Ballet was among them, and during the 2016-17 season it commissioned choreography from Crystal Pite, a Canadian choreographer previously associated with William Forsythe's ballet company in Frankfurt; she thereby became the first woman to stage a premiere for the Royal Ballet since Siobhan Davies did so in 1999.

Male dancers have had their own problems. Male ballet dancers were long accused of being homosexuals or, at least, effeminate. Willam Christensen, that tireless promoter of ballet in the American West, would recall that, during his performing days, when he appeared as the title character in *Spectre de la Rose,* he did not dare to wear anything resembling the fantastic rose-petaled costume Léon Bakst had designed for Nijinsky; instead, he wore a version of a tuxedo. If he had worn Bakst's costume, he feared he would have been hooted at and run out of town. Male modern dancers also encountered hostility. Ted Shawn was warned by supposedly well-meaning friends that "men don't dance." But men did dance, becoming increasingly accepted on and off stage.

THE RISE OF THE LGBT (Lesbian, Gay, Bisexual, and Transgender) movement has had an effect upon dance, as well as politics. Explicitly gay themes have been staged increasingly often. Equally important, theatrical gender roles have become more fluid and are not necessarily associated with any dancer's personal sexual orientation.

Sometimes gender conventions are disrupted for comic effects. Les Ballets Trockadero (familiarly known as the Trocks) certainly did so. This all-male troupe was founded in 1974 by a group of male dancers who wished to offer affectionate parodies of classical ballet. So they wore tutus and danced on pointe and, with stumbling steps and haughty or simpering expressions, mocked the mannerisms and conventions of ballerinas and danseurs. However, as time passed and the men's techniques improved, the comedy became less broad and the Trocks were able to present essentially serious revivals of works by Bournonville, Petipa, Fokine, and other choreographers with only a minimum of farcical mugging. The Trocks can also serve as a reminder that in certain dance and theatrical traditions, particularly some in Asia, all roles—male and female alike—are portrayed by performers of the same sex.

Serious defiance of gender convention has occurred in both ballet and modern dance. As far back as the 1970's, Senta Driver, a former member of Paul Taylor's company, began to experiment with choreographic weight and, reversing tradition, had women lift and carry men in some of her pieces. Later choreographers have continued such practices and their experiments have expanded dance's technical possibilities.

Choreographers have a host of movement resources on which to draw. Just as in past centuries ballet choreographers utilized such national dances as the mazurka and czardas, as well as ballroom dance forms—in particular, the waltz—so in our own time popular dance styles have found their way into both ballet and modern-dance productions.

Tap, in its origins a blending of British clog dancing and the dances of black African slaves, has been especially influential, dominating Broadway and Hollywood musicals into the 1940's and '50's, with the dapper Fred Astaire and the more athletically assertive Gene Kelly becoming much-praised stars. Ballet dancers have often been fond of tap, possibly because of its emphasis on intricate nimble footwork. For *On Your Toes,* a 1936 musical by Richard Rodgers and Lorenz Hart, George Balanchine devised *Slaughter on Tenth Avenue,* a miniature ballet about a hoofer (originally Ray Bolger) who realizes that some gangsters plan to shoot him at the end of one of his numbers and so keeps repeating it almost to the point of total exhaustion when, luckily, policemen burst in and apprehend the criminals. Detached from its original context, it entered the repertoire of the New York City Ballet as an independent item in 1968 with Arthur Mitchell as the hoofer. Tap has continued to attract ballet choreographers from Agnes de Mille to, in more recent years, Justin Peck and Christopher Wheeldon.

A form of street dance that has attracted widespread notice since the 1970s is hip-hop, which arose out of inner-city African-American and Latino communities. Characterized by swivels, unexpected balances, and locked poses that suddenly pop into life, hip-hop can be spectacular to watch and it has achieved success in the United Kingdom, Germany, and France, as well as in the United States. Several companies have made it the basis for their technique, including Compagnie Käfig, a French company of Moroccan dancers who combine it with mime, gymnastics, and capoeira, a Brazilian martial-arts dance form. A leading exponent of hip-hop in the United States is Rennie Harris, whose Rennie Harris Puremovement, founded in 1997, was America's first hip-hop company. Although hip-hop productions are usually virtuoso displays, Harris has also experimented with making hip-hop the basis for narratives, as in his *Rome & Jewels* of 2000, a hip-hop retelling of *Romeo and Juliet.*

ONE FORM TO WHICH MANY BALLET AND MODERN DANCE choreographers find themselves drawn is the multi-act or evening-length production, a single work occupying an entire program. Such creations are sometimes called full-length, a misleading designation, for any good dance, be it ten minutes or three hours in duration, is "full-length": it is as long as it needs to be.

Advocates of long forms sometimes use "full-length" not as a descriptive term, but as a value judgment, as if implying that one-act works are somehow inferior. However, from 1900 on, although there have been important evening-long works by Graham, Balanchine, Ashton, MacMillan, Cunningham, and other choreographers, most of the great ballet and modern-dance creations of our time are in one act. Historically, it can be argued that the full-evening dance was not always the norm, even in the nineteenth century. Going to the theatre then was often like settling down for a night of television today. Just as television fans may enjoy dramas, comedies, and variety shows all in the course of an evening, so a night at an opera house might include an opera, a ballet, and sometimes even a play as well.

Although choreographers may offer full-evening works on many themes, or on no specific theme at all, multi-act ballet productions are usually narratives, frequently inspired by myths, legends, history, or well-known literary works. Shakespeare is an especially popular source, with *Romeo and Juliet* and *A Midsummer Night's Dream* being often choreographed. Such narratives have the advantage of familiar, and therefore easily comprehensible, subject matter. But many multi-act narratives can seem much too long, requiring choreographic padding just to fill out an evening. Nevertheless, inventive choreographers can devise unusual multi-act ballets.

Often, when dancegoers speak of "full-length" ballets, they think of well-known nineteenth-century multiact works: for instance, the Tchaikovsky ballets *Swan Lake, Sleeping Beauty,* and *Nutcracker.* Productions of these classics can take many forms. Sometimes, producers will attempt to reproduce the original choreography as closely as possible. More often, stagings will combine sections of traditional choreography—especially, famous bits—with totally new choreography by the local ballet master. Elements of the story may even be changed, supposedly to suit the taste of contemporary audiences: thus, in our post-Freudian era, *Swan Lake* is occasionally staged as if it were the Prince's symbol-laden and psychologically fraught dream. But the problem remains of how much alteration is artistically justifiable: when is *Swan Lake* no longer really *Swan Lake?*

One 19th-century ballet that remains especially open to idiosyncratic interpretations is *Nutcracker,* for little survives of Lev Ivanov's original choreography. Choreographers have therefore felt free to alter the plot and change the setting as they please. Because *Nutcracker* celebrates communal harmony and family warmth, some companies shift the action to their own cities, especially if those locales are historically or architecturally distinctive. One elaborate example of this approach is Christopher Wheeldon's *Nutcracker*, in 2017, for the Joffrey Ballet of Chicago, which takes place at the fabled Chicago World's Fair of 1893. Other unusual *Nutcrackers* have been Donald Byrd's *Harlem Nutcracker*, which includes Duke Ellington arrangements of some of Tchaikovsky's melodies, and which Donald Byrd/The Group presented in 1996; Mark Morris's *The Hard Nut*, for the Mark Morris Dance Group in 1991, which relocates the action to suburban America in the 1950's; and Graeme Murphy's *Nutcracker—The Story of Clara,* for the Australian Ballet in 1992, in which an elderly ballerina in Australia remembers her past.

Other choreographers may borrow famous plots and make them the basis of totally original compositions, just as throughout the centuries dramatists have borrowed Greek myths and made them their own. The British choreographer Matthew Bourne has become associated with such radical revisions. Bourne has reinterpreted several ballet plots because, as he put it, "I wanted to explore characters," and his sources include *Nutcracker*, which he relocated in a Victorian orphanage resembling a Dickensian workhouse, and *La Sylphide,* which he titled *Highland Fling* and set in a modern-day Glasgow housing project. What may be his most striking creation is a version of *Swan Lake*, in which, reversing the usual characterizations, the prince is a shy young man attracted by a powerful male swan, whose flock is also all-male.

DANCE HAS NOT ALWAYS RESPECTED ITS PAST. Many works, acknowledged in their time as great, have been allowed to fade away. Balletmasters have tinkered with the classics so much as to drastically alter their choreographic content. Modern dancers, including some of the art's important pioneers, have taken a cavalier attitude toward their creations, stating that they are more interested in choreographing new works than in preserving old ones. But when it became clear that some of their finest old ones were in danger of sinking into oblivion, many choreographers or their heirs—in ballet and modern dance alike—have taken steps to insure that these works are being preserved, both through notation and through the efforts of official *régisseurs* entrusted to them.

The rugged individualists of modern dance are also increasingly welcoming pieces by other choreographers into their own repertories. Stephen Petronio has established what he terms his Bloodlines Project, enabling his dancers to dance works by choreographers who have been important to him, including Merce Cunningham, Trisha Brown, Steve Paxton, Anna Halprin, and Yvonne Rainer. Paul Taylor renamed his organization Paul Taylor American Modern Dance, and his dancers have performed works by outside choreographers, including Martha Graham, and he has invited other companies to share programs with him, performing works by Cunningham, Doris Humphrey, and Donald McKayle, among others. The results of such activities have been programs of great diversity. Of course, representatives of repertory ballet companies throughout the world, as well as many European contemporary dance groups, might point out, with more than a hint of justifiable pride, that they have long favored choreographically mixed programs.

The more diversity there is in dance, the better off the dance world may be. Defying economic woes and political tensions, dance is always on the move, coming from and going to many artistic places, simultaneously exploring new territory and viewing beloved and familiar creations with fresh eyes.

Related Reading

T. S. Eliot on Exploration

We shall not cease from exploration

And the end of all our exploring

Will be to arrive where we started

And know the place for the first time.

(T. S. Eliot, from "Little Gidding," the last poem of his *Four Quartets,* in T. S. Eliot, *The Complete Poems and Plays 1909-1950.* New York: Harcourt, Brace and Company, 1958, p. 145)

Bibliography

A selected list of books for further reading. Annotation is added for titles that do not reveal the nature of the contents. Multiple works by an author are listed alphabetically.

General

Adshead, Janet, and June Layson, eds. *Dance History: A Methodology for Study.* London: Dance Books Ltd., 1983.

Anderson, Jack. *Choreography Observed.* Iowa City: University of Iowa Press, 1989.

Au, Susan. *Ballet and Modern Dance.* New York: Thames and Hudson, 1988.

Balanchine, George, and Francis Mason. *Balanchine's Complete Stories of the Great Ballets.* Garden City, N.Y.: Doubleday & Co., Inc., 1977.

Beaumont, Cyril W. *Complete Book of Ballets.* New York: Grosset & Dunlap, 1938. Three supplements were published by Putnam in London: Supplement to *Complete Book of Ballets* (1942), *Ballets of Today* (1954), and *Ballets Past and Present (1955)*.

Bremser, Martha and Lorna Sanders, eds. *Fifty Contemporary Choreographers,* second ed. London: Routledge, 2011.

Bremser, Martha, ed, *International Dictionary of Ballet,* 2 vols. London: St. James Press, 1993.

Clarke, Mary, and Clement Crisp. *Ballet: An Illustrated History.* London: Adam & Charles Black, 1973.

———.*The Ballet Goer's Guide.* New York: Alfred A. Knopf, 1981.

Clarke, Mary, and David Vaughan, eds. *The Encyclopedia of Dance.* New York: G.P. Putnam's Sons, 1977.

Cohen, Selma Jeanne, ed. *Dance as a Theatre Art: Source Readings in Dance History from 1581 to the Present, Second Edition.* Princeton, N.J.: Princeton Book Company, Publishers, 1992.

———. *Next Week, Swan Lake: Reflections on Dance and Dances.* Middletown, Conn.: Wesleyan University Press, 1982. Studies in dance aesthetics.

Cohen, Selma Jeanne, founding ed. and Elizabeth Aldrich, managing ed. *International Encyclopedia of Dance,* 6 vols. New York: Oxford University Press, 1998.

Copeland, Roger, and Marshall Cohen, eds. *What Is Dance?: Readings in Theory and Criticism.* New York: Oxford University Press, 1983.

Denby, Edwin. *Dancers, Buildings and People in the Streets.* New York: Horizon Press, 1965.

———. *Looking at the Dance.* New York: Horizon Press, 1968.
Two unusually perceptive books of dance criticism.

Dictionary Catalog of the Dance Collection. New York: The New York Public Library, 1974.
The catalog of one of the world's great dance libraries in book form. Annual supplements are published as *Bibliographic Guide to Dance.* Boston: G.K. Hall & Company.

Emery, Lynne Fauley. *Black Dance from 1619 to Today.* 2nd, rev. ed. Princeton, N.J.: A Dance Horizons Book/Princeton Book Company, Publishers, 1988.

Fancher, Gordon, and Gerald Myers, eds. *Philosophical Essays on Dance: With Responses from Choreographers, Critics and Dancers.* New York: Dance Horizons, 1981.

Fonteyn, Margot. *The Magic of Dance.* New York: Alfred A. Knopf, 1979.

Guest, Ann Hutchinson. *Dance Notation: The Process of Recording Movement on Paper.* New York: Dance Horizons, 1984.
A history of notation systems.

Guest, Ivor. *Adventures of a Ballet Historian: An Unfinished Memoir.* New York: Dance Horizons, 1982.
The autobiography of a distinguished dance historian.

———. *The Dancer's Heritage: A Short History of Ballet.* New York: Macmillan, 1961; repro. London: The Dancing Times, 1985.

Hastings, Baird. *Choreographer and Composer: Theatrical Dance and Music in Western Culture.* Boston: Twayne Publishers, 1983.

Homans, Jennifer. *Apollo's Angels: A History of Ballet.* New York: Random House, 2010.

Jones, Susan. *Literature, Modernism and Dance.* Oxford: Oxford University Press, 2013.
Discusses relationships between dance and major modernist writers.

Jordan, Stephanie. *Stravinsky Dances: Re-Visions Across a Century.* Alton: Dance Books, 2007.

Jowitt, Deborah. *Time and the Dancing Image.* New York: William Morrow and Company, Inc., 1988.

Kirstein, Lincoln. *Dance: A Short History of Classical Theatrical Dancing.* Anniversary Edition. Princeton, N.J.: Princeton Book Company, Publishers, 1987.

—————. *Movement and Metaphor: Four Centuries of Ballet.* New York: Praeger Publishers, 1970.

Koegler, Horst. *The Concise Oxford Dictionary of Ballet.* 2nd ed. London: Oxford University Press, 1982.

Kraus, Richard, and Sarah Chapman. *History of Dance in Art and Education.* 2nd ed. Englewood Cliffs, N.J.: Prentice-Hall, Inc., 1981.
Contains a special section on the history of dance education.

Lawler, Lillian B. *The Dance in Ancient Greece.* Middletown, Conn.: Wesleyan University Press, 1964.

Lawrence, Robert. *The Victor Book of Ballets and Ballet Music.* New York: Simon & Schuster, 1950.

Migel, Parmenia. *The Ballerinas: From the Court of Louis XIV to Pavlova.* New York: Macmillan, 1972; repro. New York: Da Capo Press, 1980.

Mueller, John. *Astaire Dancing: The Musical Films.* New York: Alfred A. Knopf, 1989.

Page, Ruth. *Class: Notes on Dance Classes Around the World 1915–1980.* Edited and additional notes by Andrew M. Wentink. Princeton, N.J.: Princeton Book Company, Publishers, 1984.

Redfern, Betty. *Dance, Art, and Aesthetics.* London: Dance Books Ltd., 1983.

Reynolds, Nancy and Malcolm McCormick. *No Fixed Points: Dance in the Twentieth Century.* New Haven: Yale University Press, 2003.

Robert, Grace. *The Borzoi Book of Ballets.* New York: Alfred A. Knopf, 1946.

Robertson, Allen, and Donald Hutera. *The Dance Handbook.* Boston: G.K. Hall & Co., 1988.

Siegel, Marcia B. *The Shapes of Change: Images of American Dance.* Boston: Houghton Mifflin Company, 1979.
Analyses of significant pieces of American choreography.

Seibert, Brian. *What the Eye Hears: A History of Tap Dancing.* New York: Farrar, Straus and Giroux, 2015.
Includes discussions of tap in relation to ballet and modern dance.

The Simon and Schuster Book of the Ballet. New York: Simon & Schuster, 1980.

Sorell, Walter, ed. *The Dance Has Many Faces*. 3rd ed. Pennington, N.J.: a cappella books, 1992.
Anthology of essays by choreographers, critics, and scholars.

Sorell, Walter. *Dance in Its Time: The Emergence of an Art Form*. Garden City, N.Y.: Doubleday & Co., Inc., 1981.

Sparshott, Francis. *Off the Ground: First Steps to a Philosophic Consideration of Dance*. Princeton, N.J.: Princeton University Press, 1988.
An approach to dance aesthetics.

Stearns, Marshall and Jean. *Jazz Dance: The Story of American Vernacular Dance*. New York: Macmillan, 1968.

Steinberg, Cobbett, ed. *The Dance Anthology*. New York: New American Library, 1980.
Anthology of essays on dance history and aesthetics.

Early Ballet

Arbeau, Thoinot [pseudonym of Jehan Tabouret]. *Orchesography* [1588], translated by Mary Stewart Evans. New York: Kamin Dance Publications, 1948; repro. with a new introduction and notes by Julia Sutton, New York: Dover Publications, 1967.

Brooks, Lynn Matluck. *The Dances of the Procession of Seville in Spain's Golden Age*. Cassel, Germany: Edition Reichenberger, 1988.

Caroso, Fabritio. *Nobiltà di Dame* [1600], translated and edited by Julia Sutton, music edited by F. Marian Walker. New York: Oxford University Press, 1986.
A treatise on courtly dance.

Chazin-Bennahum, Judith. *Dance in the Shadow of the Guillotine*. Carbondale: Southern Illinois University Press, 1988.
French ballet from 1787 to 1801.

Christout, Marie-Françoise. *Le Ballet de Cour de Louis XIV*. Paris: Editions A. et J. Picard & Cie., 1967.
In French.

———. *The Ballet de Cour in the Seventeenth Century*. Geneva, Switzerland: Editions Minkoff, 1987.
In English and French. Lavishly illustrated.

Cornazano, Antonio. *The Book on the Art of Dancing* [1465?], translated by Madeleine Inglehearn and Peggy Forsyth. London: Dance Books Ltd., 1981.

Guest, Ivor. *The Ballet of the Enlightenment: The Establishment of the Ballet d'Action in France 1770–1793*. London: Dance Books, 1996.

Guthrie, John. *Historical Dances for the Theatre: The Pavan and the Minuet.* rev. ed. London: Dance Books Ltd., 1982.

Hilton, Wendy. *Dance of Court and Theater: The French Noble Style 1690–1725.* Princeton, N.J.: Princeton Book Company, Publishers, 1981.

Harris-Warrick, Rebecca and Bruce Alan Brown. *The Grotesque Dancer on the Eighteenth-Century Stage: Gennaro Magri and His World.* Madison: University of Wisconsin Press, 2005.

Jenyns, Soame. *The Art of Dancing: A Poem in Three Cantos* [1729], edited by Anne Cottis. London: Dance Books Ltd., 1978.

Lynham, Deryck. *The Chevalier Noverre: Father of Modern Ballet.* London: Sylvan Press Ltd., 1950; repro. London: Dance Books Ltd., 1972.

Magri, Gennaro. *Theoretical and Practical Treatise on Dancing,* translated and edited by Mary Skeaping, with Anna Ivanova, Irmgard E. Berry, and Annalisa Fox. London: Dance Books Ltd., 1988.

McGowan, Margaret M. *Art du ballet de Cour en France 1581–1643.* Paris: Editions du Centre National de la Recherche Scientifique, 1978. In French.

———. *Le Balet comique de Balthazar de Beaujoyeulx, 1581: A Facsimile with an Introduction.* Binghamton, N.Y.: Center for Medieval and Early Renaissance Studies, 1982. A facsimile text of, and commentary on, *Ballet Comique de la Reine.*

Noverre, Jean Georges. *Letters on Dancing and Ballets* [1803], translated by Cyril W. Beaumont. London: Cyril W. Beaumont, 1930; repr. New York: Dance Horizons, 1966.

Ralph, Richard. *The Life and Works of John Weaver.* New York: Dance Horizons, 1985.

Pappacena, Flavia. *Carlo Blasis' Il Trattato di danza (Treatise on Dance 1820–1830).* Lucca: Libreria Musicale Italiana, 2005.

Swift, Mary Grace. *A Loftier Flight: The Life and Accomplishments of Charles Louis Didelot, Balletmaster.* Middletown, Conn.: Wesleyan University Press, 1974.

Winter, Marian Hannah. *The Pre-Romantic Ballet.* New York: Dance Horizons, 1974.

Wood, Melusine. *Historical Dances, 12th to 19th Century.* London: Imperial Society of Teachers of Dancing, 1952; repro. London: Dance Books Ltd., 1982.

Nineteenth-Century Western European Ballet

Beaumont, Cyril W. *The Ballet Called Giselle*. London: Cyril W. Beaumont, 1944; repro New York: Dance Horizons, 1969.

Blasis, Carlo. *The Code of Terpsichore* [1828], translated by R. Barton. New York: Dance Horizons, 1976.
A treatise on ballet technique.

Bournonville, August. *My Theatre Life*, translated by Patricia W. McAndrew. Middletown, Conn.: Wesleyan University Press, 1979.

Bruhn, Erik, and Lillian Moore. *Bournonville and Ballet Technique*. London: Adam & Charles Black, 1961; repro. New York: Dance Horizons, n.d.

de Vanyer, Jill and Richard Kendall. *Degas and the Dance*. New York: Henry N. Abrams, 2002.
A study of the world's most famous painter of ballet and his era.

Garafola, Lynn, ed. *Rethinking the Sylph: New Perspectives on the Romantic Ballet*. Hanover: University Press of New England for Wesleyan University Press, 1997.

Gautier, Théophile. *Gautier on Dance*, translated by Ivor Guest. London: Dance Books Ltd., 1986.

———.*The Romantic Ballet*, translated by Cyril W. Beaumont. rev. ed. London: Cyril W. Beaumont, 1947; repro. New York: Dance Horizons, n.d.
A collection of Gautier's reviews.

Guest, Ivor. *The Ballet of the Second Empire 1847–1870*. 2nd ed. Middletown, Conn.: Wesleyan University Press, 1974.

———. *Ballet Under Napoleon*. Alton: Dance Books, 2002.

———. *The Divine Virginia: A Biography of Virginia Zucchi*. New York: Marcel Dekker, Inc., 1977.

———. *Fanny Cerrito: The Life of a Romantic Ballerina*. London: Phoenix House, 1956; repr. London: Dance Books Ltd., 1974.

———. *Fanny Elssler*. Middletown, Conn.: Wesleyan University Press, 1970.

———. *Jules Perrot: Master of the Romantic Ballet*. New York: Dance Horizons, 1984.

———. *The Romantic Ballet in England*. 2nd ed. Middletown, Conn.: Wesleyan University Press, 1972.

———. *The Romantic Ballet in Paris*. Alton: Dance Books, 2008.

———. *The Romantic Ballet in Paris*. Middletown, Conn.: Wesleyan University Press, 1966.

———. *The Romantic Ballet in Paris.* Alton: Dance Books, 2008.

Jurgensen, Knud Arne. *The Bournonville Ballets: A Photographic Record, 1844–1933.* London: Dance Books Ltd., 1987.

Smith, Marian. *Ballet and Opera in the Age of Giselle.* Princeton: Princeton University Press, 2000.

———, ed., *La Sylphide: Paris 1832 and Beyond.* Alton: Dance Books Ltd., 2012.

Terry, Walter. *The King's Ballet Master: A Biography of Denmark's August Bournonville.* New York: Dodd, Mead & Company, 1979.

Russian Ballet

Alovert, Nina. *Baryshnikov in Russia.* New York: Holt, Rinehart & Winston, 1984.

Anderson, Jack. *The Nutcracker Ballet.* New York: Mayflower Books, 1979.

Beaumont, Cyril W. *The Ballet Called Swan Lake.* London: Cyril W. Beaumont, 1952.

Demidov, Alexander. *The Russian Ballet: Past and Present,* translated by Guy Daniels. Garden City, N.Y.: Doubleday & Co., Inc., 1977.

Kschessinska, Mathilde. *Dancing in Petersburg,* translated by Arnold Haskell. Garden City, N.Y.: Doubleday & Co., Inc., 1961.
The autobiography of a Mariinsky ballerina.

Morrison, Simon. *Bolshoi Confidential: Secrets of the Russian Ballet from the Rule of the Tsars to Today.* New York: Liveright Publishing Corporation, 2016.

Petipa, Marius. *Russian Ballet Master: The Memoirs of Marius Petipa,* translated by Helen Whittaker. London: Adam & Charles Black, 1958; repro. New York: Dance Horizons, n.d.

Plisetskaya, Maya, trans. Antonina W. Bouis. *I, Maya Plisetskaya.* New Haven: Yale University Press, 2001.

Roslavleva, Natalia. *Era of the Russian Ballet.* New York: E.P. Dutton & Co., Inc., 1966.
A history of Russian ballet from the earliest days to the Soviet era.

Smakov, Gennady. *Baryshnikov: From Russia to the West.* New York: Farrar, Sraus & Giroux, 1981.

Swift, Mary Grace. *The Art of the Dance in the USSR.* South Bend, Ind.: University of Notre Dame Press, 1969.

Wiley, Roland John. *Tchaikovsky's Ballets: Swan Lake, Sleeping Beauty, Nutcracker.* Oxford, England: Clarendon Press, 1985.

The Diaghilev Era

Aschengreen, Erik. *Jean Cocteau and the Dance,* translated by Patricia McAndrew. Copenhagen: Gyldendal, 1986.

Beaumont, Cyril W. *Michel Fokine and His Ballets.* London: Cyril W. Beaumont, 1935; repro 1945.

Berg, Shelley C. *Le Sacre du Printemps: Seven Productions from Nijinsky to Martha Graham.* Ann Arbor, Mich.: UMI Research Press, 1988.

Buckle, Richard. *L'Après-Midi d'un Faune.* New York: Dance Horizons, 1983.

———. *Diaghilev.* New York: Atheneum, 1979.

———. *Nijinsky.* New York: Simon & Schuster, 1971; rev. ed. Harmondsworth, England: Penguin Books, 1980.

Cossart, Michael de. *Ida Rubinstein (1885–1960): A Theatrical Life.* Liverpool: Liverpool University Press, 1987.

Fokine, Michel. *Memoirs of a Ballet Master,* translated by Vitale Fokine. Boston: Little, Brown & Company, 1961.

Fonteyn, Margot. *Pavlova: Portrait of a Dancer.* New York: Viking Penguin Inc., 1984.

Garafola, Lynn. *Diaghilev's Ballets Russes.* New York: Oxford University Press, 1989.

García-Márquez, Vicente. *Massine: A Biography.* New York: Alfred A. Knopf, 1995.

Gold, Arthur, and Robert Fizdale. *Misia: The life of Misia Sert.* New York: Vintage Books, 1992.
   A friend to artists, composers and writers, she was a long-time associate and provider of funds to Diaghilev and was involved in many aspects of the Ballets Russes, even rescuing the company financially on opening night of *Petrushka.*

Grigoriev, Serge L. *The Diaghilev Ballet 1909–1929,* translated by Vera Bowen. London: Constable, 1953; repro. New York: Dance Horizons, n.d.

Karsavina, Tamara. *Theatre Street.* New York: E.P. Dutton & Co., Inc., 1931; repro. London: Dance Books Ltd., 1981.
   Autobiography of a Mariinsky-trained ballerina of Diaghilev's Ballets Russes.

Kerensky, Oleg. *Anna Pavlova.* New York: E.P. Dutton & Co., Inc., 1973.

Keynes, Milo, ed. *Lydia Lopokova.* New York: St. Martin's Press, 1983.

Kirstein, Lincoln. *Nijinsky Dancing.* New York: Alfred A. Knopf, 1975.

Krasovskaya, Vera. *Nijinsky,* translated by John E. Bowlt. New York: Schirmer Books, 1979.

Lazzarini, John and Roberta. *Pavlova: Repertoire of a Legend.* New York: Schirmer Books, 1980.

Macdonald, Nesta. *Diaghilev Observed by Critics in England and the United States 1911–1929.* New York: Dance Horizons, 1975.

Magriel, Paul, ed. *Nijinsky, Pavlova, Duncan: Three Lives in Dance.* New York: Da Capo Press, 1977.

Massine, Leonide. *My Life in Ballet.* New York: St. Martin's Press, 1968.

Money, Keith. *Anna Pavlova: Her Life and Art.* New York: Alfred A. Knopf, 1980.

Nijinska, Bronislava. *Early Memoirs,* translated and edited by Irina Nijinska and Jean Rawlinson. New York: Holt, Rinehart & Winston, 1981.

Nijinsky, Romola. *Nijinsky.* New York: Simon & Schuster, 1934; repro. 1981.

Percival, John. *The World of Diaghilev.* New York: Harmony Books, 1979.

Ries, Frank W.D. *The Dance Theatre of Jean Cocteau.* Binsted, Hampshire, UK: Dance Books Ltd, 2015.

American Ballet

Amberg, George. *Ballet in America: The Emergence of an American Art.* New York: Duell, Sloan & Pearce, 1949; repro. New York: Da Capo Press, 1983.

Ashley, Merrill. *Dancing for Balanchine.* New York: E.P. Dutton & Co., Inc., 1984. A New York City Ballet ballerina analyzes her Balanchine training.

Brooks, Lynn Matluck. *John Durang: Man of the American stage.* Amherst, NY: Cambria Press, 2011.

Chujoy, Anatole. *The New York City Ballet: The First Twenty Years.* New York: Alfred A. Knopf, 1953; repro. New York: Da Capo Press, 1982.

d'Amboise, Jacques. *I Was a Dancer.* New York: Alfred A. Knopf, 2011. Memoirs of a principal dancer of the New York City Ballet.

de Mille, Agnes. *Dance to the Piper.* Boston: Little, Brown & Company, 1952; repro. New York: Da Capo Press, 1980. An autobiography.

Duberman, Martin. *The Worlds of Lincoln Kirstein.* New York: Alfred A. Knopf, 2007.

Easton, Carol. *No Intermissions: The Life of Agnes de Mille.* Boston: Little Brown and Company. 1996.

Ewing, Alex. C. *Bravura!: Lucia Chase and the American Ballet Theatre.* Gainesville: University Press of Florida, 2009.

Jowitt, Deborah. *Jerome Robbins: His Life, His Theater, His Dance.* New York: Simon & Schuster, 2004.

Kiralfy, Bolossy. *Bolossy Kiralfy, Creator of Great Musical Spectacles: An Autobiography,* edited by Barbara M. Barker. Ann Arbor, Mich.: UMI Research Press, 1988.

Kirstein, Lincoln. *Ballet: Bias and Belief.* New York: Dance Horizons, 1983. Polemical writings on American ballet.

———. *Thirty Years: The New York City Ballet.* New York: Alfred A. Knopf, 1978.

Martin, John. *Ruth Page: An Intimate Biography.* New York: Marcel Dekker, Inc., 1977.

Martins, Peter. *Far from Denmark.* Boston: Little, Brown & Company, 1982. An autobiography.

McDonagh, Don. *George Balanchine.* Boston: G.K. Hall & Co., 1983.

Moore, Lillian. *Echoes of American Ballet.* New York: Dance Horizons, 1976. A collection of essays on aspects of American ballet history.

Payne, Charles. *American Ballet Theatre.* New York: Alfred A. Knopf, 1978.

Perlmutter, Donna. *Shadowplay: The Life of Antony Tudor.* New York: Viking, 1991.

Reynolds, Nancy. *Repertory in Review: Forty Years of the New York City Ballet.* New York: The Dial Press, 1977.

Sorley Walker, Kathrine. *Ninette de Valois: Idealist Without Illusions.* London: Hamish Hamilton, 1987.

Sowell, Debra Hickenlooper. *The Christensen Brothers: An American Dance Epic.* Amsterdam: Harwood Academic Publishers, 1996.

Steinberg, Cobbett. *San Francisco Ballet: The First Fifty Years.* San Francisco: San Francisco Ballet Association, 1983.

Swift, Mary Grace. *Belles and Beaux on Their Toes: Dancing Stars in Young America.* Washington, D.C.: University Press of America, 1980. American ballet from 1820 to 1850.

Tracy, Robert, with Sharon DeLano. *Balanchine's Ballerinas: Conversations with the Muses.* New York: Linden Press/Simon & Schuster, 1983.

British Ballet

Bland, Alexander. *The Royal Ballet: The First Fifty Years.* Garden City, New York, Doubleday & Co., Inc., 1981.

Clarke, Mary. *Dancers of Mercury: The Story of Ballet Rambert.* London: Adam & Charles Black, 1962.

————. *The Sadler's Wells Ballet*. London: Adam & Charles Black, 1955. New York: Da Capo Press, 1977.

de Valois, Ninette. *Come Dance with Me: A Memoir 1898–1956*. New York, World Publishing, 1957; repr. New York: Da Capo Press, 1980.

Findlater, Richard. *Lilian Baylis: The Lady of Old Vic*. London: Penguin Books 1975.

Fonteyn, Margot. *Autobiography*. London: W.H. Allen, 1975.

Hall, Fernau. *Modern English Ballet*. London: Melrose, 1950.

Parry, Jann. *Different Drummer: The Life of Kenneth MacMillan*. London: Faber and Faber, 2010.

Rambert, Marie. *Quicksilver: An Autobiography*. New York: St. Martin's Press, 1972.

Sorley Walker, Kathrine, and Sarah C. Woodcock. *The Royal Ballet: A Pictorial History*. London: Threshold/Corgi, 1981.

Thorpe, Edward. *Kenneth MacMillan: The Man and His Ballets*. London: Hamish Hamilton, 1985.

Vaughan, David. *Frederick Ashton and His Ballets*. New York: Alfred A. Knopf, 1977.

White, Joan W., ed. *Twentieth Century Dance in Britain*. London: Dance Books Ltd., 1985.

International Ballet

Anderson, Jack. *The One and Only: The Ballet Russe de Monte Carlo*. New York: Dance Horizons, 1981.

Aschengreen, Erik, trans. Patricia N. McAndrew. *Harald Lander: His Life and Ballets*. Alston: Dance Books, 2009.

Béjart, Maurice. *Béjart by Béjart*. New York: Congdon & Lattes, 1980.

Buckle, Richard, in collaboration with John Taras. *George Balanchine: Ballet Master*. New York: Random House, 1988.

Doeser, Linda. *Ballet and Dance: The World's Major Companies* New York: St. Martin's Press, 1977.

Franca, Celia. *The National Ballet of Canada: A Celebration*. Toronto: University of Toronto Press, 1978.

Garda-Marquez, Vicente. *The Ballets Russes: Colonel de Basil's Ballets Russes de Monte Carlo 1932–1952*. New York: Alfred A. Knopf, 1980.

Grut, Marina. *The History of Ballet in South Africa.* Cape Town: Human & Rousseau, 1981.

Guest, Ivor. *Le Ballet de l'Opéra de Paris.* Paris: Opéra de Paris-Flammarion, 1976. In French. A history of the Paris Opéra Ballet from its founding to the present.

———. *The Paris Opéra Ballet,* English ed. Alton, England: Dance Books Ltd, 2006.

Häger, Bengt, trans. Ruth Sharman. *Ballets Suédois (The Swedish Ballet).* New York: Harry N. Abrams, 1990.

Katz, Leslie George, Nancy LaSallé, and Harvey Simmonds, eds. *Choreography by George Balanchine: A Catalogue of Works.* New York: Viking Press, 1984.

Kavanagh, Julie. *Nureyev: The Life.* New York: Pantheon Books, 2007.

Naslund, Erik, trans. Roger Tanner. *Rolf de Maré: Art Collector, Ballet Director, Museum Creator.* Alton: Dance Books, 2009.

Percival, John. *Theatre in My Blood: A biography of John Cranko.* New York: Franklin Watts, 1983.

Schønberg, Bent, ed. *World Ballet and Dance.* London: Dance Books Ltd., 1989. An international yearbook published annually covering dance activity and specific themes.

Sorley Walker, Kathrine. *De Basil's Ballets Russes.* New York: Atheneum, 1983.

Souritz, Elizabeth. *Soviet Choreographers in the 1920s,* trans. by Lynn Visson; ed., with additional translation, by Sally Banes. Durham, N.C.: Duke University Press, 1990.

Taper, Bernard. *Balanchine: A Biography.* New York: Times Books, 1984.

Wolff, Stephane. *L'Opéra au Palais Garnier (1875–1962).* Paris: Editions Slatkine, 1983. In French. An account of ballet and opera productions at the Paris Opéra during the period. The production records can be understood with a minimum reading knowledge of French.

Wyman, Max. *Dance Canada: An Illustrated History.* Vancouver, B.C.: Douglas & McIntyre, 1989.

———. *The Royal Winnipeg Ballet: The First Forty Years.* Garden City, N.Y.: Doubleday & Co., Inc., 1978.

Modern Dance

Anderson, Jack. *The American Dance Festival.* Durham, N.C.: Duke University Press, 1987.

————. *Art Without Boundaries: The World of Modern Dance,* Iowa City, Iowa: University of Iowa Press, 1997.

Banes, Sally. *Democracy's Body: Judson Dance Theater* 1962–1964. Ann Arbor, Mich.: UMI Research Press, 1980.

————. *Terpischore in Sneakers: Post-Modern Dance.* Boston: Houghton Mifflin Company, 1980.

Brown, Carolyn. *Chance and Circumstance: Twenty Years with Cage and Cunningham.* New York: Alfred A. Knopf, 2007.

Brown, Jean Morrison, ed. *The Vision of Modern Dance.* Princeton, N.J.: Princeton Book Company, Publishers, 1979.
A collection of statements and writings by pioneer to contemporary modem dance choreographers.

Clark, VèVè and Sara E. Johnson, eds. *Kaiso!: Writings by and about Katherine Dunham.* Madison: University of Wisconsin Press, 2005.

Clarke, Mary, and Clement Crisp. *London Contemporary Dance Theatre: The First 21 Years.* London: Dance Books Ltd., 1989.

Cohen, Selma Jeanne. *Doris Humphrey: An Artist First.* Middletown, Conn.: Wesleyan University Press, 1972.
An autobiography by Humphrey, left incomplete at her death, supplemented with a biographical study by Cohen.

Cohen, Selma Jeanne, ed. *The Modern Dance: Seven Statements of Belief.* Middletown, Conn.: Wesleyan University Press, 1966.
Seven choreographers discuss their art.

Cunningham, Merce. *Changes: Notes on Choreography.* New York: Something Else Press, 1968.

Cunningham, Merce, in conversation with Jacqueline Lesschaeve. *The Dancer and the Dance.* New York: Marion Boyars Publishers, 1985.

Duncan, Isadora. *My Life.* New York: Boni & Liveright, 1927; often reprinted.

Escoffier, Jeffrey, and Matthew Lore, eds. *Mark Morris'L'allegro, il penseroso ed il moderato: A celebration.* New York: Marlowe and Company, 2002.

George-Graves, Nadine. *Urban Bush Women: Twenty Years of African American Dance Theater, Community Engagement, and Working It Out.* Madison: University of Wisconsin Press, 2010.

Hodgson, John, and Valerie Preston-Dunlop. *Rudolf Laban: An Introduction to His Work and Influence.* Plymouth, England: Northcote House, 1990.

Horosko, Marian. *Martha Graham: The Evolution of Her Dance Theory and Technique,* rev. ed. Gainesville, University Press of Florida, 1991.

Horst, Louis, and Carroll Russell. *Modern Dance Forms in Relation to the Other Modern Arts.* San Francisco: Impulse Publications, 1961; repro. Princeton, N.J.: Princeton Book Company, Publishers, 1987.

Humphrey, Doris. *The Art of Making Dances.* New York: Rinehart & Co., Inc., 1959; repro. Princeton, N.J.: Princeton Book Company, Publishers, 1990. The Horst and Humphrey volumes sum up two famous approaches to teaching dance composition.

———. *New Dance: Writings on Modern Dance.* Sel. and ed. by Charles H. Woodford. Hightstown, NJ: Princeton Book Company, Publishers, 2008.

Jordan, Stephanie. *Mark Morris: Musician-Choreographer.* Binsted: Dance Books, 2015.

Kendall, Elizabeth. *Where She Danced.* New York: Alfred A Knopf, 1979. A study of the social and cultural background out of which modern dance emerged.

King, Eleanor. *Transformations: A Memoir/The Humphrey-Weidman Era.* New York: Dance Horizons, 1978.

Klosty, James, ed. *Merce Cunningham.* New York: E.P. Dutton & Co., Inc., 1975.

Koner, Pauline. *Solitary Song.* Durham, N.C.: Duke University Press, 1988. An autobiography.

Kriegsman, Sali Ann. *Modern Dance in America: The Bennington Years.* Boston: G.K. Hall & Co., 1981.

Laban, Rudolf. *A Life for Dance,* translated by Lisa Ullmann. London: Macdonald & Evans Ltd., 1975. An autobiography.

Limón, José, ed. Lynn Garafola. *An Unfinished Memoir.* Hanover: University Press of New England for Wesleyan University Press, 1999.

Livet, Ann, ed. *Contemporary Dance.* New York: Abbeville Press, 1978. Comments on contemporary dance by choreographers and critics.

Lloyd, Margaret. *The Borzoi Book of Modern Dance.* New York: Alfred A Knopf, 1949; repro. New York: Dance Horizons, 1974.

Louis, Murray. *Inside Dance.* New York: St. Martin's Press, 1980.

Martin, John. *The Modern Dance.* New York: A.S. Barnes & Co., Inc., 1933; repro. New York: Dance Horizons, 1965; Princeton, N.J.: Princeton Book Company, Publishers, 1989. Printed version of lectures originally delivered in 1931 and 1932 that sum up the philosophy of early modern dance.

Mazo, Joseph. *Prime Movers: The Makers of Modern Dance in America*. New York: William Morrow & Company, 1977; repro. Princeton, N.J.: Princeton Book Company, Publishers, 1982.

McDonagh, Don. *The Complete Guide to Modern Dance*. Garden City, N.Y.: Doubleday & Co., Inc., 1976.

———. *Martha Graham: A Biography*. New York: Praeger Publishers, 1973.

———. *The Rise and Fall and Rise of Modern Dance*. New York: New American Library, 1970.
Discusses experimental and "postmodern" dance since the 1950s.

Morgan, Barbara. *Martha Graham: Sixteen Dances in Photographs*. Dobbs Ferry, N.Y.: Morgan & Morgan, 1980.

Preston-Dunlop, Valerie. *Rudolf Laban: An Extraordinary Life*. London: Dance Books Ltd., 1998.

Preston-Dunlop, Valerie, and Susanne Lahusen, eds. *Schrifttanz: A View of German Dance in the Weimar Republic*. London: Dance Books Ltd., 1990.
Articles from a German magazine of Expressionist dance, 1928–1931.

Rainer, Yvonne. *Work 1961–73*. Halifax: The Press of the Nova Scotia College of Art and Design, 1974.
Autobiographical and aesthetic statements by an important choreographer of the Judson Dance Theatre.

Rogosin, Elinor. *The Dance Makers: Conversations with American Choreographers*. New York: Walker & Company, 1980.

Ross, Janice. *Anna Halprin: Experience As Dance*. Berkeley: University of California Press, 2007.

Ruyter, Nancy Lee Chalfa. *Reformers and Visionaries: The Americanization of the Art of Dance*. New York: Dance Horizons, 1979.
The social, cultural, and educational background out of which early American modem dance emerged.

St. Denis, Ruth. *An Unfinished Life: An autobiography*. New York: Harper & Brothers, 1939; repro. New York: Dance Horizons, 1971.

Schlundt, Christena L. *The Professional Appearances of Ruth St. Denis and Ted Shawn*. New York: The New York Public Library, 1962.

———. *The Professional Appearances of Ted Shawn and His Men Dancers*. New York: The New York Public Library, 1967.

———. *Tamiris: A Chronicle of Her Dance Career*. New York: The New York Public Library, 1972.

Seroff, Victor. *The Real Isadora*. New York: Dial Press, 1971.

Servos, Norbert. *Pina Bausch—Wuppertal Dance Theater, or The Art of Training a Goldfish: Excursions into Dance.* Trans. by Patricia Stadie. Cologne: Ballett-Biihnen-Verlag, 1984.

Shelton, Suzanne. *Divine Dancer: A Biography of Ruth St. Denis.* Garden City, N.Y.: Doubleday & Co., Inc., 1981.

Sherman, Jane. *The Drama of Denishawn Dance.* Middletown, Conn.: Wesleyan University Press, 1979.

Siegel, Marcia B. *Days on Earth: The Dance of Doris Humphrey.* New Haven: Yale University Press, 1988.

Soares, Janet Mansfield. *Martha Hill and the Making of American Dance.* Middletown: Wesleyan University Press, 2009.

———. *Louis Horst: Musician in a Dancer's World.* Durham: Duke University Press, 1992.

Sorell, Walter. *Hanya Holm.* Middletown, Conn.: Wesleyan University Press, 1979.

Spector, Irwin. *Rhythm and Life: The Work of Émile Jaques-Dalcroze.* Stuyvesant, N.Y.: Pendragon Press, 1990.

Steegmuller, Francis, ed. *Your Isadora: The Love Story of Isadora Duncan and Gordon Craig.* New York: Random House and The New York Public Library, 1974.

Stodelle, Ernestine. *The Dance Technique of Doris Humphrey and Its Creative Potential, Second Edition.* Princeton, N.J.: Princeton Book Company, Publishers, 1991.

———. *Deep Song: The Dance Story of Martha Graham.* New York: Schirmer Books, 1984.

Taylor, Paul. *Private Domain.* New York: Alfred A. Knopf, 1987. An autobiography.

Terry, Walter. *Ted Shawn: Father of American Dance.* New York: The Dial Press, 1976.

Vaughan, David. *Merce Cunningham: Fifty Years.* New York: Aperture, n.d.

Warren, Larry. *Anna Sokolow: The Rebellious Spirit.* Princeton, N.J.: Princeton Book Company, Publishers, 1991.

———. *Lester Horton: Modern Dance Pioneer.* New York: Marcel Dekker, Inc., 1977; repro. Princeton, N.J.: Princeton Book Company, Publishers, 1991.

Wigman, Mary. *The Language of Dance,* trans. by Walter Sorell. Middletown, Conn.: Wesleyan University Press, 1966.

Periodicals

Articles on dance history appear in such magazines as the American *Ballet Review* and *Dance Magazine* and the British *The Dancing Times*. Important American and British periodicals of the past that prove useful to dance historians are *Dance and Dancers, Dance Index, Dance News,* and *Dance Perspectives*. Periodicals currently devoted to dance history include *Dance Chronicle: Studies in Dance and the Related Arts, Dance Research Journal,* and *Studies in Dance History,* all published in the United States, and *Dance Research,* published in England.

Short Profiles

People and companies mentioned in the text are briefly described, indicating place of origin and dates.

Adam, Adolphe (France, 1803–1856). Composer of many well-known ballets, notably *Giselle* (1841).

Ailey, Alvin (U.S., 1931–1989). Dancer, choreographer, and director; protégé of Lester Horton and other pioneer modern dancers; formed his own company to present his works—blending tribal, jazz, and modern dance—and those of other choreographers.

Allan, Maud (sometimes, incorrectly, Maude Allan; Canada, 1880–1956). "Exotic" dancer in the Greek revival style; best known in role of *Salome*.

Alonso, Alicia (Cuba, b. 1921). Ballerina with American Ballet Theatre and other companies; founded own company in Cuba, 1948, out of which grew the National Ballet of Cuba; a notable *Giselle*.

Alston, Richard (England, b. 1948). Dancer and choreographer; performed and choreographed for London Contemporary Dance Theatre and other companies; resident choreographer, then director of Rambert Dance Company (Ballet Rambert).

Alvin Ailey American Dance Theatre, New York, 1958–. Founded and directed by Alvin Ailey.

Amagatsu, Ushio (Japan, b. 1949). Dancer, choreographer, and director of the third-generation Butoh company, Sankai Juku.

American Ballet, *see* New York City Ballet

American Ballet Company, *see* Feld Ballets/NY

American Ballet Theatre, New York, 1939–. Outgrowth of the Mordkin Ballet (1936–1939); founded by Lucia Chase and Richard Pleasant as Ballet Theatre; later codirected by Lucia Chase and Oliver Smith, then by Mikhail Baryshnikov, until late 1992 by Jane Hermann and Oliver Smith, since then by Kevin McKenzie.

Anderson, Lea (England, b. 1959). Dancer, choreographer, director; trained in ballet, art, music, and movement analysis; formed her own companies the Cholmondeleys (female) and the Featherstonehaughs (male)—to create abstract, symbolical, often humorous works inspired by diverse sources.

Angiolini, Gaspero (Italy, 1731–1803). Dancer and choreographer of *ballets d'action,* especially in Vienna and St. Petersburg; conducted an epistolary polemic with Noverre.

Arbeau, Thoinot (Jehan Tabourot; France, 1519–1596). Writer; published *Orchésographie* (1588), a manual of ballroom dancing and deportment.

Armitage, Karole (U.S., b. 1954). Dancer, choreographer; performed for Geneva Ballet and Merce Cunningham Company; formed Armitage Ballet to choreograph avant-garde ballets to experimental-rock music; often collaborates with artist David Sallé.

Arpino, Gerald (U.S., 1928–2008). Dancer, choreographer, director, and teacher; collaborator with Robert Joffrey since the inception of the Joffrey Ballet; associate director, principal choreographer, became director in 1988; made both classical and topical ballets.

Ashton, Sir Frederick (English, b. Ecuador, 1904–1988). Dancer and choreographer, principally for Ballet Rambert and the Royal Ballet; his works noted for a lyrically musical classical style.

Bakst, Leon (Russia, 1866–1924). Artist and designer; provided notable decor for a number of Diaghilev's Ballets Russes productions.

Balanchine, George (Russia, 1904–1983). Dancer and choreographer for Diaghilev's Ballets Russes; seminal figure in the creation of American ballet and the Neoclassical style; founder of New York City Ballet.

Ballet Caravan, *see* New York City Ballet

Ballet Club, *see* Ballet Rambert

Ballet Folklorico de Mexico, Mexico City, 1952–. Founded and directed by Amalia Hernandez.

Ballet Rambert, London, 1930–. Founded and directed by Marie Rambert and Ashley Dukes as the Ballet Club at the Mercury Theatre; outgrowth of productions staged by Rambert since 1926; later directors have included Norman Morrice, John Chesworth, Robert North, and Richard Alston; since 1987 called Rambert Dance Company.

Ballet Russe de Monte Carlo, 1938–1962. Founded and directed by Sergei Denham and René Blum with Leonide Massine; Denham the sole director after 1942.

Ballet Society, *see* New York City Ballet

Ballet Theatre, *see* American Ballet Theatre

Ballet of the 20th Century, Brussels, 1960–1987. Outgrowth of performances at the Theatre de la Monnaie; director-choreographer Maurice Bejart. In 1987 the company moved to Lausanne as Béjart Ballet Lausanne, now directed by Gil Roman.

Ballet West, Salt Lake City, Utah, 1963–. Founded and directed by Willam Christensen as the Utah Civic Ballet in 1951; succeeding directors were Bruce Marks, John Hart, Jonas Kåge and, since 2004, Adam Sklute.

Les Ballets des Champs-Elysées, Paris, 1945–1952. Founded by Boris Kochno and Christian Bérard with Roland Petit.

Ballets Jooss, Essen, Germany, then Dartington Hall and Oxford, England, 1933–1953. Outgrowth of the Essen-based Folkwang Tanzbuhne; founded and directed by Kurt Jooss.

Les Ballets de Monte Carlo, 1936–1938. Founded and directed by René Blum with Michel Fokine.

Les Ballets de Paris, erratically 1948–1959. Founded and directed by Roland Petit.

Ballets Russes (Diaghilev), Paris, 1909–1929. Founded and directed by Sergei Diaghilev to bring Russian art to western Europe; profoundly influential by producing original ballets using foremost artists and composers of the era.

Ballets Russes de Monte Carlo, 1932–1952. Founded and directed by René Blum and Col. Wassili de Basil, with Serge Grigoriev as regisseur; successor to Diaghilev's Ballets Russes; later called Original Ballet Russe.

Les Ballets Suédois, Paris, 1920–1925. Founded and directed by Rolf de Mare with Jean Börlin.

Balon, Claude (also known as Jean, sometimes Ballon; France, 1671–1744). Dancer at the Paris Opéra; appeared with Mlle Prévost in *Les Horaces* (1714); noted for exceptional legerity.

Barberina, *see* Campanini

Baronova, Irina (Russia, 1919–2008). Dancer, film and musical actress; one of the trio of "baby ballerinas" (with Tatiana Riabouchinska and Tamara Toumanova); performed with the Ballet Russe companies and Ballet Theatre; became an active member of England's Royal Academy of Dancing.

Barr, Margaret (b. India of English mother and American father, 1904–1991). Studied in late 1920s with Martha Graham and at Denishawn; founder of the Dance Drama Group at Dartington Hall, England, in 1931; later settled and choreographed in Australia.

Baryshnikov, Mikhail Nikolayevich (Latvia, b. 1948). Dancer, director, stage and film actor; one of the leading male dancers of the twentieth century; performed with Leningrad Kirov Ballet, American Ballet Theatre, and New York City Ballet; noted for brilliant and seamless virtuosity; former director of American Ballet Theatre. Founded White Oak Dance Project with Mark Morris, 1990–2002.

Baum, Morton (U.S., 1905–1968). Managing director of the New York City Center of Music and Drama from 1943; invited Ballet Society (New York City Ballet) and later the Joffrey Ballet and the Alvin Ailey Company to be resident companies.

Bausch, Pina (Germany, 1940–2009). Dancer, choreographer, and director of the Wuppertal Dance Theatre (now Tantztheater Wuppertal Pina Bausch) for which she choreographed Neo-Expressionist works examining human relationships.

Bayanihan Dance Company, Manila, Philippines, 1956–. Director-choreographer Lucrecia Reyes Urtula (1929–1999), pioneer in the study of Philippine folk and ethnic dances.

Baylis, Lilian (England, 1874–1937). Director in charge of the Old Vic and Sadler's Wells theatres; invited Ninette de Valois to choreograph and develop a ballet company, which became the Royal Ballet.

Beatty, Talley (U.S., 1918–1995). Dancer and choreographer; performed with Katherine Dunham; choreographed works based on jazz-and black dance for his own and other companies.

Beauchamps, Pierre (France, 1631–1705). Dancer and ballet master; formulated a notation system and codified ballet's five positions.

Beaujoyeulx, Balthasar de (Italy, d.ca. 1587). Composer and ballet master; in the service of Catherine de Medici in France, he produced several court dance spectacles, including *Ballet Comique de la Reine (1581)*.

Beccari, Filippo (Italy, fl. late 18th century). Dancing master; founded the Moscow Ballet School (1793), forerunner of the Bolshoi Ballet School.

Béjart, Maurice (France, 1927–1995). Dancer, choreographer, and director; founded his own company, Les Ballets de l'Etoile, which became the Ballet Théâtre de Paris, presenting his choreography; in 1960 established the Ballet of the 20th Century company in Brussels, then Lausanne, choreographing experimental ballets.

Benois, Alexander (Russia, 1870–1960). Artist and designer; provided notable decor for a number of Diaghilev's Ballets Russes productions and for various companies thereafter.

Benserade, Isaac de (France, 1612–1691). Poet and librettist; author of *Ballet de la Nuit* (1653), *Le Triomphe de l'Amour* (1681), and others.

Bérain, Jean-Louis (France, 1638–1711). Designer, especially of costumes; designed *Le Triomphe de l'Amour (1681)*.

Bérard, Christian (France, 1902–1949). Artist and designer; provided designs for ballets by Balanchine, Massine, Petit, and Lichine; cofounder with Petit and Boris Kochno of Les Ballets des Champs-Élysées.

Bernstein, Leonard (U.S., 1918–1990). Composer and conductor; wrote scores for a number of ballets and musicals choreographed by Jerome Robbins; his concert music was also choreographed.

Bettis, Valerie (U.S., 1920–1982). Dancer and choreographer; her solo and group modern dance works are highly dramatic, often based on poetry and plays.

Birmingham Royal Ballet, England, 1990–. Founded in 1946 in London as apprentice company to the Royal Ballet; called Sadler's Wells Opera Ballet, Sadler's Wells Theatre Ballet, from 1976 Sadler's Wells Royal Ballet; founded by Ninette de Valois, it is directed by David Bintley.

Blair, David (England, 1932–1976). Principal dancer with the Royal Ballet and a partner of Margot Fonteyn.

Blasis, Carlo (Italy, 1797–1878). Dancer and teacher; finest teacher of the era, at the academy of La Scala, Milan; published treatises on his theories of ballet technique.

Blum, René (France, 1878–1942). Impresario; after Sergei Diaghilev's death, founded Ballets Russes de Monte Carlo with Col. Wassili de Basil, Ballets de Monte Carlo with Michel Fokine, and Ballet Russe de Monte Carlo with Léonide Massine.

Bodenwieser, Gertrud (Austria, 1890–1959). Dancer, teacher; developed a style of movement both mechanistic and lyrical for her own performing group; emigrated to Sydney at the outset of World War II and there established modern dance for Australian dancers.

Bolm, Adolph (Russia, 1884–1951). Dancer, choreographer, and teacher at St. Petersburg's Mariinsky Theatre, for Diaghilev's Ballets Russes, and for Anna Pavlova's company; choreographed and taught extensively in America; director of Chicago Opera Ballet and founder of San Francisco Ballet.

Bolshoi Ballet, Moscow, 1773–. Began with classes at Moscow orphanage; company formally initiated in 1776 with performances by students of the orphanage; established itself at the Petrovsky Theatre in 1780; twentieth century directors have included Alexander Gorsky, Leonid Lavrovsky, and Yuri Grigorovich.

Bonfanti, Marie (Italy, 1847–1921). Dancer and teacher; trained by Carlo Blasis; enjoyed a long American career, especially in spectacles like *The Black Crook* (1866).

Börlin, Jean (Sweden, 1893–1930). Dancer, choreographer; trained and performed in Sweden and with Fokine; named by Rolf de Maré as principal dancer and choreographer of Les Ballets Suédois.

Bourne, Matthew (England, b. 1960). Choreographer and director. Started studying dance at twenty-two at what is now called Trinity Laban Conservatoire of Music and Dance. Formed companies of his own, including New Adventures in 2002. Known for idiosyncratic reinterpretations of classic ballets and films, including *Nutcracker, La Sylphide* (renamed *Highland Fling), Swan Lake* (with all-male swans), and *The Red Shoes.*

Bournonville, August (Denmark, 1805–1879). Dancer, choreographer, and teacher; created *La Sylphide* (1836) and many other ballets still performed today, and a distinctive style that is perpetuated in Denmark.

Boyce, Johanna (U.S., b. 1954). Choreographer whose works, often for untrained dancers, make use of ordinary movements.

Bozzacchi, Giuseppina (Italy, 1853–1870). Dancer who created the role of Swanilda in *Coppélia* (1870) in Paris.

Braque, Georges (France, 1882–1963). Artist; provided decor for Diaghilev's Ballets Russes, notably *Les Fâcheux (1924).*

Brianza, Carlotta (Italy, 1867–1930). Dancer who performed in Russia, creating the role of Aurora in Petipa's *The Sleeping Beauty (1890).*

Brown, Trisha (U.S., 1936–2017). Dancer and choreographer; experimental works, often set in alternative spaces; founder-member of the Judson Dance Theatre.

Bruce, Christopher (England, b. 1945). Dancer and choreographer; performed and choreographs for various companies; resident choreographer for Ballet Rambert and director 1994–2002.

Butler, John (U.S., 1918–1993). Dancer, choreographer; performed with Martha Graham company; formed own company and toured internationally; major portion of career spent as freelance ballet and modern dance choreographer for dance companies, opera, and television.

Cage, John (U.S., 1912–1992). Composer; long-time collaborator of Merce Cunningham; created experimental collage scores that often contain "prepared" instruments, recitation, tape, and natural and electronic sounds.

Cahusac, Louis de (France, 1700 [1706?]–1759). Author of librettos and treatises on dance history; published *La Danse Ancienne et Moderne* (1754).

Camargo, Marie Anne de Cupis de (France, of Spanish-Italian descent, 1710–1770). Dancer at the Paris Opéra; one of the first to shorten the ballet skirt.

Camargo Society, London, 1930–1933. Formed to further the cause of British ballet; sponsored performances by important artists; superseded by Ballet Rambert and the Vic-Wells Ballet.

Campanini, Barberina ("La Barberina"; Italy, 1721–1799). Dancer at the Paris Opéra and in Berlin; noted for brilliant technique.

Camryn, Walter (U.S., 1903–1984). Dancer, teacher, and choreographer; performed and choreographed for various companies, including the Page-Stone Ballet; opened the Stone-Camryn School (1941) in Chicago with Bentley Stone.

Carlson, Ann (U.S., b. 1954). Dancer, choreographer; often uses unlikely starting points (animals, untrained performers) for her experimental works on the human condition.

Carlson, Carolyn (U.S., b. 1943). Dancer, choreographer; performed with Nikolais and Anne Béranger companies; dancer/choreographer of avant garde works for Paris Opéra Ballet; also active as choreographer in Italy, Finland, and Sweden.

Caroso, Fabritio (Italy, b.ca. 1553 d. 1605). Dancer, dance master, writer; taught Rome's elite; published technical treatise *Il Ballarino* (1581; retitled *Nobiltà di Dame,* 1600).

Castle, Irene (Foote; U.S., 1893–1969) and Vernon (England, 1887–1918). Exhibition ballroom dancers; established standard for inventiveness and elegance; popularized ballroom dancing and a number of dances (*Maxixe, Castle Walk, Hesitation Waltz*).

Cecchetti, Enrico (Italy, 1850–1928). Dancer and ballet master; principally noted as a teacher in St. Petersburg, London, and elsewhere; formulated a syllabus of ballet training.

Cerrito, Fanny (Italy, 1817–1909). Dancer, wife of Arthur Saint-Léon; fiery Romantic ballerina.

Charrat, Janine (France, b. 1924). Dancer, choreographer, and director; appeared as a child in the film *Ballerina* (1937); dancer and choreographer with Roland Petit and many companies, including her own.

Chase, Lucia (U.S., 1897–1986). Dancer and director; performed with the Mordkin Ballet and in dramatic roles for American Ballet Theatre, creating roles in de Mille and Tudor ballets; backer of Ballet Theatre and co-director of the company from 1945 to 1980.

Childs, Lucinda (U.S., b. 1940). Dancer and choreographer; creates experimental works, often for Robert Wilson; was a member of the Judson Dance Theatre.

Chirico, Giorgio de (Greece, 1888–1978). Artist; provided decor for several companies, notably Le *Bal* (1929) for Diaghilev's Ballets Russes.

Chladek, Rosalia (Czechoslovakia, 1905–1995). Dancer, teacher, choreographer, principally in Austria; longtime teacher and director at Dalcroze Institute in Hellerau, developing her own system of modern dance training; created many and diverse Expressionist works.

Christensen, Harold (U.S., 1904–1989). Dancer and teacher; performed with various companies; former director of the San Francisco Ballet School.

Christensen, Lew (U.S., 1909–1984). Dancer, choreographer, and director; principal dancer, ballet master, and teacher with Balanchine's early companies and school; former director of San Francisco Ballet, he choreographed *Filling Station* (1938), one of the early all-American ballets.

Christensen, Willam (U.S., 1902–2001). Dancer, choreographer, teacher, and director; performed and choreographed for the San Francisco Opera Ballet, staging the first American productions of full-evening classics; founded Ballet West in Utah.

City Center Joffrey Ballet, *see* Joffrey Ballet

Clark, Michael (England, b. 1962). Dancer, choreographer; trained at Royal Ballet School and with experimental choreographers; began as soloist and then formed small company to present his iconoclastic works.

Clayton, Bessie (U.S., fl.1895–1915). Dancer; ballet-acrobat in *Ziegfeld Follies* and other revues.

Cocteau, Jean (France, 1889–1963). Writer, designer, and filmmaker; contributed librettos and decor for a number of ballets for various companies in France, especially Diaghilev's Ballets Russes; wrote extensively on dance and other arts.

Cohan, Robert (U.S., b. 1925). Dancer, choreographer, teacher, and director; performed with Martha Graham and other companies; director of London School of Contemporary Dance founding artistic director of The Place and London Contemporary Dance Theatre, and artistic adviser to the Israel-based Batsheva Dance Company.

Copland, Aaron (U.S., 1900–1990). Composer; wrote important scores for ballet and modern dance, notably *Rodeo* (1942) and *Appalachian Spring* (1944); his concert music often choreographed.

Coralli, Jean (Italy, 1779–1854). Dancer and choreographer of the Romantic ballet era at the Paris Opéra; his Le *Diable Boîteux* (1836) featured Fanny Elssler in "The Cachucha"; co-choreographer of *Giselle* (1841).

Cranko, John (South Africa, 1927–1973). Dancer, choreographer, and director; choreographed for Sadler's Wells and Royal Ballet; invited to Stuttgart, where he developed a major company famous for his full-length dramatic works; influenced German ballet.

Cuevas, Marquis George de (Chile, 1885–1961). Benefactor and director; founded Ballet International and principally Le Grand Ballet de Marquis de Cuevas with Bronislava Nijinska; the company drew ranking stars and choreographers, especially American.

Cunningham, Merce (U.S., 1919–2009). Dancer, choreographer, teacher, and director; performed with the Martha Graham company; formed his own company to experiment in pure-dance and chance choreography, collaborating with foremost artists of the era.

Dafora, Asadata (Sierra Leone, 1890–1965). Dancer, choreographer, and director; pioneer in presenting black African dance and culture; formed his own touring company in America, the Federal Theater African Dance Troupe.

Dalcroze, *see* Jaques-Dalcroze

Dance Notation Bureau, New York, 1940–. Founded by Eve Gentry, Janey Price, Ann Hutchinson (Guest), and Helen Priest Rogers, with Hanya Holm and John Martin as advisers, as a central clearinghouse for notation information and teaching, principally Labanotation.

Dance Theatre of Harlem, New York, 1971–. Founded by Arthur Mitchell and codirected with Karel Shook as a classical ballet company composed of black dancers.

Danilova, Alexandra (Russia, 1903–1997). Dancer and teacher; performed with Diaghilev's Ballets Russes, and prima ballerina with successive Ballet Russe companies and others; danced the major classical as well as soubrette roles; longtime teacher at the School of American Ballet.

Dauberval, Jean (France, 1742–1806). Dancer and choreographer; early exemplar of the use of simple and humorous subjects in his *La Fille Mal Gardée* (1789); teacher of Didelot and Viganò.

Davies, Siobhan (England, b. 1950). Dancer, choreographer, and teacher; performer and associate choreographer for the London Contemporary Dance Theatre and her own group.

Dean, Laura (U.S., b. 1945). Dancer and choreographer; experimental works, early ones in collaboration with Steve Reich, have explored movement based on continuous turning and use of space.

de Basil, Col. Wassili (Russia, 1888–1951). Director with Rene Blum of Ballets Russes de Monte Carlo; continued as sole director of his own Ballets Russes, later known as Original Ballet Russe.

Debussy, Claude (France, 1862–1918). Composer; wrote *Jeux* (1913) for Diaghilev's Ballets Russes; his *Prelude a l'Après-Midi d'un Faune* famously choreographed by Nijinsky.

Degas, Hilaire Germain Edgar (France, 1834–1917). Impressionist painter, noted especially for depictions of dancers.

de Hesse, Jean-Baptiste François (Holland, 1705–1779). Ballet master, dancer, principally in France; noted character dancer and influential early choreographer of *ballets d'action* at Versailles and the Opéra-Comique.

Delibes, Léo (France, 1836–1891). Composer; for the Paris Opéra wrote scores for *La Source* (1866), *Coppélia* (1870), and *Sylvia* (1876).

Delsarte, François (France, 1811–1871). Musician and theorist; formulated a system of analyzing human expression by dividing the body into three controlling areas—head, torso, and limbs; greatly influenced early modern dance.

de Mille, Agnes (U.S., 1909–1993). Dancer, choreographer, writer, and lecturer; early work in England; choreographed important ballets, especially on American themes, for American Ballet Theatre and Ballet Russe de Monte Carlo; revitalized choreography for the musical theatre; founded Heritage Dance Theatre at the North Carolina School of the Arts.

Denham, Sergei (Russia, 1897–1970). Impresario; founder with René Blum of Ballet Russe de Monte Carlo in 1938, sole director from 1942; founded the Ballet Russe School in New York.

Denishawn (school and company), Los Angeles and New York, 1915–1931. Founded by Ruth St. Denis and Ted Shawn; first large American company to present modern dance.

Derain, André (France, 1880–1954). Artist; provided decor for Diaghilev's Ballets Russes—notably *La Boutique Fantasque* (1919), and other companies.

de Valois, Dame Ninette (Ireland, b. 1898–2001). Dancer, choreographer, teacher, and director; performed with Diaghilev's Ballets Russes; opened a school in England and formed Vic-Wells Ballet, which became the Royal Ballet under her direction; notable as founder of English ballet.

Diaghilev, Sergei (Russia, 1872–1929). Arts impresario; founded and directed the Ballets Russes; noted for catalyzing collaboration among the foremost artists of the era and producing sensational and vanguard ballets.

Didelot, Charles (France, 1767–1837). Dancer, choreographer, and teacher; introduced new stage mechanisms in his *Flore et Zéphyre* (1796); made important reforms in St. Petersburg.

Dolin, Sir Anton (England, 1904–1983). Dancer, choreographer, teacher, and writer; noted especially as a dancer for Diaghilev's Ballets Russes, the Markova-Dolin company, London Festival Ballet (also artistic director, 1950–1961), and many other companies.

Dowell, Anthony (England, b. 1943) Dancer and director; performed with the Royal Ballet as a *danseur noble,* especially with Antoinette Sibley; director of the Royal Ballet 1986–2001.

Driver, Senta (U.S., b. 1942). Dancer, choreographer, and director; created experimental works for her own company, Harry.

Duncan, Isadora (U.S., 1877–1927). Dancer, choreographer, and teacher; seminal figure in modern dance; reduced costume to draperies and bare feet for ease of movement; interpreted concert music in free movement style.

Dunham, Katherine (U.S., 1912–2006). Dancer, choreographer, anthropologist, and teacher; first to examine indigenous black dances of the West Indies and to present them in theatrical form with her own company; director of the performing arts department at Southern Illinois University.

Dunn, Robert Ellis (U.S., 1928–1996). Musician and dance theorist; formed a workshop in experimental dance composition, out of which grew the Judson Dance Theatre.

Duport, Louis (France, 1781–1853). Dancer, choreographer; principal rival of Auguste Vestris at the Opéra; performed to great acclaim in Didelot's ballets in St. Petersburg, and in Naples and London; choreographed for and directed a theatre in Vienna.

Dupré, Louis (France, 1697–1774). Dancer and teacher at the Paris Opéra; may have appeared in John Weaver's *The Loves of Mars and Venus* (1717).

The Dutch National Ballet, *see* The National Ballet of Holland.

Durang, John (U.S., 1768–1822). Dancer and choreographer; first American born dancer to gain acclaim; noted especially for his hornpipe.

DV8 Physical Theatre, London, 1986–. Founded and directed by Lloyd Newson; presents experimental works that explore physical extremes with artistry.

Eiko and Koma (Japan, b. 1952 and b. 1948). Dancers, choreographers, principally in the U.S.; present dances of exceedingly slow movement, physical and often erotic, and symbolically layered; first appeared, and have lived, in the U.S. in 1976.

Elgar, Sir Edward (England, 1857–1934). Composer; wrote one commissioned ballet score; his concert music often used for choreography, notably *Enigma Variations*.

Ellington, Edward ("Duke"; U.S., 1899–1974). Jazz-based composer and band leader; his music frequently choreographed, especially by Alvin Ailey.

Elssler, Fanny (Austria, 1810–1884). Dancer; sensuous and dramatic Romantic ballerina; achieved international acclaim.

Elssler, Theresa (Austria, 1808–1878). Dancer; sister and frequent partner of Fanny; noted for *travesti* roles.

English National Ballet, London, 1989–. Founded by Anton Dolin and Alicia Markova in 1950 as London Festival Ballet, under the direction of Julian Braunsweg; other directors followed including Tamara Rojo in 2012.

Fagan, Garth (Jamaica, b. 1940). U.S. dancer, choreographer, director; amalgamated his Afro-Caribbean and modem dance training to form a student, later professional, company, now called Garth Fagan Dance, presenting sleek, energetic, personable works. He also choreographed the record-breaking musical *The Lion King* (1997).

Falla, Manuel de (Spain, 1876–1946). Composer; wrote *El Amor Brujo* (1915) and *Le Tricorne* (1919) for Diaghilev's Ballets Russes.

Favier, Jean (France, 1648–1719). Dancer, dancing master, choreographer; versatile dancer in Louis XIV court and at Opéra under Lully's direction; choreographed dances for nobility and professionals, notably *Le Mariage de la Grosse Cathos.*

Feld, Eliot (U.S., b. 1943). Dancer, choreographer, and director; performed with New York City Ballet and principally American Ballet Theatre, for which he began to choreograph; formed his own companies and has choreographed for a number of other companies.

Fenley, Molissa (U.S., b. 1954). Dancer and choreographer; experimental works of vigorous, energetic movement.

Feuillet, Raoul-Auger (France, ca. 1660–1710). Dancer and choreographer; formulated early notation system.

Fiocre, Eugénie (France, 1845–1908). Dancer at the Paris Opéra; known for *travesti* roles, notably Franz in *Coppélia* (1870).

Fokine, Michel (Russia, 1880–1942). Dancer and choreographer at St. Petersburg Mariinsky Theatre, for Diaghilev's Ballets Russes, and in America; one of the Ballets Russes' seminal choreographers; noted for choreographic reforms.

Fonteyn, Dame Margot (England, 1919–1991). Dancer; one of the great twentieth-century ballerinas, principally with the Royal Ballet; noted for her pure line and musicality.

Forsythe, William (U.S., b. 1949). Dancer, choreographer; performed with Joffrey Ballet and Stuttgart Ballet; began choreographing for Stuttgart and since 1984 has made Frankfurt his choreographic base.

Forti, Simone (Italy, b. 1935). Dancer, choreographer in U.S.; created experimental works, presented in alternative spaces, based on natural movement, sound cues, or simple instructions; early collaboration with her then husband, the artist Robert Morris.

Franklin, Frederic (England, 1914–2013). Dancer, choreographer, teacher, and director; performed with Ballet Russe de Monte Carlo and various other companies, frequently partnering Alexandra Danilova; director and ballet master of several American companies; noted for restagings of the classics.

Fuller, Loïe (U.S., 1862–1928). Dancer; experimented with the effect of stage lighting on voluminous costumes of silk, manipulated by movement.

Galeotti, Vincenzo (Italy, 1733–1816). Dancer and choreographer; especially in Denmark, where his *The Whims of Cupid and the Ballet Master* (1786) still survives.

Gardel, Pierre (France, 1758–1840). Dancer, choreographer, and ballet master at the Paris Opéra; director of its ballet school and teacher of Carlo Blasis.

Garnier, Jacques (France, 1940–1989). Dancer, choreographer, director; performed for the Paris Opéra Ballet; formed Ballet Théâtre du Silence to present modern dance works; returned to the Opéra to direct G.R.C.O.P.

Garth Fagan Dance, Rochester, N.Y., 1970/71–. Founded, and still directed, by Garth Fagan as Bottom of the Bucket BUT . . . Dance Theatre, then Bucket; begun as a training company, now professional, for mostly black modern dancers.

Gautier, Théophile (France, 1811–1872). Poet, librettist, and critic; wrote the libretto for *Giselle* (1841); his reviews offer a lively account of the Romantic ballet era.

Geltzer, Yekaterina Vassilyevna (Russia, 1876–1962). Dancer at the Moscow Bolshoi Theatre; noted for demi-caractère roles and as the creator of the principal role in the first Soviet realist ballet, *The Red Poppy* (1927).

Genée, Dame Adeline (Denmark, 1878–1970). Dancer at London's Empire Theatre and in the U.S.; president of Royal Academy of Dancing, 1920–1954.

Gerdt, Pavel Andreyevich (Russia, 1844–1917). Dancer and teacher; most famous *premier danseur* of his time in the Imperial Theatres; became noted teacher in St. Petersburg.

Gert, Valeska (Germany, 1892–1978). Dancer, actress; performed as solo dancer in cabarets and recital works based in mime that were satirical, grotesque, socially conscious; later career as a film actress.

Ginner, Ruby (France, 1886–1978). Teacher, historian, dancer in England; explored and taught ancient Greek dance in her own school; wrote *The Revived Greek Dance* (1933).

Glass, Philip (U.S., b. 1937). One of the most influential of 20th century composers; composed experimental works based on unusual tonalities and repetition used frequently for performance art productions and ballets.

Glière, Reinhold Moritsovich (Russia, 1876–1956). Composer; wrote scores for a number of ballets, notably *The Red Poppy* (1927) and *The Bronze Horseman* (1949).

Gluck, Christoph Willibald (Germany, 1714–1787). Composer; wrote *Don Juan* (1761) and *Semiramis* (1765) for Angiolini; early *ballets d'action*.

Goleizovsky, Kasian Yaroslavovich (Russia, 1892–1970). Dancer and choreographer; performed and choreographed for St. Petersburg Mariinsky Theatre and Moscow Bolshoi Ballet as well as in cabarets and music halls; his experimental choreography was considered controversial.

Gordon, David (U.S., b. 1936). Dancer and choreographer; creates experimental works, often in collaboration with his wife, Valda Setterfield; member of the Judson Dance Theatre; has choreographed for ballet companies including American Ballet Theatre.

Gorsky, Alexander Alexeyevich (Russia, 1871–1924). Dancer and choreographer, principally in Moscow; sought choreographic reform by creating works of dramatic realism.

Graham, Martha (U.S., 1894–1991). Dancer, choreographer, and teacher; pioneer in American modern dance; performed with Denishawn until forming her own company and school to explore movement based on "contraction" and "release"; extensive repertoire ranges from psychologically intense to lighthearted works; a major influence on successive generations.

Grahn, Lucile (Denmark, 1819–1907). Dancer and ballet mistress; one of the famous Romantic ballerinas.

Grand Ballet de Marquis de Cuevas, Paris, 1947–1962. Founded by Marquis George de Cuevas with Bronislava Nijinska.

G.R.C.O.P. (Groupe de Recherche Chorégraphique de l'Opéra de Paris), Paris, 1980–1989. Formed by Rosella Hightower during her Opéra Ballet directorship, comprised of about twelve company volunteers to develop and perform experimental works at the Opéra-Comique and on tour; directed by Jacques Garnier.

Grigorovich, Yuri Nikolayevich (Russia, b.1927). Dancer, choreographer, and director; *demi-caractère* dancer at the Leningrad Kirov Ballet, where he did his first choreography, *The Stone Flower* (1957); choreographer and director of Moscow's Bolshoi Ballet, producing many elegant and powerful ballets, notably *Spartacus* (1968).

Grisi, Carlotta (Italy, 1819–1899). Dancer; the first Giselle—she created the title role in *Giselle*. Romantic ballerina of strength and lightness.

Guimard, Marie-Madeleine (France, 1743–1816). *Première danseuse* at the Paris Opéra; appeared in ballets of Noverre and Gardel.

Guy, Edna (U.S., fl. 1930s). Dancer, choreographer; early pioneer, with Hemsley Winfield and her own group, of blacks in modern dance.

Halprin, Anna (Ann; U.S., b. 1920). Choreographer, dancer, teacher; early modern dancer and West Coast pioneer of avant-garde experiments and happenings, often in alternative spaces created by her husband, architect Lawrence Halprin; groomed many avant-garde choreographers; develops body/movement therapy workshops at her Tamalpa Institute (Marin County, California).

Hamburg Ballet, 17th century–. Originally the opera ballet; the company flourished after 1959 with Peter van Dyk and, since 1973, John Neumeier as directors.

Hansen, Joseph (Belgium, 1842–1907). Dancer and choreographer in Moscow, London, and Paris.

Harkness, Rebekah (U.S., 1915–1982). Composer and benefactor; early sponsor of Jerome Robbins and Robert Joffrey; formed her own company, school, and theatre in New York.

Harkness Ballet, New York, 1964–1975. Founded by Rebekah Harkness under the direction of George Skibine, then Brian Macdonald, Benjamin Harkarvy, Lawrence Rhodes, Ben Stevenson, and Vincente Nebrada.

Hawkins, Erick (U.S., 1909–1994). Dancer, choreographer, and director; early performances with the American Ballet and Ballet Caravan; turned to modern dance in the Martha Graham company; formed his own company to explore "normative" movement and to create experimental works.

Hay, Deborah (U.S., b. 1941). Dancer and choreographer; creates experimental works accessible to performance by untrained dancers; member of the Judson Dance Theatre.

Haydée, Marcia (Brazil, b. 1937). Dancer and director; prima ballerina of the Stuttgart Ballet, later its director; noted especially as a dancer/actress.

Helpmann, Sir Robert (Australia, 1909–1986). Dancer, choreographer, director, and film actor; notable performing career as both noble and dramatic dancer for Vic-Wells and Sadler's Wells Ballets; choreographed a number of important works for these companies and the Australian Ballet, which he directed.

Hijikata, Tatsumi (Japan, 1928–1986). Dancer, choreographer, teacher; developer of the Expressionist theatre-dance form, Butoh; trained most of its best-known exponents.

Hilverding, Franz Anton Christoph (Austria, 1710–1768). Dancer, ballet master at Viennese court and in Russia; early choreographer of *ballets d' action,* influencing Noverre; trained Gaspero Angiolini.

Hoctor, Harriet (U.S., 1905–1977). Dancer and teacher; a technical virtuoso and ballet-acrobat; performed in revues, including the Ziegfeld Follies, and films; opened a ballet school in Boston.

Hoffmann, Reinhild (German, b. 1943). Dancer, choreographer; product of Jooss's Folkwang School; innovator in *Tanz-theater* works; directed companies in Bremen, Bochum, and Berlin.

Holm, Hanya (Germany, 1898–1992). Dancer, choreographer, teacher; protégée of Mary Wigman; opened important schools in New York and Colorado Springs; set modern dance works on her own and other companies; choreographer of several long-running musicals.

Honegger, Arthur (France, 1892–1955). French/Swiss composer; wrote scores for Börlin, Nijinska, Massine, Fokine, and others.

Horst, Louis (U.S., 1884–1964). Composer, teacher, and writer; musical collaborator and adviser in modern dance, especially with Martha Graham; notable influence as teacher of dance composition.

Horton, Lester (U.S., 1906–1953). Dancer, choreographer, and notable teacher; significant influence on modern dance, especially on the West Coast; formed his own company to present his strong and energetic works. His was the first racially integrated dance company.

Howard, Robin (England, 1924–1989). Director; early champion of Graham-based modern dance in England; founded the school at The Place out of which emerged the London Contemporary Dance Theatre.

Hoyer, Dore (Germany, 1911–1967). Dancer, choreographer; protégée of Jaques-Dalcroze and Gret Palucca; created her own austere and Expressionist solo works; briefly ballet mistress at Hamburg State Opera.

Humphrey, Doris (U.S., 1895–1958). Dancer, choreographer, director, and teacher; pioneer in American modern dance; performed with Denishawn until forming her own school and company with Charles Weidman to explore movement based on "fall" and "recovery"; created many important works and was a notable teacher of choreography.

Humphrey-Weidman Company, New York, 1928–1945. Founded and directed by Doris Humphrey and Charles Weidman.

Ivanov, Lev Ivanovich (Russia, 1834–1901). Dancer and choreographer; his principal works include *The Nutcracker* (1892) and Acts Two and Four of *Swan Lake* (1895) at St. Petersburg Mariinsky Theatre.

Jaques-Dalcroze, Émile (Switzerland, 1865–1950). Musician and theorist; developed a system of expressing musical rhythm through bodily movements called *eurhythmics,* which greatly influenced early modern dance.

Jeanmaire, Renée ("Zizi"; France, b. 1924). Dancer; performed with the Paris Opéra Ballet and Original Ballet Russe; principal career with her husband, Roland Petit, in his Ballets de Paris—creating her noted role in his *Carmen* (1949)—and in revues and films.

Joffrey, Robert (U.S., 1930–1988). Dancer, choreographer, director, and teacher; formed his own company in association with Gerald Arpino to present an eclectic repertoire, including important revivals (Jooss' *The Green Table*, for example); he helped launch the Jackson International Ballet Competition with its founder Thalia Mara.

Joffrey Ballet, New York, 1954–. Founded and codirected by Robert Joffrey and Gerald Arpino; after 1966 also known as City Center Joffrey Ballet; moved to Chicago, 1995; Ashley Wheater has been artistic director since 2007.

Johanssen, Christian (Sweden, 1817–1903). Dancer and seminal teacher in St. Petersburg's Imperial Ballet School.

Jones, Bill T. (U.S., b. 1952). Dancer and choreographer; creates athletic modern dance works principally for men, with partner Arnie Zane (1948–1988), and for other companies; director of Bill T. Jones/Arnie Zane & Co.; acquired New York City's Dance Theater Workshop in 2011, renaming it New York Live Arts.

Jooss, Kurt (Germany, 1901–1979). Dancer, choreographer, teacher, and director; founded his own company in Germany and later in England, where his school was established; choreographed strong works synthesizing ballet and modern dance, notably *The Green Table* (1932); in 1949 returned to Essen to reestablish the Folkwang School and Ballet.

José Limón Dance Company, New York, 1947–. Founded and directed by José Limón, succeeded by Carla Maxwell, then Colin Connor.

Judson Dance Theatre, New York, established 1962 (dormant since late 1970s). Founded collaboratively by Yvonne Rainer, Steve Paxton, David Gordon, Deborah Hay et al. at the Judson Memorial Church; outgrowth of Robert Ellis Dunn's composition workshop.

Karsavina, Tamara (Russia, 1885–1978). Dancer at the Mariinsky Theatre and for Diaghilev's Ballets Russes, for which she created many principal roles; instrumental as influence in formation of British ballet.

Keeler, Ruby (Nova Scotia, 1910–1993). Tap dancer, film star in the U.S.; performed in clubs, *Ziegfeld Follies,* and on Broadway; she had a long film career, notably *42nd Street* (1933).

Keersmaeker, Anne Teresa de (Belgium, b. 1960). Dancer, choreographer; trained at Béjart's MUDRA School; began choreographing in 1982 and formed Rosas dance company in 1983 to tour worldwide; presents experimental works both highly structured and emotive.

Kiralfy, Bolossy (Hungary, 1848–1932) and Imre (Hungary, 1845–1919). Dancers, choreographers, impresarios; as self-trained children, performed and toured theatrical national dances; produced and staged major spectacles in the U.S. and England, respectively.

Kirov Ballet, Leningrad, 1738–. Originally at the Bolshoi Theatre in St. Petersburg, thence to the Mariinsky Theatre; noted directors have been Marius Petipa, Fyodor Lopukhov, Konstantin Sergeyev, and Oleg Vinogradov; now known as Mariinsky Ballet.

Kirstein, Lincoln (U.S, 1907–1996). Writer and director; brought George Balanchine to America; founded the School of American Ballet with Edward M.M. Warburg, the American Ballet, Ballet Caravan, and Ballet Society (later New York City Ballet); has published many important books of dance history.

Kochno, Boris (Russia, 1904–1990). Writer, librettist, and impresario; supplied librettos and artistic advice to Diaghilev's Ballets Russes, the Ballet Russe de Monte Carlo, and the Ballets des Champs-Elysées, which he founded with Roland Petit and Christian Bérard.

Koralli, Vera Alexeyevna (sometimes Karalli; Russia, 1889–1972). Dancer at Moscow's Bolshoi Ballet and for Diaghilev's Ballets Russes.

Kresnik, Johann (Hans); Germany, b. 1939). Dancer, choreographer, ballet master; performed in West Germany; a *Tanztheater* exponent, he has choreographed for companies in Bremen and   Heidelberg and for state opera houses; known for vehement political satire.

Kreutzberg, Harald (Germany, 1902–1968). Dancer, choreographer, and teacher; protege of Mary Wigman; created his own starkly dramatic works for solo recitals, and with his partners Yvonne Georgi and briefly Ruth Page; best-known male modern dancer of his era.

Kschessinska, Mathilde (Russia, 1872–1971). Dancer at St. Petersburg Mariinsky Theatre, where she was named *prima ballerina assoluta;* noted for brilliant technique and *demi-caractère* roles.

Kylian, Jiri, also Jiři Kylián (Czechoslovakia, b. 1947). Dancer, choreographer, director; performed and began choreographing for Stuttgart Ballet; became director of the Netherlands Dance Theatre in 1976, creating movement-imbued modern ballet works; also established NDT II, for young dancers, and NDT III, for older dancers.

Laban, Rudolf von (Hungary, 1879–1958) Dancer, choreographer, and theoretician; best known for his analysis of human bodily motion, formulated in his system of dance notation.

La Fontaine, Mlle de (France, ca.1655–ca.1738). First professional female dancer; appeared at the Paris Opéra in *Le Triomphe de l'Amour* (1681).

Landé, Jean Baptiste (France, d. 1748). A French dancer and ballet master who danced in Holland, Sweden, Denmark and Russia; founded a ballet school in 1738 that was precursor of the St. Petersburg Imperial Ballet School.

Lander, Harald (Denmark, 1905–1971). Dancer, choreographer, director, and teacher; had a long and distinguished career as a character dancer and then choreographer-director of the Royal Danish Ballet; catalyzed revival of August Bournonville's ballets; became director of Paris Opéra School in 1956.

Laschilin, Lev Alexandrovich (Russia, 1888–1955). Dancer and choreographer at Moscow's Bolshoi Ballet; choreographed with Vassily Tikhomirov the seminal Soviet-style ballet, *The Red Poppy* (1927).

Lasso, Orlando di, also known as Orlande de Lassus (Flanders, 1532–1594). Composer, principally of motets, madrigals, and chansons, who collaborated on *Le Ballet des Polonais* (1573) with Beaujoyeulx.

Lavrovsky, Leonid Mikhailovich (Russia, 1905–1967). Dancer, choreographer, and teacher; *premier danseur* at the Leningrad Kirov Ballet and choreographed there the first Russian production of *Romeo and Juliet* (1940); thereafter, choreographer and school director at Moscow's Bolshoi Ballet.

Lee, Mary Ann (U.S., 1823–1899). Dancer; first American-born ballerina to gain acclaim; performed many Romantic ballet roles abroad and with her own company, cofounded with George Washington Smith.

Léger, Fernand (France, 1881–1955). A Cubist/Futurist artist; provided decor for several companies, notably *La Création du Monde* for Les Ballets Suédois.

Legnani, Pierina (Italy, 1863–1923). Dancer; performed principally in St. Petersburg, where she was named *prima ballerina assoluta;* introduced the virtuosic thirty-two *fouettés.*

Lemon, Ralph (U.S., b. 1952). Dancer, choreographer; performed for Nancy Hauser, Meredith Monk, Blondell Cummings; began choreographing in 1975; formed his own collaborative company in 1985 to create stylistically eclectic experimental works that probe the human condition.

Lifar, Serge (Russia, 1905–1986). Dancer, choreographer, director, and writer; noted dancer with Diaghilev's Ballets Russes; became *premier danseur* and director-choreographer at the Paris Opéra; produced many ballets; author of books and manifestos; his collection of Ballets Russes designs is now at the Wadsworth Atheneum, Hartford, Connecticut.

Limón, José (Mexico, 1908–1972). Dancer, choreographer, and teacher; performed with the Humphrey-Weidman Company and his own trio; formed his own company to produce many important works displaying drama, musicality, and his own forceful personality; influential as a long-time teacher at the Juilliard School.

Linke, Susanne (German, b. 1944). Dancer, choreographer; trained at the Wigman and Jooss schools; longtime director of the Folkwang School's performing Tanzstudio; since 1985 an independent choreographer of *Tanztheater* solo and duet works.

Littlefield, Catherine (U.S., 1904–1951). Dancer, choreographer, teacher, and director; founded The Littlefield (later Philadelphia) Ballet in 1935, a pioneering American ballet company.

Littlefield, Dorothie (U.S., 1912–1953). Dancer and ballet mistress, the first American teacher hired by Balanchine for the School of American Ballet; performed with various companies and collaborated with her sister, Catherine, at The Littlefield Ballet.

Livry, Emma (France, 1842–1863). Dancer; protégée of Marie Taglioni; victim of a fatal on-stage accident.

London Contemporary Dance Theatre, 1967–1994. Founded by Robin Howard; originally directed by Robert Cohan. Pioneering company that did much to introduce modern dance to Great Britain. It is now part of The Place.

London Festival Ballet, *see* English National Ballet

Lopukhov, Fyodor Vasilievich (Russia, 1886–1973). Dancer, choreographer, and teacher; performed in character roles with the Mariinsky Theatre ballet; director and notable choreographer of experimental ballets as well as restagings of classics in Leningrad; brother of ballerina Lydia Lopokova.

Loring, Eugene (U.S., 1911–1982). Dancer, choreographer, and teacher; performed and choreographed for the American Ballet, Ballet Caravan—notably *Billy the Kid* (1938), one of the early all-American ballets—and Ballet Theatre; choreographed for films and established a school in Los Angeles.

Louis XIV (France, 1638–1715). King of France and champion of dance; founded the royal academies of dance and music, merged in 1672; known as "Le Roi Soleil" after his role in the *ballet de cour, Ballet de la Nuit* (1653).

Louis, Murray (U.S., 1926–2016). Dancer, choreographer, teacher, and director; early collaborator with Alwin Nikolais at the Henry Street Settlement Playhouse and later the Chimera Foundation in New York; formed his own company to explore movement based on body "isolations."

Løvenskjold, Herman Severin (Denmark, 1815–1870). Composer; wrote scores for Bournonville, notably *La Sylphide* (1836).

Lubovitch, Lar (U.S., b. 1943). Dancer, choreographer; performed with diverse ballet and modern dance companies; formed his own company in 1968 to create experimental, then increasingly classical modern dance works; also choreographs regularly for other companies and Broadway shows.

Lully, Jean-Baptiste (Italy, 1632–1687). Composer in France; supervisor of royal music for Louis XIV from 1661; director of l'Académie Royale de Musique from ballet 1672.

Lunacharsky, Anatoly (Russia, 1875–1933). First Soviet Commissar of
Education.

MacMillan, Kenneth (Scotland, 1929–1992). Dancer, choreographer, and
director; choreographed for various companies, principally the Royal
Ballet, of which he was director for several years; also produced works
for American Ballet Theatre.

Magri, Gennaro (Italy, ca. 1737–1789). Ballet master, author;
choreographed in Italy and Austria before publishing his book on
technique, *Trattato Teoretico-Prattico di Ballo* (1779).

Mahler, Gustav (Austria, 1860–1911). Composer; his concert music often
choreographed, notably by Antony Tudor in *Dark Elegies* (1937),
Kenneth MacMillan, *Song of the Earth* (1965) and John Neumeier (1975)
in *Third Symphony.*

Makarova, Natalia Romanovna (Russia, b. 1940). Dancer; performed
with Leningrad Kirov Ballet; a major ballerina in the West, she has
performed with many companies, notably American Ballet Theatre, and
in musicals.

Manen, Hans van (Holland, b. 1932). Dancer, choreographer, director;
original member of the Netherlands Dance Theatre and its co-director;
later, co-director of the National Ballet of Holland; he choreographs for
both companies and others.

Manzotti, Luigi (Italy, 1835–1905). Choreographer; created mammoth
spectacles, notably *Excelsior* (1881).

Marin, Maguy (France, b. 1951). Choreographer, dancer; performed for
Strasbourg Opera Ballet and Béjart's Ballet du XXe Siècle; choreographs
works of high theatricality and social awareness for her own company,
Compagnie Maguy Marin, and others, notably Lyon National Opéra
Ballet.

Markova, Dame Alicia (England, 1910–2004). Dancer; major twentieth-
century ballerina for Diaghilev's Ballets Russes, her own company with
Anton Dolin, and many others; she was noted especially for dancing
Giselle.

Marshall, Susan (U.S., b. 1958). Dancer, choreographer; Juilliard-trained modern dancer; her choreography early won several awards; formed her own company in 1983 to produce works of highly risky physicality, exploring anomalous details of human behavior and relationships. She is chairman of the dance department at Princeton.

Martin, John (U.S., 1893–1985). Writer and critic, mainly for *The New York Times*; enjoyed a long career as analytical observer of the American dance scene; championed early American modern dance.

Martins, Peter (Denmark, b. 1946) Dancer, choreographer, and director; principal dancer with the Royal Danish Ballet and the New York City Ballet; he was a choreographer for the NYCB and responsible for its leadership as director of the company as well as its School of American Ballet from 1990 until 2018.

Massine, Leonide (Russia, 1896–1979). Dancer, choreographer, and teacher; one of the seminal choreographers for Diaghilev's Ballets Russes and Ballet Russe de Monte Carlo; noted for *demi-caractère* and symphonic ballets.

Matisse, Henri (France, 1869–1954). Artist; provided decor for Diaghilev's Ballets Russes *Le Chant du Rossignol* (1920) and Massine's *Rouge et Noir* (1939).

Maywood, Augusta (U.S., 1825–1876). Dancer; American ballerina at the Paris Opéra and throughout Europe; the first American dancer to win international acclaim.

Mazilier, Joseph (France, 1801–1868). Dancer and choreographer of the Romantic ballet era at the Paris Opéra; created many popular ballets, several to music by Adolphe Adam.

McGregor, Wayne (England, b. 1970). British modern-dance choreographer, studied at Bretton Hall College of University of Leeds and in New York at the José Limón School, appointed resident choreographer of Royal Ballet in 2006. His choreography is known for its contrasts between sharp fragmented phrases and fluid movements and for its concern with technology and scientific theory, including brain research.

McIntyre, Dianne (U.S., b. 1946). Dancer and choreographer; creates modern dance works in both lyrical and dramatic styles.

McKayle, Donald (U.S., b. 1930). Dancer, choreographer, and teacher; formed his own company to choreograph concert works based on black themes, particularly *Rainbow 'Round My Shoulder* and *District Storyville*. He has taught at UC Irvine, Connecticut College, Sarah Lawrence and Bennington.

Ménéstrier, Père (France, 1631–1705). Jesuit priest, author of *Des Ballets Anciens et Modernes selon les Règles du Thèâtre* (1682).

Meyerbeer, Giacomo (Germany, 1791–1864) Composer; wrote *Robert le Diable* (1831) for the Paris Opéra; ballet music from his other operas also used for Ashton's *Les Patineurs.*

Milhaud, Darius (France, 1892–1974). Composer; wrote a number of scores, notably *The Creation of the World* (1923), for Les Ballets Suédois and other companies; often used popular dance rhythms from France, Brazil, and the United States.

Miller, Marilyn (U.S., 1898–1936) Dancer, actress; child prodigy, became most noted star of musicals and revues in the 1920s; also made three films.

Minkus, Leon (Austria, 1826–1917). Composer of ballets, principally for Marius Petipa.

Miró, Joan (Spain, 1893–1983). Artist; provided decor to several companies, notably *Jeux d'Enfants* (1932) for de Basil's Ballets Russes.

Mitchell, Arthur (U.S., b. 1934). Dancer, choreographer, teacher, and director; long-time principal dancer with New York City Ballet; formed his own company, Dance Theatre of Harlem, with Karel Shook in New York.

Moiseyev, Igor Alexandrovich (Russia, 1906–2007). Dancer, choreographer, and director; performed and choreographed at Moscow's Bolshoi Ballet; developed his State Folk Dance Ensemble to perform his choreography of scenes from daily life.

Molière, Jean-Baptiste Poquelin; (France, 1622–1673). Playwright and librettist; collaborated with Lully on *comédies-ballets.*

Monk, Meredith (U.S., b. 1942) Dancer and choreographer, singer and composer; experimental choreographer with a strong theatrical sensibility; favors use of alternative performing spaces.

Mordkin, Mikhail Mikhailovich (Russia, 1880–1944). Dancer, choreographer, teacher, and director; performed with Moscow's Bolshoi Ballet and as Anna Pavlova's partner with her company; formed his own company and school in America.

Mordkin Ballet, *see* American Ballet Theatre

Morrice, Norman (Mexico, 1931–2008). British dancer, choreographer, and director; performed in, choreographed for, and directed Ballet Rambert; was director of the Royal Ballet; strongly influenced by American modern dance, he forwarded the modern dance movement in England.

Morris, Margaret (Scotland, 1891–1980). Dancer and teacher; early disciple of modern dance in London and Scotland; perpetuated her style through a number of publications.

Morris, Mark (U.S., b. 1956). Dancer, choreographer, director; performed ballet and ethnic dance, especially flamenco and Balkan dance; formed his own company to create movement-filled, energetic, often humorous modern dance works; choreographs works for other ballet and modern dance companies and as director of the Brussels Theatre de la Monnaie company, 1987–1991; founded White Oak Dance Project with Mikhail Baryshnikov 1990–2002; and in 2001 established the Mark Morris Dance Center in Brooklyn.

Moscow Art Theatre, 1898–. Russian repertory theatre founded by Stanislavsky and Nemirovich-Danchenko; later named Stanislavsky and Nemirovich-Danchenko Music Theatre, incorporating a ballet company.

Murphy, Graeme (Australia, b. 1950). Choreographer, dancer, director; performed for the Australian Ballet, Sadler's Wells Royal Ballet and others; choreographed for various companies, and since 1976 as director of the Sydney Dance Company.

National Ballet of Holland, Amsterdam (now the Dutch National Ballet), 1961–. Formed by the merger of the Amsterdam Ballet and the Netherlands Ballet; directed by Sonia Gaskell, then Rudi van Dantzig, Wayne Eagling, and Ted Brandsen.

Netherlands Dance Theatre, The Hague, 1959–. Begun as a splinter group from the Netherlands Ballet; its repertoire especially strong in modern ballets; directed by Benjamin Harkarvy, Glen Tetley, both with Hans van Manen, Jiri Kylian and, since 2012, Paul Lightfoot.

Neumeier, John (U.S., b. 1939. Dancer, choreographer, and director; performed and choreographed for many companies; director-choreographer of the Hamburg Ballet, especially producing large-scale symphonic ballets.

New Negro Art Theatre Dance Group, New York, 1927–1934. Founded by Hemsley Winfield as the Negro Art Theater; continued as first black modern dance company; its name was changed in 1931 for the first concert in New York.

New York City Ballet, 1948–. Outgrowth of the American Ballet (1934–1938, 1941), Ballet Caravan (1936–1941), and Ballet Society (1946–1948), all founded by Lincoln Kirstein with George Balanchine, its director from 1948 to 1983. One of the world's great companies, it has the largest repertoire of any American ballet company.

Newson, Lloyd (England, b. 1957). Dancer, choreographer; director of DV8 Physical Theatre.

Nijinska, Bronislava Fominichna (Russia, 1891–1972). Dancer at the Mariinsky Theatre and choreographer for Diaghilev's Ballets Russes; sister of Vaslav Nijinsky; created roles in her brother's ballets and choreographed a number of important experimental ballets for Ballets Russes and other companies, notably *Les Noces* (1923).

Nijinsky, Vaslav Fomich (Russia, 1890–1950). Dancer at the Mariinsky Theatre and notably for Diaghilev's Ballets Russes; before succumbing to mental illness, he was one of ballet's greatest male dancers, known especially for *ballon,* and a choreographer of several experimental ballets.

Nikolais, Alwin (U.S., 1912–1993). Dancer, choreographer, teacher, and director; early advocate of dance as total theatre; created all the elements of his highly experimental works; influential as a teacher-director in collaboration with Murray Louis at Henry Street Playhouse and their own theatre in New York.

Noguchi, Isamu (U.S., 1904–1988). Sculptor of abstract works, provided notable sets especially for Martha Graham.

North, Robert (U.S., b. 1945). Dancer, choreographer, and director; principal career in England with London Contemporary Dance Theatre and choreography for other companies; became director of Ballet Rambert.

Northern Ballet, Manchester, England, 1969–. Founded and directed by Laverne Meyer as Northern Dance Theatre, then Northern Ballet Theatre; directed by David Nixon since 2001.

Noverre, Jean Georges (France, 1727–1810). Dancer and choreographer; greatest exponent of *ballet d'action,* expounded in his *Lettres sur la Danse et sur les Ballets* (1760).

Nureyev, Rudolf (Russia, 1938–1993). Dancer, choreographer, and director; one of the leading male dancers of the twentieth century; performed with the Leningrad Kirov Ballet and the Royal Ballet as a foremost partner of Margot Fonteyn. He restaged the classics for many other companies; directed the Paris Opéra Ballet; noted for feline virtuosity and commanding stage presence.

Ohno, Kazuo (Japan, 1906–2010). Dancer, choreographer, teacher; developer with Tatsumi Hijikata, and exponent of the Expressionist theatre dance form, Butoh; represents an elegant, gentle, androgynous style within the grotesquerie.

Original Ballet Russe, 1939–1952. Later title of Col. Wassili de Basil's Ballets Russes de Monte Carlo.

Oukrainsky, Serge (Russia, ca.1885–1972). Dancer, teacher, and director; performed with the Anna Pavlova company; founded a school (1917) and company in Chicago with Andreas Pavley; directed the Chicago, Los Angeles, and San Francisco opera ballets.

Page, Ruth (U.S., 1899–1991). Dancer, choreographer, and director; toured extensively with Adolph Bolm's company, Harald Kreutzberg, and others; formed the Page-Stone Ballet (1938) with Bentley Stone in Chicago, then her own company, later called the Chicago Ballet.

Palucca, Gret (Germany, 1902–1993). Dancer, choreographer, teacher; protégée of Mary Wigman; developed her own formal, lyrical style in solo and group works; opened long-lived school in 1925 in Dresden and taught there until well into her 80s.

Panov, Valery Matveyevich (Russia, b. 1938) and Galina Ragozina (Byelorussia, b. 1949). Dancers; performed with the Leningrad Kirov Ballet; in the West, they have performed and choreographed for a number of companies; preeminent exemplars of the Russian style.

Pavley, Andreas (Holland, 1892–1931). Dancer, teacher, and director; performed with the Anna Pavlova company; founded a school (1917) and company in Chicago with Serge Oukrainsky.

Pavlova, Anna Pavlovna (Russia, 1881–1931). The leading ballerina of the early twentieth century; performed at the Mariinsky Theatre and as principal of her own company, which toured extensively and introduced classical ballet internationally; noted for her compelling on-stage presence.

Paxton, Steve (U.S., b. 1939). Dancer and choreographer; creates experimental works exploring "contact improvisation"; founder-member of the Judson Dance Theatre.

Peck, Justin (U.S., b. 1987). Dancer and choreographer with New York City Ballet and other companies; appointed NYCB's resident choreographer 2014. Known for choreographically cheeky ballets reflecting various aspects of contemporary life.

Pécour, Louis (France, 1653–1729). Dancer and ballet master at the Paris Opéra; appeared in *Le Triomphe de l'Amour* (1681) and other Lully ballets; many of his dances were notated by Feuillet.

Perez, Rudy (U.S., b. 1929). Dancer, choreographer, and teacher; experimental choreographer and creator of taped sound-collages; member of the Judson Dance Theatre.

Perrot, Jules (France, 1810–1882). Dancer and choreographer of the Romantic ballet era; created many ballets, notably *Giselle* (1841, with Jean Coralli).

Petipa, Lucien (France, 1815–1898). Dancer and ballet master; brother of Marius Petipa; best *danseur noble* of the Romantic era at the Paris Opéra, where he created the role of Albrecht in *Giselle* (1841).

Petipa, Marius (France, 1818–1910). Dancer and choreographer; enjoyed a long reign in St. Petersburg as the premier ballet master, creating many of the best-known classical ballets, notably *The Sleeping Beauty* (1890).

Petit, Roland (France, 1924–2011). Dancer, choreographer, and director; performed with the Paris Opéra Ballet and in recitals with Janine Charrat; helped found Les Ballets des Champs-Elysées, later founded Les Ballets de Paris; choreographed many works for his own and other companies, films, and revues, often starring his wife, Renée Jeanmaire.

Petronio, Stephen (U.S., b. 1956). Dancer, choreographer; performed for Trisha Brown company; his own high-powered, physically demanding work involves modern dance, body/movement techniques, and improvisational forms.

Philidor, Andre Danican (France, 1647–1730). Musician, archivist; court musician for Louis XIV; composed balls and ballets, notably *Le Mariage de la Grosse Cathos;* collected and copied the scores of court music from 1570s onward.

Picabia, Francis (France, 1878–1953). Dadaist and Surrealist painter; collaborated with Les Ballets Suédois, notably the libretto and decor for *Relâche.*

Picasso, Pablo (Spain, 1881–1973). Artist; provided decor for Diaghilev's Ballets Russes—notably his collaboration on *Parade* (1917)—and other companies.

Pilobolus, 1971–. Founded as a collaborative at Dartmouth College, Hanover, New Hampshire, by Moses Pendleton and Jonathan Wolken, joined by Lee Harris, Robby Barnett, Alison Chase, and Martha Clarke. Its roster now varies. The company, that explores movement produced from gymnastics, athletic contact, and contortions, has performed in concert, on Broadway, and on television.

Pleasant, Richard (U.S., 1906–1961). Director and publicity agent; cofounded Ballet Theatre with Lucia Chase.

Plisetskaya, Maya Mikhailovna (Russia, b.1925). Dancer and film actress; one of the great ballerinas of the twentieth century; performed with Moscow's Bolshoi Ballet in classical and dramatic roles; noted for brilliant virtuosity and suppleness.

Pomare, Eleo (U.S., b. 1937). Dancer and choreographer; performed in Holland and America; formed his own company, which presents his modern dance works of stark realism based on the black experience.

Poulenc, Francis (France, 1899–1963). Composer; wrote scores for Diaghilev's Ballets Russes, notably *Les Biches* (1924).

Prévost, Françoise (France, ca.1680–1741). Dancer and teacher at the Paris Opéra; choreographed *Les Caractères de la Danse* (1715).

Priest, Josias (England, d.1734). Dancer and dancing master; choreographer of Henry Purcell's masques.

Primus, Pearl (U.S., 1919–1994). Dancer, choreographer, anthropologist, and teacher; performed with the New Dance Group; examined indigenous dances of Africa and the West Indies and choreographed in these forms for various companies.

Prokofiev, Sergei Sergeyevich (Russia, 1891–1953). Composer; wrote scores for a number of important ballets, notably *The Prodigal Son* (1929) and *Romeo and Juliet* (1940).

Pugni, Cesare (Italy, 1805[1802?]–1870). Composer of ballets for Jules Perrot, Arthur Saint-Léon, and Marius Petipa.

Purcell, Henry (England, 1659–1695). Composer; wrote music for many early English masques; his concert music also choreographed.

Rainer, Yvonne (U.S., b. 1934). Dancer and choreographer; experimental choreographer; founder-member of the Judson Dance Theatre.

Rambert, Dame Marie (Poland, 1888–1982). Dancer, teacher, and director; worked with Diaghilev's Ballets Russes; enjoyed a long career in England, where she opened a school and formed a company that pioneered in English ballet, producing important dancers and notable English choreographers.

Rambert Dance Company, London, 1987–. Continuation of Ballet Rambert as a modern dance group, directed by Richard Alston. In 2013 its name was shortened to Rambert; Mark Baldwin became director in 2002.

Rameau, Jean-Philippe (France, 1683–1764). Composer; his many *opéra-ballets* include *Les Indes Galantes* (1735).

Rasch, Albertina (Austria, 1896–1967). Dancer and choreographer, especially in America, where she formed technically well-grounded touring troupes of women; she choreographed for films and musicals.

Ratmansky, Alexei (Russia, b. 1968). Choreographer, trained Moscow's Bolshoi Ballet School, danced with Ukrainian National Ballet, Royal Winnipeg Ballet, Royal Danish Ballet; directed Bolshoi Ballet, 2004–2008, and artist in residence at the American Ballet Theatre. Choreographer of productions ranging from ballets to Shostakovich, commenting on conditions in Russia, to new versions of Soviet-era works, including *Bright Stream* and *The Bolt.* Also staged scrupulously researched revivals of 19th-century classics, among them *Paquita, Swan Lake,* and *Sleeping Beauty.*

Ravel, Maurice (France, 1875–1937). Composer; wrote *Daphnis and Chlöe* (1912) for Diaghilev's Ballets Russes; and his most famous piece, *Bolero* (1928) for dancer/actress Ida Rubinstein.

Reich, Steve (U.S., b. 1936). Composer; creates avant-garde scores based on repetition used by experimental choreographers, especially Laura Dean, with whom he collaborated.

Reisinger, Julius (Austria, 1828–1892). Choreographer of the first production of *Swan Lake* (1877) in Moscow.

Riabouchinska, Tatiana (Russia, 1917–2000). Dancer and teacher; one of the trio of "baby ballerinas" (with Irina Baronova and Tamara Toumanova); performed with the Ballet Russe companies and a number of others; opened a school in Los Angeles.

Robbins, Jerome (U.S., 1918–1998). Dancer, choreographer, and director; performed and choreographed extensively for American Ballet Theatre and New York City Ballet; important work in musical theatre (a five-time Tony award winner); codirected New York City Ballet with Peter Martins, 1983–1989.

Roerich, Nicholas (Russia, 1874–1947). Painter and archaeologist; collaborated with Diaghilev's Ballets Russes, notably the decor for *Le Sacre du Printemps.*

Ronsard, Pierre de (France, 1524–1585). Writer, especially of poetry, who collaborated on *Le Ballet des Polonais* (1573) with Beaujoyeulx.

Rosati, Carolina (Italy, 1826–1905). Dancer, principally at the Paris Opéra; created the title role in Petipa's *The Daughter of Pharaoh* (1862) in St. Petersburg.

Rouault, Georges (France, 1871–1958). Artist; provided decor for Diaghilev's Ballets Russes production of *The Prodigal Son* (1929).

The Royal Ballet, London, 1931–. Founded by Ninette de Valois and Lilian Baylis, and directed by de Valois, as the Vic-Wells Ballet, later called Sadler's Wells Ballet; received Royal Charter, 1956; directed by Kevin O'Hare since 2012.

Royal Danish Ballet, Copenhagen, ca.1722–. Principal director-choreographers were Vincenzo Galeotti, August Bournonville; since 2000, Nikolaj Hübbe.

Rubinstein, Ida (Russia, 1885–1960). Dancer, actress, director; created principal roles in Fokine ballets for Diaghilev's Ballets Russes, notably *Cléopâtre* and *Schéhérazade;* formed her own company, commissioning major artists to create star-vehicle works, notably *Le Martyre de St. Sebastien* (1911) and *Boléro* (1928).

Sadler's Wells Ballet, *see* The Royal Ballet

Sadler's Wells Royal Ballet, *see* Birmingham Royal Ballet

St. Denis, Ruth (U.S., 1878–1968). Dancer, choreographer, and teacher; a modern dance pioneer, who experimented with "music visualizations" (direct interpretation of music into movement) and created lavish productions based on ethnic dances for the Denishawn company, cofounded with Ted Shawn.

Saint-Léon, Arthur (France, 1821–1870). Dancer, choreographer, and teacher of the Romantic ballet era; husband of Fanny Cerrito; created a notation system and many ballets, notably *Coppélia* (1870).

Sallé, Marie (France, 1707–1756). Dancer at the Paris Opéra and in London; made important costume reforms; her dance style prefigured the *ballet d'action.*

San Francisco Ballet, 1933–. Outgrowth of the San Francisco Opera Ballet under the direction of Adolph Bolm, succeeded by Serge Oukrainsky, Willam Christensen, Lew Christensen—who increased the company's autonomy—Michael Smuin, and currently Helgi Tomasson; Harold Christensen was director of the affiliated school.

Sangalli, Rita (Italy, 1850–1909). Dancer; toured extensively in Europe, and in America in *The Black Crook* (1866); became a prima ballerina at the Paris Opéra.

Sankai Juku ("school of mountain and sea"), Tokyo, 1970s–. Third-generation Butoh company, directed by Ushio Amagatsu.

Satie, Erik (France, 1866–1925). Composer; wrote *Parade* (1917) for Diaghilev's Ballets Russes and *Relâche* (1924) for Les Ballets Suédois; his concert music often choreographed.

Schlemmer, Oskar (Germany, 1888–1943). Painter, experimentalist, designer; pioneered Abstract Dance, notably in *Triadic Ballet* (1922); member of the Bauhaus.

Schneitzhoeffer, Jean-Madeleine (France, 1785–1852). Composer at the Paris Opéra; wrote *La Sylphide* (1832) for Taglioni and *La Tempête* (1834) for Coralli.

Scott, Sir Walter (England, 1771–1832). Poet and novelist, known especially for his romantic novels.

Scottish Ballet, Bristol, then Glasgow, 1957–. Founded and directed by Elizabeth West and Peter Darrell as Western Theatre Ballet in Bristol, then relocated in Scotland.

Shawn, Ted (U.S., 1891–1972). Dancer, choreographer, teacher, director, and writer; with Ruth St. Denis, formed the Denishawn school and company; champion of male dancing with his Men Dancers company (1933–1939); founded Jacob's Pillow Dance Festival.

Smith, George Washington (U.S., 1820–1899). Dancer, ballet master, and teacher; performed in and staged Romantic ballets for American theatres and touring companies; first American to dance Albrecht in *Giselle*.

Smith, Oliver (U.S., 1918–1994). Painter, stage designer, director; provided decor for many landmark ballets and musicals, especially for American Ballet Theatre; codirector of the company 1945–1980 and again after 1990.

Smuin, Michael (U.S., 1938–2007). Dancer, choreographer, and director; performed with American Ballet Theatre; former director-choreographer of San Francisco Ballet; has also choreographed musicals for Broadway and films.

Sokolova, Lydia (England, 1896–1974). Dancer, especially with Diaghilev's Ballets Russes; noted for vivacity, she created a number of *demi-caractère* roles.

Sokolow, Anna (U.S., 1910–2000). Dancer, choreographer, and teacher; performed with the Martha Graham company and assisted Louis Horst; choreographed for her own and various companies works of sometimes scathing social commentary.

Somes, Michael (England, 1917–1994). Dancer, director, and teacher; notable career with the Royal Ballet as *danseur noble* and partner of Margot Fonteyn; was assistant director of the company.

Staats, Léo (France, 1877–1952). Dancer, choreographer, ballet master, and teacher; dancer at the Paris Opéra, partnering Carlotta Zambelli, where he choreographed many ballets and revived the classics.

Stanislavsky, Konstantin Sergeyevich (Russia, 1863–1938). Theatrical actor, director, and teacher; developed an acting method based on inner identification with a role and natural use of the body and voice; cofounder of the Moscow Art Theatre.

Stepanov, Vladimir Ivanovich (Russia, 1866–1896). Dancer and teacher; after studying anatomy, published his dance notation system based on musical notation in *Alphabet des Mouvements du Corps Humain* (1892); used for restaging many Mariinsky classics.

Stone, Bentley (U.S., 1908–1984). Dancer, teacher, and director; formed the Page-Stone Ballet (1938) in Chicago with Ruth Page; founded an important school (1941) in Chicago with Walter Camryn.

Strauss, Richard (Germany, 1864–1949). Composer; wrote *The Legend of Joseph* (1914) for Diaghilev's Ballets Russes; his concert music often choreographed.

Stravinsky, Igor Fyodorovich (Russia, 1882–1971). Composer; wrote important scores for Diaghilev's Ballets Russes and New York City Ballet and other companies, including *Firebird* (1910), *Petrouchka* (1911), *Le Sacre du Printemps* (1913), *Les Noces* (1923), *Apollon Musagete (Apollo,* 1928), *Orpheus* (1948), and *Agon* (1957).

Stuttgart Ballet, ca.1759–. Principal early directors were Jean Georges Noverre and Filippo Taglioni; contemporary renown began under John Cranko in 1961; continues to encourage new choreography.

Sydney Dance Company, Australia, 1969–. Founded as The Dance Company of New South Wales, directed by Jaap Flier; Graeme Murphy became director in 1976. The company became known for provocative Australian-made works; name changed in 1979.

Taglioni, Filippo (Italy, 1777–1871). Dancer and choreographer; father of Marie; early creator of Romantic ballet with *La Sylphide* (1832), which established his daughter's preeminence.

Taglioni, Marie (Italy, 1804–1884). Dancer; daughter of Filippo; the foremost Romantic ballerina, noted for an ethereal on-stage presence.

Takei, Kei (Japan, b. 1946). Dancer, choreographer, and teacher; principally in America, where her Moving Earth company explores movement through an obstacle-laden course in the unfinished cycle *Light.*

Tamiris, Helen (U.S., 1902–1966). Dancer, choreographer, and teacher; modern dance recitalist; choreographed works of social significance as well as several important musicals; noted as a teacher.

Tanaka, Min (Japan, b. 1945). Dancer, choreographer; early training in ballet and modem dance; became exponent of his own form of Butoh, called BuTai, which is expressed in vibrating, pulsating "hyper-dance"; considered third-generation Butoh.

Taylor, Paul (U.S., b. 1930). Dancer, choreographer, and director; performed with various modern dance companies, especially the Martha Graham company; formed his own company in 1993; unusually versatile, his choreography ranges from the humorous and sardonic to the lyrical.

Tchaikovsky, Peter Ilyich (Russia, 1840–1893). Composer; wrote scores for *Swan Lake* (1877, 1895), *The Sleeping Beauty* (1890), and *The Nutcracker* (1892); his concert music often choreographed.

Tchelitchev, Pavel (Russia, 1898–1957). Artist and designer; provided decor for Diaghilev's Ballets Russes and later several other companies.

Tetley, Glen (U.S., 1926–2007). Dancer, choreographer, and director; performed and choreographed for many companies, first in modem dance, then in ballet; directed the Netherlands Dance Theatre and the Stuttgart Ballet.

Tharp, Twyla (U.S., b. 1941). Dancer, choreographer, and director; experimentalist in avant-garde dance; formed her own company to explore movement that is often loose, quirky, and humorous, superimposed on careful structure; also choreographs for Broadway, television, ballet and ice skating companies. Her dance *Push Comes to Shove* (1976) was created for Baryshnikov.

Thomson, Virgil (U.S., 1896–1989). Composer; wrote *Filling Station* (1938) for Ballet Caravan.

Tikhomirov, Vassily Dimitrievich (Russia, 1876–1956). Dancer, choreographer, and teacher; performed, especially with his wife, Yekaterina Geltzer, and choreographed principally for Moscow's Bolshoi Ballet, of which he became director; produced with Lev Laschilin the seminal Soviet-style ballet *The Red Poppy* (1927); notable as a teacher.

Tomasson, Helgi (Iceland, b. 1942). Dancer, choreographer, and director; principal dancer with New York City Ballet; currently director of the San Francisco Ballet.

Torelli, Giacomo (Italy, 1608–1678). Stage designer in France during the reign of Louis XIV.

Toumanova, Tamara (Russia, 1919–1996). Dancer and film actress; one of the trio of "baby ballerinas" (with Irina Baronova and Tatiana Riabouchinska); performed with the Ballet Russe companies and Ballet Theatre, and toured extensively thereafter; appeared in a number of American films.

Tudor, Antony (England, 1908–1987). Dancer, choreographer, and teacher; early work for Ballet Rambert and his own companies in England; since 1940 had a close connection with American Ballet Theatre; his works express deep psychological insight through classical ballet movement.

Turnbull, Julia (U.S., 1822–1887). Dancer; performed in America all the foremost Romantic ballet roles.

Ulanova, Galina Sergeyevna (Russia, 1910–1998). Dancer and teacher; one of the great ballerinas of the twentieth century; performed with Leningrad Kirov Ballet and Moscow's Bolshoi Ballet, creating many important roles, notably Juliet in *Romeo and Juliet* (1940); noted for sensitivity and drama of interpretation.

Utrillo, Maurice (France, 1883–1955). Artist; designed Balanchine's *Barabau* (1925) for Diaghilev's Ballets Russes.

Vaganova, Agrippina Jakovlevna (Russia, 1879–1951). Dancer, teacher, and director; performed with Leningrad Mariinsky Ballet; best known as a teacher and formulator of the Russian system of training; the Leningrad Choreographic School named for her.

Vainonen, Vassily Ivanovich (Russia, 1901–1964). Dancer and choreographer; performed and choreographed principally in Leningrad, where his first ballet caused controversy; his *Flames of Paris* (1932) is a successful example of Soviet-style choreography.

Valberkh, Ivan Ivanovich (Russia, 1766–1819). Dancer, choreographer, and teacher; first well-known Russian ballet master; director of the St. Petersburg and Moscow ballet schools.

van Manen, Hans, *see* Manen, Hans van

Van Vechten, Carl (U.S., 1880–1964). Writer and music and dance critic; early analyst of the dance scene in America.

Verdon, Gwen (U.S., 1925–2000). Dancer, actress; star, especially of jazz dance, in musicals and film, notably *Can-Can* (1953), and *Damn Yankees* (1955).

Vernoy de Saint-Georges, Jules Henri (France, 1801–1875). Writer; co-author with Théophile Gautier and Jean Coralli of *Giselle* (1841).

Véron, Dr. Louis-Desire (France, 1798–1867). Physician and innovative director of the Paris Opéra.

Vestris, Auguste (France, 1760–1842). Dancer and teacher at the Paris Opéra; son of Gaetan; best-known dancer of his time, noted for his virtuosity.

Vestris, Gaetan (Italy, 1729–1808). Dancer and choreographer at the Paris Opéra; called "Ie dieu de la danse."

Vic-Wells Ballet, *see* The Royal Ballet

Viganò, Salvatore (Italy, 1769–1821). Dancer, choreographer, and composer; ballet master at Milan's La Scala Opera; creator of *coreodrammi.*

Vsevolozhsky, Ivan Alexandrovich (Russia, 1835–1909). Diplomat and designer, director of the Imperial Theatres during part of the tenure of Marius Petipa.

Warhol, Andy (U.S., 1928–1987). Artist and filmmaker; progenitor of "Pop Art" and contributor of designs for Merce Cunningham.

Waring, James (U.S., 1922–1975). Dancer, choreographer, and teacher; created modern dance works of quick wit and intelligence for a number of ballet and modern dance companies.

Weaver, John (England, 1673–1760). Dancer and choreographer; pioneer of *ballet d'action,* notably in *The Loves of Mars and Venus* (1717).

Webster, Clara (England, 1821–1844). Dancer; victim of a fatal on-stage accident.

Weidman, Charles (U.S., 1901–1975). Dancer, choreographer, director, and teacher; performed with Denishawn until he and Doris Humphrey formed their own company; choreographed works of both high humor and powerful drama; also choreographed for musicals; notable teacher.

Wheeldon, Christopher (England, b. 1977). Dancer (until 2000, when he decided to concentrate on choreography) and choreographer who, after dancing with Royal Ballet, joined New York City Ballet in 1993 and became its resident choreographer, headed his own troupe Morphoses, 2006–2010. Created two notable multiact works for Royal Ballet based on literary classics, *Alice's Adventures in Wonderland* and *The Winter's Tale.*

Wigman, Mary (Germany, 1886–1973). Dancer, choreographer, and teacher; seminal figure in modern dance, developing the form *Ausdruckstanz* (Expressive Dance); her influence felt worldwide principally through her disciples.

Wilson, Billy (U.S., 1935–1994) Dancer, choreographer, teacher, and director; performed with ballet companies in America and abroad; choreographed in various genres and as artistic director of Dance Theatre of Boston.

Wilson, Robert (U.S, b. 1941). Artist and producer; initiated massive, slowmoving, multiarts productions that have influenced experimental choreographers.

Winfield, Hemsley (U.S., 1906–1934). Dancer, choreographer, director; self-trained early pioneer of blacks in modern dance; formed, with Edna Guy, company ultimately called New Negro Art Theatre Dance Group, with works derivative of Denishawn; also appeared on Broadway and in opera.

Zakharov, Rostislav (Russia, 1907–1984). Dancer, choreographer, teacher; performed for Kharkov and Kiev ballet companies; founded the choreographic training school at the State Theatre Institute in Moscow; choreographed many works, principally for the Bolshoi Ballet, notably *The Fountain of Bakhchisarai.*

Zambelli, Carlotta (Italy, 1875–1968). Dancer and teacher at the Paris Opéra and in St. Petersburg.

Zorn, Friedrich Albert (Germany, fl. late 1800s). Teacher and writer; noted for publication of a textbook on dancing, *Grammatik der Tanzkunst* (1887), in which he developed his own system of notation.

Zucchi, Virginia (Italy, 1847–1930). Dancer and teacher; performed principally in St. Petersburg; her expressiveness influenced Russian training.

Index